Wraysbury Then and Now

A village in time

By

Graham R Morley

With additional contributions from
Diana Hughes, Tony Kimber and Margaret Lenton

Published by
Wraysbury Parish Council

First published in the United Kingdom 2018
by

©Wraysbury Parish Council
The Village Hall
41 The Green
Wraysbury TW19 5NA

A CIP catalogue record for this book is available from the British Library

ISBN: 978-1-9996635-0-6

This is a 'Not for Profit' publication and all proceeds will go to help and support Wraysbury local charities.

All information deemed to be correct at time of printing

Printed and bound in Great Britain
By
Print2Demand Ltd.
1 Newlands Road
Westoning
Bedfordshire, MK45 5LD

Wraysbury – A Geographical Introduction

Wraysbury (population 4011 in the 2011 census) is in the Royal Borough of Windsor and Maidenhead, some 18 miles west by south-west of London on the east bank of the River Thames. It's approximately 6 miles from Heathrow airport, nestling in the Thames Valley, adjacent to the villages of Datchet and Horton. With excellent road and rail connections, it was historically part of Buckinghamshire but transferred to Berkshire in 1974. It is a village with pre-Saxon roots and very close connections to the Kings and Queens of England, in particular, King John and the Magna Carta, and Henry VIII.

The village's geographical spread hasn't really changed much over the generations, stretching from the county ditch that runs across the Wraysbury Road on the way to Staines, the last house being number 115, to in the opposite direction, the Horton Road and Horton Village. But you will see as we go on through the centuries in this book, how prosperity and the Industrial Revolution has transformed it.

The first part of Wraysbury nearest Staines, that now encompasses Gloucester Drive and Lammas Drive and ends roughly where the M25 bridge crosses the Wraysbury Road, was all open land in Tudor times and better known as Queensmead (and for many more senior residents, it still is). For, whilst all the countryside was owned by the Crown, the lands here were always used as marriage or dower settlements by the King for his Queens. This practice was common and continued, right from Edward III in 1327, through Richard I, Henry IV, Edward IV, Henry VII and finally to three of Henry VIII's Queens, Catherine of Aragon, Anne Boleyn and Jane Seymour. It is said that Jane Seymour had a house in Queensmead, furnished with goods and chattel, which were the property of Anne Boleyn that she 'robbed' from Ankerwycke. Wifely enmity ran deep even then!

The village then follows the Wraysbury Road into Hythe End by the bridge over the River Colne, once home to a thriving (for a while) paper mill which is mentioned in the Domesday Book. After the bridge, the village then sits either side of the road before becoming the Staines Road, passing all the land that once belonged to Ankerwycke (in 1885 it had 700 acres!) and Ankerwycke Priory all the way to the shops where the road forks left to Windsor Road and straight on into the High Street.

Continuing through the High Street, the road follows seamlessly into Station Road, passing the sites of some great old houses that have been demolished: Chelston House, Old Bowry House, The Vicarage and lastly, the site of Wraysbury House, home to the Gylls and later the Herring family, which is now under a gravel pit! The road then crosses over the railway and then the River Colne at a place that used to be called 'Whitehall'. This is the site of another large house, lived in by Francis Buckland at the end of the 19th century and later the home of Mr. White of R. White's Lemonade fame. More about these lovely old houses later in this book.

The village finally ends at the site of Wraysbury Mill (again also mentioned in the Domesday Book), originally an iron mill and then a copper mill, finally becoming a paper mill, which lasted until 1972. The whole mill site was later demolished and became a small residential development. This is the western end of Wraysbury where it becomes the village of Horton.

Going back to Windsor Road from the fork with the High Street, the village then crosses the Long Bridge and straddles the road passed the Village Green and The Grange, thankfully one of the village's finer old houses that still remains. Opposite lies the old pub, The George, dating from the 16th century and where Henry Cooper, the great boxer, used to train in his heyday. Behind The George used to be another grand house called Glenmore, sadly demolished as most have been, this time to make way for a telephone exchange and other dwellings. The road carries on past St. Andrew's Close where St. Andrew's church stands. There has been a church on this site since about Saxon times. The road then continues and becomes Welley Road with its numerous side roads - some leading to the river and riverside houses (and, in the 19/20th century, wharfage and ferries), others to quiet residential housing in private or unadopted areas.

Nearing the end of Welley Road is The Avenue, another private and unadopted road, now a very pleasant residential area with, in a lot of cases, direct access to the river. All this part of the village used to be open farmland, which was redeveloped from 1923 to c1930s, up to and including Brookside Avenue, Acacia Avenue and Welley Avenue, again all unadopted roads. This area is now known as Sunnymeads and has the benefit of its own railway station.

Welley Road took its name it is believed, from Welley House, of which more later in this History. From here Welley Road continues over the railway line down to the junction with Horton Road and thus reaches the far end of our beautiful village.

This then is Wraysbury, a village of History

--oo00O00oo--

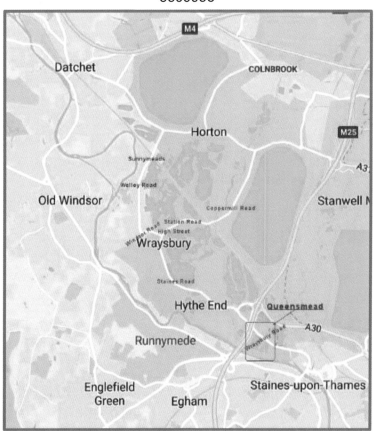

The village of Wraysbury
Source: © Google Maps

Preface

This is a look at our village from ancient times until the more modern era, something I hope will be read and enjoyed and is not too stuffy. For some it will be an evocation, whilst for others it will be completely new.

I have tried to tell the story of our village in a way that is light-hearted, entertaining and factual and, where necessary, the relevant proofs and sources of information are both detailed and shown. It is the story of village life and it is, in part, about its people.

It has not been possible to mention everyone nor indeed every facet of village life or activity, it is an overview, a snapshot if you will, looking at the various aspects of village life that make up our daily living.

The quality of some photographs reproduced is less than would be liked, but is due to being taken from faded originals and old newspapers, some of which were almost see through!

It has not been my intention to omit, suppress or upset anyone in the compilation of this work and if by chance there are errors or omissions, I sincerely apologise.

In some points in this work, I have challenged Gyll's History of Wraysbury on its facts. I would point out that at time of publication in 1862[1], the whole work was subject to heavy criticism by his peers as being - *'a strange medley of useful facts, useless ornamentation and suppositious learning'* - and further - *'it is necessary to caution its readers against its errors and in particular, to see that its elucidations of history not only are correct but that they do not diverge from, or flicker impertinently round, the points on which they ought to concentrate their light'*

Graham R. Morley

---

[1] The Morning Post 22nd January 1862

Contents

The George c.1950s
Source: Wraysbury Archives

Thanks and Acknowledgements

I would like to thank all those villagers who allowed me unqualified access to their personal stories, diaries and photographs, without which it would not have been possible to write this work.

Sources and Acknowledgements
Wraysbury Parish Archives, Ancestral Research Archives & Library, Spartacus Educational, British Newspaper Archives, National Archives, Pam and Ray Alletson, Anne Blake, Rita Brutnell, Maureen and Frank Burr, Frank Burry, Henry Butt, Roger Chapman, Andy Clemance, Giovanna Cochrane, Elsie Joan Cole, Julie Coram, Janet Crame BEM, Marcelle Cresto, Elizabeth Dean, Tom Dibley, History notes of Joan Dick, 'Eddie' Elderfield, Shirley Fairbairn, Marilyn Ferguson, Revd. Joseph Fernandes, Lucy Foster, Jennie Francis, Pam and Dennis Gabriel, Margaret Gardiner, Revd. Colin Gibson, Janet Graham, Barbara Hearne, Tony Hermes, Joyce Histead, Jill Hopkins, Diana and Carl Hughes, Carolyn Humphries, 1988 notes of Nancy Klarman, Peter Knott, Glyn Larcombe, Memoirs of Basil Masterson 1997, John Mellor, Joan Mitchell, Katie Morgan, Ros Nockles, Vic and Ruby Oliver, Fred Parsons, Len and Avril Pearce, Brian Reeves, John Rice, Margaret Rooks, Graham Sinclair, John Sleep Leg. D'Hon, Rosemary Smith, John Stephenson, Revd. Carolyn Urwin, Reg and June Watmore, Lesley West, Memoirs of Christie Willatts, W. I. Memoirs of Peggy Willatts, Robert and Linda Willatts, Roger Willatts, Rosalind Willatts, Mike G. Williams.

Grateful thanks are extended to Wraysbury Parish Council, Wraysbury Parochial Charities and Wraysbury Village Trust for their support with this work
and to
Mark and Jackie Keynes for always making me welcome at the Village Hall

Since the compilation of this book, the author acknowledges the contribution to village life of Len Pearce and his subsequent death on the 13th July 2017 and of Jack Pengelly who died on the 21st February 2018

The Splash
Source: Wraysbury Archives

In the Beginning

Early Man to the Normans - 1066 and all that!

Early Man!
Thanks to ©Aardman
Animation

The Normans
Source: ©English Heritage

What was Wraysbury like? Tony Kimber finds out.

Part 1
of
The Wraysbury History Project

Early Man to the Normans

First settlers

The History of the Wraysbury area goes back far beyond the modern geographical boundaries. Around 3 million years ago the geological upheavals and continental movements of planet earth had settled and early humans were evolving in Africa. Wraysbury was sited towards the southern end of a promontory on the north west of 'Europe' almost surrounded by sea but still joined to the main European land mass. Rain was falling, and rivers were flowing across this land to the seas, gradually creating hills and valleys. It is possible that, in the next few thousand years, some of the early humans travelled on foot and by boat along the rivers to Wraysbury living off the abundance of fruit and wildlife that evolved in the forests that would have covered the land in the period known as 'The Old Stone Age' or Upper Palaeolithic era 30,000 BCE - 10,000 BCE.

When an ice mass slowly moved from the north on to this area at the beginning of the last Ice Age humans will have retreated in front of it back to the continent, only returning as the ice receded some 12,000 years ago. The ice will have rounded valleys and smoothed jagged hills, creating an environment suitable for humans. In time more forests will have covered the fertile ground in what is known as the Mesolithic period - 10,000 BCE to 4,000 BCE - and once again human kind will have visited Wraysbury. The Mesolithic period was the era of hunter-gatherers but also in this period they may have commenced settling in communities, clearing land by the rivers, growing crops and farming livestock. When the melt waters of the ice built up pressure sufficient to force through from the North Sea and separate this Island from the continent about 8,000 years ago there was already a spread of farming settlements throughout England, initially located by the navigable rivers such as the Thames and the Colne, but as territory became culturally important and friction between communities developed, there will have been movements to settlements on higher ground or islands which could be more easily defended against acquisitive neighbours – particularly as weapons developed during the later Bronze and Iron Ages.

We know that the area now known as Wraysbury was visited and occupied, by peoples going back well before this period some five to six thousand years ago. Although outside the modern boundaries of Wraysbury, Kingsmead Quarries, south east of Horton, is one of the most important archaeological sites in the UK where they have found flints from the Old Stone Age and other remains showing visitation and occupation from then through to the present day. The main evidence for their presence in this period are flint tools, including hand-axes, which have been found in the area. Evidence for this period mainly consists of worked flint, including distinctive small 'microliths'. In 2008 the site of a Mesolithic house was found at Kingsmead thought to be over 5000 years old which is one of the oldest found in the UK. The pictures on the next page show the site in its modern context and a modern reconstruction plus some of the flint arrowheads and pottery found in the house and some nearby pits which are consistent with this dating.

The next period, 4000 BCE to 2500 BCE is known as the New Stone Age or Neolithic. This was the era when agriculture became established and monumental stone structures were erected including long barrows. From this era onwards, pottery becomes an important part of the archaeological record.

Reconstruction done by Will Foster and Tom Goskar of Wessex Archaeology

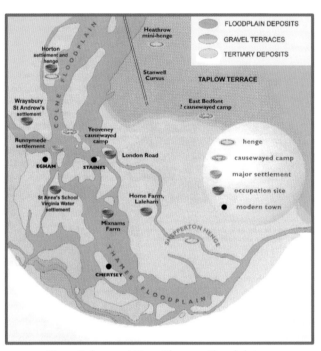

River Colne and River Thames Floodplains
© [1]Based upon an Image produced by the
Surrey County Archaeology Unit (part of Surrey County Council)

Over thousands of years rivers carving a path in their flood plain meander from side to side. Humans who settled next to rivers had to move as the rivers moved. At Kingsmead they have found signs of a wide watercourse which is shown opposite as the Horton settlement on an analysis from Surrey as part of the Colne Floodplain. It would explain the presence of a settlement in that place. The Kingsmead site includes a Neolithic cursus, thought possibly to be a ritual processional way, and a 'henge'.

To the West of Wraysbury just into Staines there is Yeoveney. The map on the next page shows the location relative to Wraysbury. In 1959 an aerial photograph showed indications of archaeological remains and a Causewayed Enclosure from the Neolithic Age was identified. The aerial photograph from 1959, also on the next page, has the oval outline of the outer ring of the enclosure marked and there are indications of other rings within it. In 1961-3, in advance of Gravel extraction at Yeoveney, rescue archaeology investigated the site. The area enclosed was about 2.4 hectares or 6 acres. It is thought that the enclosure was constructed between 3600 BCE and 3200 BCE and finds from the site, also shown on the next pages, suggest occupation from then through later prehistoric times, the Roman occupation, and the Saxon and medieval periods.

[1] Taken from the publication - 'Hidden Depths - An Archaeological Exploration of Surrey's Past'

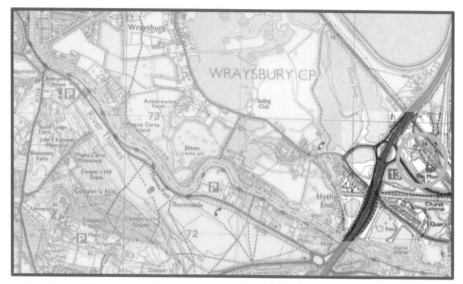

Above: Location of Yeoveney. © Crown copyright and database rights 2018 OS 100051581

1959 aerial photograph of the same site

The diagram above shows an artist's impression of a Causwayed Enclosure by water

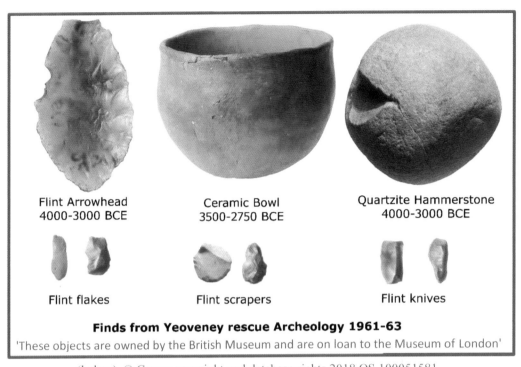

Flint Arrowhead
4000-3000 BCE

Ceramic Bowl
3500-2750 BCE

Quartzite Hammerstone
4000-3000 BCE

Flint flakes

Flint scrapers

Flint knives

Finds from Yeoveney rescue Archeology 1961-63

'These objects are owned by the British Museum and are on loan to the Museum of London'

(below) © Crown copyright and database rights 2018 OS 100051581

Superimposing the photograph on to the local map (above) shows clearly the location and size of the area. It just comes into Wraysbury. The site is unusual in the UK, being at a low level in the delta of the Colne River as it entered the Thames. The site was quarried away in 1963/64 and lies, as can be seen, south of the A30 as it approaches Junction 13 on the M25.

The period from c. 2500BCE to c. 800BCE is known as the Bronze Age when man discovered that metals could be extracted from rock by heating with fire, and a particular mixture of coper and tin made a really useful strong material, now known as Bronze. In Berkshire there was an expansion of settlements and an increasingly sophisticated exploitation of the landscape, including large-scale field systems found locally. Finds from this period also include metalwork for the first time. A Bronze Age Beaker burial has also been found at Kingsmead (artist's impression on the next page) as well as two Bronze Age farmsteads with Round Houses and a substantial Romano British Farmstead.

Artist's impression of the Horton beaker Burial

© Wessex Archaeology

© Wessex Archaeology

Among the Bronze age finds at Kingsmead from around 2000 BCE was a large Penangular ring ditch shown above

Excavations in advance of the construction of Terminal 5 at Heathrow Airport and at Virginia Water have confirmed that there were many Neolithic and Bronze Age Settlements close to water in other areas around Wraysbury. At Heathrow there was uncovered a complex settlement and farming landscape spanning later Neolithic to Saxon periods. Fragments of Neolithic cursus and a few other structures and pits attest to Neolithic activity before and associated with the Stanwell Cursus complex. By around 1700 BCE, the landscape had been apportioned and divided into field systems traversed by double-ditched trackways and incorporating small farmsteads.

The various archaeological discoveries in the area surrounding Wraysbury paint a picture of communities living in Enclosures or Villages, communicating and trading with each other with traditions and beliefs which involve Cursus activity. In particular the Neolithic Stanwell Cursus which crosses the site of Heathrow Terminal 5, shown on the next page, is large enough to draw in people from many nearby communities including Wraysbury.

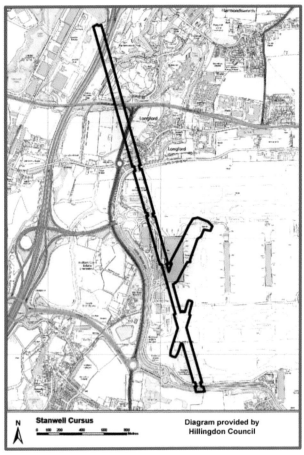

Stanwell Cursus Complex © Crown copyright and database rights 2018 OS 100051581

Much of the surface soil of Wraysbury has been removed during Gravel extraction processes which were done at a time before regular archaeological surveys of sites were done. It is therefore possible, that much archaeological evidence for prehistoric life within the modern Wraysbury boundaries has been lost because of this.

One successful excavation in Wraysbury was on a site just west of St Andrew's Church. This was excavated by The Wraysbury History Group, with Victor Marchant as the overseeing Archaeologist, between 1974 and 2008. The History group had been founded in 1972 by the late village historians Arthur Walters and Dennis Pitt who also wrote the Wirecesberie Chronology published in 2011. The location of this and other significant Wraysbury sites are shown on a following page.

Around 750 BCE humans managed to increase the temperature at which they controlled fire and discovered an even more useful metal, now known as Iron. This was the start of the Iron Age which continued until the Romans arrived in 43 CE. While there have not been specific archaeological finds in Wraysbury relating to occupation in the Iron Age, there is evidence of such occupation in many of the known prehistoric sites in the area and it is a reasonable assumption that the site next to St Andrew's Church was also occupied at this time. This site may have been the nearest to the river in Wraysbury that a permanent settlement could be established that was not at risk of flooding. Certainly pottery finds from that site indicate that it was occupied throughout the first millennium, and it was reported that there was evidence which showed the presence of earlier peoples.

Sometime during the Iron Age – perhaps around 600 BCE or even earlier - a small berry from a yew tree settled in the earth at Ankerwycke in Wraysbury and grew into a tree. As it grew older it became a spiritual place for our ancestors and a meeting point. That tree is now thought to be around 2½ to 3 thousand years old and is still growing in Wraysbury – more about the Ankerwycke Yew later in this History.

Kingsbury
Saxon Palace

Wraysbury
Archaeological
Sites

The Ankerwycke
Yew

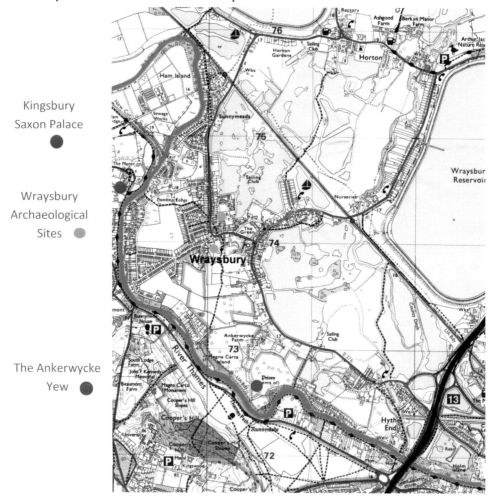

© Crown copyright and database rights 2018 OS 100051581

In the Heathrow Terminal 5 area there seems to have been little activity in the Iron Age until the emergence of a nucleated settlement of roundhouses, four-post structures and livestock enclosures in the Middle Iron Age. That settlement continued in use through to the end of the Roman period, with various modifications and realignments of the accompanying field systems.

In CE43 Britain was invaded by the Romans led by the Emperor Claudius. The Romans quickly spread throughout most of Britain, sometimes occupying and expanding the larger existing Iron Age settlements. One of these was Calleva Atrebatum – Roman Silchester – which was an important crossroads with routes to London, Bath, Gloucester and Old Sarum (Southampton). A major barrier on the road from London to Silchester (the Devil's Highway) was the River Thames and the most convenient crossing point between London and Silchester was Staines, which had an island allowing the river to be crossed using two shorter bridges. This became an important Roman residential and trading centre known as Pontes (The Bridges).

There is no evidence that Romans ever lived in Wraysbury, but we do know that they traded with the locals here as some Roman artefacts were found in the settlement near St Andrew's Church. They included a late Roman coin minted in Arles in France in the reign of Valens and Valentinian 364-378 CE shown here.

Late Roman coin – showing obverse and reverse sides
minted in Arles c.364-378CE
Source: Wraysbury History Society

The period from 410 CE, when the Romans left Britain, through to 1066 CE is known as the Anglo-Saxon period. It is known that the civilisation that had grown up around the occupying people gradually changed as the indigenous British people developed their own cultures and were augmented by immigrants arriving from the near continent. These were collectively known as the Saxons.

Along with the Roman Roads, the Rivers were still the major routes of travel at this time so it is near the River Thames in Wraysbury that items showing occupation by the Saxons have also been found. Saxon burials were found near the Primary School in Welley Road, discovered in 1984 when the swimming pool was being dug. The site is shown on the map on the previous page. The burials have been dated to the 7th Century and finds included a Saxon single edged dagger or seax. The picture below shows an example - not the one from Wraysbury - and a reconstruction of what it was probably like.

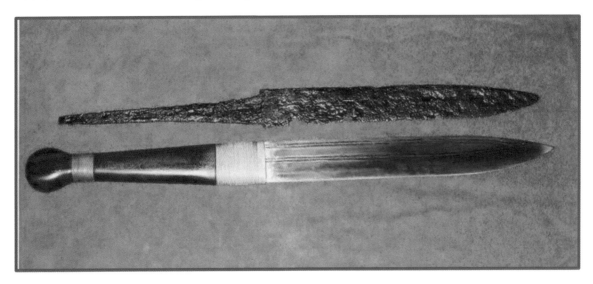

Saxon single edged dagger as found and a reconstruction
Source: Wraysbury History Society

Other dateable objects found near St Andrew's Church include a small silver Sceatta coin from 680 CE to 720 CE and a bone comb dated at around 800 CE, shown below.

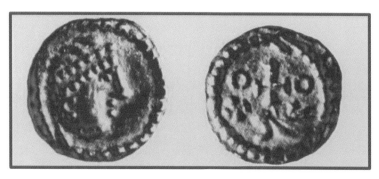

The Finds from the Dig west of St. Andrew's Church
Source: Wraysbury History Society

At Heathrow Terminal 5 the remains of an early Saxon settlement were revealed to the north-west of the earlier Bronze Age site and, after a period of apparent abandonment, new fields and stock enclosures were established in the mid-Saxon period; the area remaining as farmland into the 20th century.

It is thought that Christianity was introduced to the Anglo-Saxons in this area of the Thames Valley in about 635 CE and sometime after this a Church was established at the highest point

in the Village of Wraysbury, close to the Saxon settlement, so that it too would not be flooded when the River Thames overflowed. This is the modern site of St Andrew's Church. St Andrew was one of Christ's first disciples and a popular name for early Churches so it is possible that the Church in Wraysbury has had that name from Saxon times. The oldest artefact now in St Andrew's Church is the font, seen in the picture on the left. While the lower portion is thought to be the inverted top of a 13th Century pillar and the centre piece slightly later, the rim is thought to be pre-Norman dating from the Saxon period.

The Font in St. Andrew's Church, Wraysbury
Source: Tony Kimber

In the 9th Century King Alfred, who reigned from 871 CE to 899 CE and the Saxon and Viking Kings who followed him brought the country together so by the end of the first millennium – 1000 CE – England was a single and relatively peaceful country.

From 900 CE onwards a major influence on Wraysbury was the siting on the far side of the river Thames of the Saxon Palace at Kingsbury - what is now Old Windsor – marked on the map included earlier. It was linked to Wraysbury by a ferry across the river. In the 5th Century this small village developed into a farm with a weir and a watermill, and perhaps attracted Royal attention in the 8th Century. Certainly through the 9th and 10th Centuries it became a Royal residence and the river and Wraysbury were part of the Royal Estates. Wraysbury was good hunting ground and the nearby ferry gave the palace residents access to these grounds. Finds from excavations at Kingsbury from 1953 to 1958 included a Saxon gilt bronze sword guard.

Royal patronage increased, and lands were distributed to Royal favourites, and in 1041 CE we know that the 'Manor of Wirecesberie' as it was then known, roughly covering the current area of the village, was held by Edmund – a Thegn or Thane, who was a Land-owner by Royal Charter in return for his military service.

This all changed when England was invaded by William of Normandy in 1066 CE.

King William Ist - The Conqueror
Source: © National Portrait Gallery – Unknown Artist
1597 - 1618

The Ankerwycke Yew

Ankerwycke
Source: ©National Trust

From its seed sown in c.1500BCE to the present day
'Our Tree' has seen it all.

The trouble is, it's loved by all - and visitors come from far and wide just to see it. They leave votive offerings and strangle its branches with fertility symbols in their search for peace, love, forgiveness and who knows what else!

Will it last another 1000 years?

Wraysbury's Tree Warden and Parish Councillor
Diana Hughes, tells its story.

Part 2
of
The Wraysbury History Project

dhi

The Ankerwycke Yew and the Magna Carta Connection

Ankerwycke Farm was bought by Bucks County Council as a result of the 1937 Green Belt Act and later transferred to the Royal Borough. In 1991 Wraysbury Villagers became aware that the Borough had received an application from London Securities plc for an 18-hole 'pay as you play' golf course at Ankerwycke Farm, and a private meeting was arranged for 7th February 1991 to object to this application by concerned villagers who formed an action group. Plans included converting the existing buildings to provide changing rooms, a refreshment bar and pro-shop. Parking for 134 cars was also being sought and the applicants expected the majority of traffic movement, 400 vehicles a day in summer, to use Magna Carta Lane for access. Ankerwycke Farm comprised 170 acres of agricultural land, farm cottages and buildings as well as woods, riverside walks and Old Priory ruins and earthworks.

The Council's lease terms enforced agricultural use of the land valued at £150 per acre but the lease was not put on the open market by either the lessee or the council, and there was the likelihood that the golf facilities would be expanded still further.

Villagers were invited to a public meeting on 12th February 1991 to give their opinions on the plan. This was the beginning of the fight to save our precious heritage and it ended with the Borough Council handing over Ankerwycke Estate to the National Trust on 7th March 1998. The 99 acres of Runnymede meadows across the Thames had already been passed on to the Trust in 1931 by Lady Fairhaven, who purchased the meadows in 1929, as there had been a risk of them being sold to reduce the public debt after the war.

The magnificent 3000/4000-year-old Ankerwycke Yew owes its salvation and fame to one man, Allen Meredith, an expert on yew trees, who produced the Gazetteer of Ancient Yews in 1994, but realised their significance as early as 1974 when he was told by children that the

yew tree in Broadwell churchyard, Oxford was 200 years old. He knew instantly that this was not right and that it was much older. Even the 1983 Encyclopaedia Britannica dismissed the idea that the yew could live for thousands of years, saying that the notion was based on the fusion of close-growing trunks, none of which was more than 250 years old. He felt he that he was banging his head against a brick wall, as no-one would listen.

In 1980 Allen contacted Alan Mitchell, one of the country's leading tree experts, who eventually supported Allen's ideas about yews' great age and said 'We've now more or less agreed that these trees can be more than 4000 years old. In fact, there appears to be no theoretical end to this tree, no reason for it to die.' This is because

Allen Meredith, Russel Ball and John Sleep

if the tree is left undisturbed its branches spread

along the ground until they find suitable soil and root producing a widening circle or grove of new trees, forming what early man believed was a sacred place. Allen believes that other sacred sites such as Stonehenge might have been based on the yew groves since yew trees are believed to be 200 million years old, the oldest living things.

David Bellamy presented Allen's long study of ancient yews to the Conservation Foundation in London in 1988, and Robert Hardy, a leading actor and an expert of the yew longbow, wrote 'This extraordinary man got in touch and pointed out that the yew is the oldest living thing in the country. I decided to lend what help I could. These trees need tender loving care.'

David Bellamy (L) & Robert Hardy (R)
at the Yew

Patrick Curry, whose input was invaluable, by badgering the local council and anyone else who would listen, formed a group called Friends of Ankerwycke Yew (FAY) on 23rd May 1993, after he had met Allen who had pointed out the threat to the Ankerwycke Estate and the yew tree which was at risk of being felled to make room for the envisaged golf course. With John Sleep's vital local knowledge and through their dedication, a Tree Preservation Order was placed on the Ankerwycke Yew in April 1990 and a gathering and blessing was held on 21st June 1998 to commemorate Ankerwycke Estate and the Yew being taken into the guardianship of the National Trust.

The Blessing at the Ankerwycke Yew

Allen wrote that he first saw the tree on 23rd December 1981 when he walked along a frozen track and crossed over a stream. The trees were thick with frost, and a mist floating near the river added a certain magic to the afternoon. The tree appeared unreal since most were on high ground or in churchyards. It seemed almost part of a dream to him. He had a strong sense of its importance because in 1989, after revisiting the site, he began to receive a series of disturbing messages and dreamt about a coronation ceremony at Ankerwycke. He felt that somehow the tree was at risk and found that the area was planned for development so he also researched the area, the tree and the history of the site.

He discovered that at the time of the sealing of the Magna Carta at Runnymede in 1215, Ankerwycke was then part of Runnymede water meadows, as the River Thames changed its meandering course about 10,000 years ago according to Dr Andrew Brookes, a geomorphologist from the National Rivers Authority, and the old course of the Thames is still visible at the base of Cooper's Hill.

Matthew Paris describes the island near Staines in his document of 1236 where Henry III and William Marshal among others met to set out the Peace Treaty (Treaty of Kingston), and to reissue the Magna Carta. He said the site was off a stream near the Thames. Because of flooding, a causeway was built on the Egham side of the river during Henry's reign in about 1250, which could have led to another change in the river's course, leaving Ankerwycke on the north bank of the Thames and the wet meadows of Runnymede on the south.

Gordon Gyll, our local historian, wrote in 1861 that Runnymede was called the meadow of the Runes, or magical charms, the field of mystery, and the field of council. In Saxon times it was known as Rune-mede, implying a place of council or Witan where, originally, the runes would have been consulted. Allen has discovered that Anglo-Saxon and old Irish words for yew are found in many place names indicating that these yews were important in many areas of Britain, and were perhaps universally regarded as sacred sites. Strangely the word Ankerwycke might reveal an earlier connection with Egypt where the Ankh was a symbol of the Tree of Life and there are many place names such as Monkey Island, which could be a corruption of mo-onk or mu-ankh, meaning the water of life. Other words connected with Egypt are Khent (Kent) where it is believed the Egyptians landed, and the Isle of Thanet was thought to be derived from the Field of Tchanet in the Egyptian Delta according to Rendel Harris (Cambridge scholar)

The key to Longevity
Layering of the branches
on ground contact

Runes have deep associations with yew trees as runes were made from yew sticks and Rune-mede or Runnymede probably referred to the presence of the Ankerwycke Yew as ru/run also means yew in Saxon. Even before the Saxons the Neolithic site was of significant importance and was known as a Nemodon or Nemeton, a sacred grove or tree enclosed or protected by a ditch or water in the Celtic religion.

Allen suggested that a meeting on the Runnymede water meadow would have been risky as the hated King John would have been vulnerable to the long bows of his enemies in the armed camp so he thought that the safest place would have been the island of Ankerwycke on which stood the old yew tree, with its magnificent spread of protecting foliage, which for many centuries had been venerated by ancient tribes as a sacred central focus or Axis Mundi and a 'deva daru', an ancient guardian of wisdom.

On the island of Ankerwycke there was also a Benedictine Priory, endowed by Wraysbury's Baron Gilbert de Monfichet (Muntfichet) and his son Richard, Lord of the Manor, in about 1160, during the reign of Henry II. Wraysbury was a Crown Manor used as dower lands for the Queens of England until 1627, when it was sold by Charles 1st. The priory has been shown to be a fairly substantial building from recently-discovered foundations. The priory would have been sacred, having been built on a site already venerated, and it is possible that King John may have used it during the week before the actual sealing of the Magna Carta, which probably took place under the sacred yew tree since he would have followed the customs of chieftains and kings before him. The Ankerwycke Yew is in the centre of ancient Saxon territory, and the Witan or council of the Anglo-Saxon kings from the seventh to eleventh centuries, was held sometimes at Wraysbury, which was part of Runnymede, especially during the reign of Alfred the Great.

A Saxon-Norman manuscript, the Ancren Riwle, dated around the thirteenth century, gives evidence of a hermitage tree at Ankerwycke (ankerage meaning place of retreat or anchorite, person of secluded habits or a hermit).

When Christianity arrived in England, missionaries began to cut down the sacred yews to drive people away from paganism. Although the veneration persisted as a natural religion, the pragmatic Christian fathers then sanctified the sites and built their churches close to these sacred yews to wean people away from their ancient religion, although there can be no doubt that for some time after the conversion, people continued to light candles and offer small sacrifices under particular holy trees, and candles in Christmas trees probably hark back to those earlier times. The Benedictine Priory was founded close to the Ankerwycke Yew and there is still a little bit of the old magic in some churches with the carved heads of the Green Man, a representative of the old religion in human shape.

I know of no other conifer which sends out shoots from the whole bole of the tree as does the yew. As well as the fact that to the ancients, yew trees seemed never to die, it was possible that groves of these trees may also have caused hallucinations on warm days, since they emit a gaseous alkaloid toxin that lingers in the shade of the tree, which would appear to enhance their magic properties. Yews are also known to be toxic, apart from the flesh of the arils (red berries) and were more so when cut and withered.

To reinforce the importance of the Ankerwycke Yew and the granting of freedoms under the law, there was another celebration in 1992, on the 777th anniversary of the sealing of the Magna Carta drawn up by David Bellamy to try and protect our planet. It read "We the free people of the islands of Great Britain on the 777th anniversary of the signing of Magna Carta do: Look back and give thanks for the benefits that the signings, sealings and swearings of oaths on that document handed down to us. Look forward to new age of freedom through sustainability by granting the following rights to all the sorts of plants and animals with which we share our islands and our planet". Let us now look more closely at the Yew to see why it was so important to early man and us today.

It is notoriously difficult to date yews as they all become hollow after a thousand years or so, and in 1806 Dr. Samuel Lysons recorded Ankerwycke girth as 30ft, and in 1994, it was measured by Allen at 31ft. A girth of this size indicates a 3000-4000-year-old tree.

Oil Painting of Ankerwycke Yew
Source: Alan Bennett-Brunel University

John Lowe, who wrote a standard work on yews, said, "The base was a good deal broken away, and hollow up to 5 ft. The trunk above this point, which at one time was hollow, is now filled with a mass of trunk-like roots, to a degree more remarkable than any I have ever seen". Trees within a tree. Allen Meredith has suggested that if a core were taken from the ground near the tree, pollen grains might indicate a more precise age for the tree as with ice cores.

It has been found that rather than the girth increasing every year, in some adverse weather conditions it could actually shrink and that the girth might remain unchanged for hundreds of years. In 2005, the Ankerwycke Yew was featured on the cover of the Tree Guardian, published by the Tree Council, celebrating the 15th Anniversary of the Tree Warden Scheme, and is considered to be a green monument.

It is believed that the tree was planted rather than grown naturally as it was on ground that never flooded. It used to be thought that a group or ring of yews had been bundle-planted but with further research is has been found that when the lower branches touch the ground, as previously mentioned, they root as can be seen from the photo so that when these trees reach thousands of years of age they die and leave a copse or ring of trees, some of which may act like flying buttresses as in large cathedrals. One might ask, "Which came first?" In Allen Meredith's Gazetteer of Ancient Yews published in "The Sacred Yew" by Anand Chetan and Diana Brueton, there were about 16 trees of 3000+ years of age, and eight of four thousand years or more. Allen has only recorded the age of those yews he has actually seen, I quote as follows:

"Bettws Newdd, Gwent 33ft (est. 4000 years); Crowhurst, Surrey 32ft (4,000 years); Discoed Powys 37ft (5,000 years); Fortingall, Tayside, 56ft (at least 5,000 years); Langernyw, Clwyd, 5,000 years (this being impossible to measure, as it was a circle of yews on a prehistoric site and there was an oil tank inside an old yew); Linton, Hereford & Worcester 33ft (4,000 years); Payhembury, Devon 46ft 6in (impossible to age; old trunk split and separated); Tisbury, Wiltshire 31ft (4,000 years)."

Looking at some of these measurements it seems that our Ankerwycke Yew could well be 4,000 years of age. The average growth for most of the oldest trees was less than half inch a year and some may not have increased for hundreds of years. The oldest tree in Europe could be the Fortingall Yew, last measured 200 years ago, and believed by many to be 8,000 years old. It has split in two and appears as two trees but both portions are male and from the same root and as late as the early eighteenth century it was recognisably a vast though split whole. Some of its branches have turned female, with berries.

The cover of the Tree Guardian
Source: Diana Hughes

The writer asked the Tree Council not to publicise the Ankerwycke Yew as footfall could cause compaction of the soil around the tree causing stress and curtailing its life but the National Trust reported that because it has strong spiritual value people are leaving tokens in the tree and even resorting to putting coins into the bark. The National Trust Head Warden Robin Lewis told the members of FAY that they would put a fence around the tree to protect it. From an old photo there appears to be a portion of chestnut paling originally surrounding the tree. Guardians such as the NT should be protecting such a very venerable, much loved tree. I, as a Tree Warden, hoped that our magnificent yew would survive for another 1000 years but it is being sorely mistreated. Without man's interference, these trees would never die but continue to produce new trees through layering provided they were given the time and space.

Moving on to Ankerwycke House, there is a little book which is free from copyright, entitled 'Reminiscences of Eton' by Henry John Crickitt Blake, born in 1791, whose grandfather lived at Ankerwycke and I would like to relate some of his reminiscences in his own words set down in 1831.

Henry wrote "At 8 years of age I was entered at Eton, that little world of life and happiness, and was placed, as was then considered high for my years, in the Lower Greek. At this time my father left Upton, and constantly made Doctors' Commons his place of residence for many years. Though I lost the near neighbourhood of my father by his removal, still it was amply compensated by the kindness of my maternal Grandfather, who resided at Ankerwyke (sic) House, only five miles distant from Windsor, not far from the Bells of Ousley (*sic*), a romantic public house on the Thames and directly opposite to the far-famed Runnymede. Upon the grounds attached to the venerable old Mansion was a majestic yew tree, under which, among the old inhabitants of the Hamlet, in contradiction to History, the tradition was, that the celebrated signature of England's liberty, the Magna Carta extorted from King John by the independent Barons, was there signed, by that hitherto tyrannical prince."

"It was certainly one of the finest specimens of that almost antiquated species of tree, which is anywhere to be found in this country: and admirably adapted to the purpose for which it was then supposed to have been used. How frequently in the Holidays, have I, together with my cousins and perhaps friend from Eton, whom with kind Grandfather's permission I had invited to pass a few days with us, given the old Gardener the slip; and then, by placing our sentinels, have we received the peaches and the various productions of a luxuriant garden, handed over to us by our confederate on the other side, and enjoyed a noble feast, seated on the branches of this venerable tree. Here ensconced among its foliage, we bade adieu to the cares of school, regardless of all except the present pleasure".

He goes on to say "A few pages in this place to a description of Ankerwyke (sic) House, may not perhaps be uninteresting. It was an ancient nunnery of vast extent, and approached from the high road by a noble avenue of cedars and yew trees, which imported to it that gloom, which mostly environed the houses attached to religious education. To us boys, an indescribable awe was excited in our minds, when traversing its long and shadowy chambers and frequently, even in midday, have we dreaded to explore its upper chambers, where the refractory nuns were accustomed to be confined, and where the iron rings in the wall, recalled to the mind the harrowing punishments, which too often, in those days, were inflicted on the deluded inmates of monkish ignorance and barbarity. Not one of us younkers would have volunteered to have ascended to the upper rooms after nightfall without a light on any account: this foolish dread originated, I imagine in a scheme of the servants, who, to deter us boys from trespassing on their orgies in the servant's hall used to give out that certain noises were heard at night: that chains rattled in the cellars; and that the ghosts of nuns, displaying their unearthly shapes, were then to be seen."

"At any rate the desired object was gained: the great hall, and the long and dreary passage from thence to the servant's hall, were not traversed except by compulsion or mandate from the governor, and then with fear and trembling. At any rate, with all this mixture of boyish fears, those days were the happiest; and though long gone by, and the place of them levelled to the ground, by a new proprietor, and Indian Nabob, whose estate adjoined, and who purchased the property when my grandfather left it: and though this venerable fabric was destroyed with almost sacrilegious hand; and the only reason given for this spoliation was, that an interesting ruin might be visible from his own gew-gaw modern mansion."

"I mentioned the great hall, of course it was the entrance to the house, and situated between the dining and drawing rooms, and was about forty feet long, with lofty stone windows, in several compartments of which, were some beautifully enriched specimens of painting: more particularly family arms, bishops and their crosiers, and nuns praying to their ghostly fathers. It was often the scene of frolic to us, when a wet day would not allow us to have our sports externally: battledoor (sic) and shuttlecock, leap frog, in short, an anything to while away the time, was enacted in the great hall."

Later on, we read "A few words respecting my most excellent and generous grandfather. For some service performed for Admiral Keppel, united to an intimacy with the minister, William Pitt he had obtained the lucrative situation of Marshall of the High Court of Admiralty, a situation which in the time of war, produced upwards of fifteen thousand pounds per annum.

As I had the good fortune to be his favourite grandson, I very frequently experienced the fruits of it. He it was that sent me to Eton, and was at the sole expense of my education." We can see from his little book the richness of Wraysbury's history and that Ankerwycke House was probably the Benedictine Priory founded by the Montfichets and dissolved by Henry VIII. Henry would have taken the land but not necessarily had the house destroyed.

Henry's description of the setting of the Ankerwycke Yew is similar to that feeling of mystery felt by Allen Meredith when he first encountered the Ankerwycke Yew over 100 years later.

Looking a little more deeply into the history of the Magna Carta and the reasons for the revolt of the barons, we need to mention Professor David Carpenter of King's College London who has thoroughly researched what I believe to be the definitive history of our famous Magna Carta, which helps us to really understand the hatred for King John who carried out fines, disseisins (dispossession of land) and taxed his tenants-in-chief heavily and arbitrarily for his wars in France, and took the children of barons as hostages when he suspected their loyalty or they owed him money.

Corfe Castle
Source: Wikipedia

One of his most hideous acts was the starvation of Matilda, the daughter of Henry II, who married William de Briouze, a baronial lord of Ireland. She had previously refused to hand over her sons to John as hostages, although her younger son Richard did become a hostage. As William de Briouze owed John a great deal of money, some 5,000 marks (a mark, common currency, was two-thirds of a pound i.e. 160 old pence), for the grant of Limerick, which he could not pay, his lands were taken and he became a refugee, leaving his wife Matilda and eldest son William in Ireland. They escaped to Scotland but were captured and imprisoned in Corfe Castle for the husband's debt. Matilda was described as the most beautiful and famous lady of her age. When the king's ministers came to the prison to demand the first instalment of a debt of 50,000 marks for the life and limbs of herself and her family, she only had £16 and a little gold, so she and her son were starved to death in 11 days, and it was reported that Matilda had eaten her dead son's cheeks in desperation. John used this as a threat to others who defaulted. This case alone would have revolted his subjects and turned England against their monarch, but he also cruelly starved to death twenty-two French knights captured at Mirebeau in 1207.

Around 19th October 1214 at Bury St Edmunds the earls and barons met and agreed to make war on the king unless he accepted the coronation charter of Henry I and the laws of Edward the Confessor who were more benign Kings.

On his refusal William Marshal, the King's leading knight and Earl of Pembroke, and the barons seized the city of London and would not disarm, eventually forcing the King to agree to the terms of the Articles of the Barons, which were the basis of the Magna Carta sealed at Ankerwycke, then part of Runnymede. Magna Charta was not so named at the time as there was also a later Forest Charter of 1217. It was during the copying of the charter by scribes that the term greater charter was first recorded to differentiate it from the lesser or Forest Charter.

It was of course written in Latin and then translated into French since this was the language of the Court. It was not until later that an English version was produced. The Forest Charter was an important document in that some of the newly-planted forests were to be cut down to free the land for agriculture and grazing, and weirs were to be removed to permit navigation. Forests were important to Kings as their main sport was hunting - evidently King John was an addict - the hunters crossing the river Thames on rafts together with their dogs to hunt in Wraysbury where stands a house called King John's Hunting Lodge (once Place Farm) which might have been built on the original site.

On 15th June 1215 the twenty-five barons[1], including seven earls, who were to execute the charter were not yet chosen by the signatories mentioned in the Magna Carta but they all had to take the oath. In John's letter of 19 June, the sheriffs were to publicly read the charter throughout their bailiwicks and obey the orders of the twenty-five barons. John dragged his feet over distributing the charter and his letter, as he hoped that the peace would remain and that he could continue his usual practices. It was believed that King John's aim was to obstruct the taking of the oath by the four knights elected by county courts who were to circulate the Charter. However, on 24th August 1215, King John asked Pope Innocent to release him from his oath because it was obtained under duress so the barons raised military forces, which included some 1,082 knights.

King John knew he was defeated when the barons and knights invited Prince Louis of France, to become King of England. He landed at Kent on 21st May 1216 with an army and was ready to become king but John placed his kingdom and his son Henry under the Pope's protection on 15th October 1216 and died of dysentery during the night of 16th October, so Henry III at the tender age of nine was under the trusted guardianship of William Marshal, the regent, until he reached the age of majority at 21. A revised charter was reissued as the young King's coronation charter on 12th November. The battle of Lincoln took place on 20 May 1217 as Prince Louis still had aspirations to become king, but his Anglo-French forces were defeated by William Marshal, and the fleet bringing reinforcements from France was destroyed on 24th August 1217. In September 1217 Louis resigned his claim to the throne of England, though he very nobly did his best to help his followers recover their lands.

The forest or coronation charter of 1217 was identical to the definitive 1225 charter, which had a long list of witnesses, headed by Stephen Langton, Archbishop of Canterbury, who took a leading role in the negotiations for the charter, eleven bishops and twenty abbots, plus many earls and magnates, and eight members of the original twenty-five barons who took the oath of the 1215 charter, but it omitted the security clause (61) of 1215 which gave the barons the right to distrain and distress the king in every way they could until a wrong had been righted. The 1217 charter included benefits for the unfree, which for the first time

---

[1] Of these 25 barons, one William de Lanvellei III is a direct ancestor of Graham Sinclair. William's grandfather married Gunnora St. Clair.

meant the ordinary villein, stating that no-one was to suffer death or mutilation punishments for offences against beasts of the forests. This of course enabled free men to use the forests and create new arable land. It also helped widows in that their dower was defined as a third of the land their husbands had held in his lifetime unless less had been agreed in the marriage settlement. One can still see this reflected nowadays in 'pre-nups'. There was never another new charter issued but just a reaffirmation of the 1225 charter, many parts of which are on the statute book today, and it also forms the basis of law in western civilisation. It is the heart of the American Constitution, and in England the Accession Council, which will convene in St James's Palace when Charles is proclaimed King, long predates parliament. The meeting, of the Lords Spiritual and Temporal of this Realm, derives from the Witan, the Anglo-Saxon feudal assembly of more than 1,000 years ago.

We hope that the Ankerwycke Yew does not become just another item of idle curiosity on the tourist trail or a place for empty rituals, and most importantly that it continues to flourish for thousands of years to come. It is now believed that under its boughs the sealing of the Magna Carta was enacted which shielded everyone from arbitrary rule, and that it would last 'in perpetuity'. We hope this will also be true for our treasured Yew.

----ooo0ooo---

Old engraving of the Ankerwycke Yew - early 19th century

The Wraysbury Crest

ARMS: *Chevronny of six Or and Gules a Swan rousant proper gorged with a Saxon Crown Or with Chain reflexed over the back Or in base wavy barry wavy of four Azure and Argent.*

CREST: *On a Wreath Or and Vert an Oak Tree eradicated proper*

Incorporating the shield of Monfichet (Muntfichet), Wraysbury's Baron, who would have known of the Ankerwycke Yew and its importance to the Priory which he endowed.
Crest Designed by Carl Hughes

The red and yellow chevron background is from the arms of Monfichet, one of the Barons at the sealing of the Magna Carta and Lord of the Manor of Wraysbury.

The main area is occupied by the traditional White Swan of Buckingham, which is common to the arms of the County Council and the former Borough of Buckingham in which Wraysbury used to lie. In the formers arms the swan has a gold ducal crown about the neck, with a gold chain attached, (though in the Buckingham arms recorded at the Visitations the crown has no chain). Here the swan's neck is encircled by the gold Saxon crown from the County crest referring to the fact that Wraysbury was once the home of the Saxon kings' hunting lodge.

The white and blue waves represent the River Thames in its course across the county's southerly parts. The whole shield thus indicates the historic nature of Wraysbury once in the southern most part of Buckinghamshire and watered by the Thames.

The colours of the wreath indicate the green of the forests with the oak representing the Royal Forests of Windsor.

The word Wyrardisbury in the motto is the old spelling of Wraysbury.

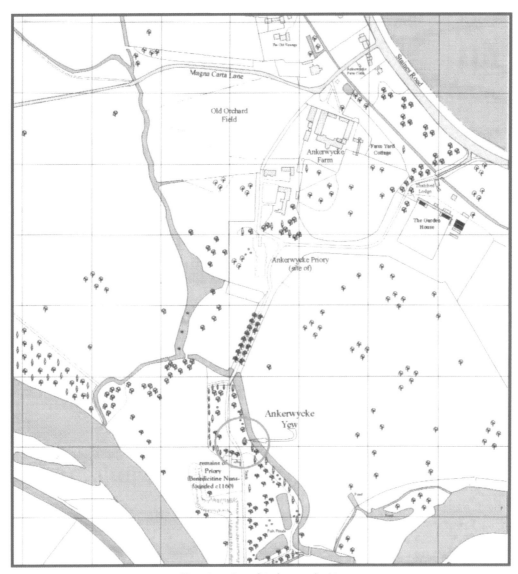

Showing site of Ankerwycke Yew

Bibliography & References:

'The Sacred Yew' by Anand Chetan and Diana Brueton – Rediscovering the ancient Tree of Life through the work of Allen Meredith. Penguin/Arkana (1994).

'Magna Carta' - With a new commentary by Professor David Carpenter of King's College London, Penguin Classics (2015)

'The Ankerwycke Yew – Living Witness to the Magna Carta' by Janis Fry with research by A. Meredith Pro Print, Carmarthen (2014)

'Reminiscences of Eton' by Henry John Crickitt Blake. BiblioLife, LLC (1831)

Personal communication with Allen Meredith

'Egypt in Britain' – Rendel Harris (1927)

Photographs supplied by John Sleep and Diana Hughes (Tree Warden – Ankerwycke Yew)

The Middle Bit

The Normans to the 20ᵗʰ Century

From those French speaking Normans to the Industrial Revolution
and the start of the 20ᵗʰ century, Wraysbury was here.
None of your 'New Town' business for us!

King Harold's defeat at Hastings - Scene 57 - Bayeux Tapestry
Source: ©Myrabella@Wikipedia Commons

Weaving her way through the years, lady Mayoress and leader of the
Parish Council, Margaret Lenton, tells us all about it.

Part 3
of
The Wraysbury History Project

The Normans to the 20th Century

This chapter takes the history of Wraysbury from the Norman Conquest to the beginning of the twentieth century. The story of Wraysbury is that it connects with historical events and in this chapter with the developments that are affecting Britain as a nation. Some aspects of this history are being included in a separate chapter about the final demise of Ankerwycke House and its lands.

Through the centuries, Wraysbury was a largely agricultural village beside the Thames which over the period changed its course. The villagers worked the land and paid dues to the church and to their lord. They were affected by climate and by events such as the 'Black Death'. Wraysbury features in the Domesday Book compiled in 1086 by William the Conqueror to survey his new realm. The spelling appears as Wirecesberie and is listed under Buckinghamshire villages. It is shown as owned by Robert Gernon, one of William I conquering barons and also a cousin, and as having 2 mills, hay for the cattle of the court and four fisheries. The land belonged to the Crown or King and it was granted by the King to people for various services, i.e. military, personal or as the King saw fit. Initially such grants were made on the commitment to provide men and/or to lead them in battle for the King. These were known as Knights' Fees. They were eventually replaced by an obligation to provide money and became the forerunner of taxation. Hence the manor of Wraysbury was at the King's disposal to grant to individuals for life, or their successors, or for the King to use as dower land for his Queen's marriage settlements.

Robert Gernon also held land in Stanstead Montfichet, Essex, from which, according to Gyll's History, Robert's son William took the name Montfichet. The next descendant was Sir Gilbert who founded the Benedictine Priory at Ankerwycke in 1157. This is the earliest known building in Wraysbury, pre-dating the current St. Andrew's church by about 60 years. It is known however, that a church had existed on this site since about 1112, with the rector being the Abbot of St. Peter, Gloucester. Although the priory was destroyed during the Dissolution of the Monasteries under Henry VIII, a length of wall still exists. The Montfichet line died out in 1268 with the death of Sir Richard Montfichet, who was one of the Barons present at the sealing of the Magna Carta in 1215. This is the most famous event in Wraysbury's history and whilst Egham asserts that the sealing took place in Runnymede and lays claim to the event, Runnymede was in the parish of Wraysbury at this time and for hundreds of years after.

The right to hold Wraysbury lands then passed through Sir Richard's sister, Aveline, who was portrayed in the Wraysbury Legend, Son et Lumiere, part of 1977 Silver Jubilee celebrations, and then to her granddaughter also called Aveline. She married Edmund, Earl of Lancaster in 1269 who was the second son of Henry III and they are both buried in Westminster Abbey.

It is thought that at around this time Place Farm House, or King John's Hunting Lodge as it is now called, was built. This very early date applies only to a small part of the house standing today, as it was greatly extended later in the 16th century and it was for this reason that it was always thought to be of Elizabethan origin. It is not recorded who built the house but around 1289 is the possible build date, a John de Remenham is recorded as holding land in Wraysbury and it is possible that he commissioned the house to be built. The present Remenham House

Place Farm House
(aka King John's Hunting Lodge)
Source: wraysbury.net

and the estate that King John's Hunting Lodge used to be part of, therefore derives its name from this Remenham family. This part of Wraysbury then became known as the Manor of Remenham. This same family also gave their name to the village of Remenham, just outside Henley where they owned substantial land.

King John's Hunting Lodge is a listed building and on examination in 1973, Buckinghamshire County Planning Committee, recorded the following: *'The timber framed medieval hall is of exceptional interest and outstanding national importance. Many of the features in the hall are without known parallel in medieval timber framed buildings, and others are highly unusual. The simultaneous combination of several such distinctive carpentry techniques in a singular structure is completely without precedent. Although built on land belonging to the Crown in the Middle Ages, there is nothing in the hall as it now stands, early enough to be ascribed to the reign of King John (1199-1216), but it is unlikely to have been built later than about 1275. It is by far the oldest secular building in Buckinghamshire and amongst the oldest remaining minor domestic residences in the country as a whole.'*

Wraysbury people were well connected and Place Farm House as it was then called, was inherited by Sir Walter Stonor b.1479, through his mother, Sybil Brecknock, the daughter and heiress of David Brecknock of Wraysbury. He was the son of Henry VI's treasurer who had acquired the manors of Wraysbury and Remenham around the beginning of the 16th century. Sir Walter lived there until 1512 and it is believed that it was he who had the considerable extension carried out. He took part in the wars in the early part of Henry VIII's reign and was knighted on the field at the Battle of Flodden in 1513. He was charged to take his ten tallest soldiers and three horses and attend on the Queen, Catherine of Aragon, at the famous Field of the Cloth of Gold in 1520. Towards the end of Henry VIII's reign in 1545, Henry rewarded Sir Walter for his years of faithful service by making him Lieutenant of the Tower of London. Sir Walter's only son John, died as a child and is buried in St. Andrew's church. He is depicted on a brass* under the carpets, dressed it is believed, as an Eton scholar. *See Page ML12

Sir Walter's daughter, Elizabeth, now Elizabeth Hoby[1] outlived three husbands and she returned to Wraysbury where she died in 1560 and is also buried in St. Andrews. It is worth noting that in King John's Hunting Lodge, there were some stained-glass windows depicting a shield of the Royal arms of Henry VIII and Catherine of Aragon, and another showing the Arms of the Stonor family, these were removed when the Hargreaves family moved to Fulmer Grange around 1930. [1]See also page ML5

Other important events in the history of Wraysbury occurred in the year 1347, in the reign of Edward III and his victorious battles, culminating with his victory at the Battle of Crecy. He likened his battles to those of legend and the Knights of the Round Table and, to give thanks

for his victory, he established The Most Noble Order of the Garter, and to show his humility he set up a new religious foundation. This was The Royal Free Chapel of St. George's, Windsor Castle, and to fund this foundation he endowed it by appropriating the income from eleven churches, the first of which was St. Andrew's, Wraysbury in 1348. This changed the status of St. Andrew's from a Rectory to a Vicarage and under this ancient right, it gave the chapel the right to appoint vicars and to collect the tithes that were payable to St. Andrew's. Apart from this short period 1350 – 1355, the Wraysbury lands were let out to farm and the rents were payable direct to St. Georges Chapel.

Arms of The Noble Order of the Garter
Source: Wikipedia

Another house of medieval date is Welley House, built in 1460 by Sir Richard Willy, on a stretch of the Thames reputed to be called The Welley, certainly there are plenty of references to Welley (Welly) on the map shown here. It is believed that this association caused the naming of the house and Welley Road, although what really came first is unclear. Sir Richard was granted land in Wraysbury by Edward IV in 1460 and according to Gyll's History, it was once used as a wharf and beer house before the Bells of Ouseley was established. It was a substantial house with large grounds which according again to Gyll was demolished around 1830, this was due to the old Windsor Lock Cut made in 1822 which isolated the house. In researching Place Farm, a document was traced to the Bodleian Library and there was found a map dated 1756 which clearly showed Welley House and its location in what is now The Avenue. With the aid of the map is was possible to pinpoint the house as being close to No.25 and at this address there is gap between the houses that is now believed to be the old entrance way to Welley House.

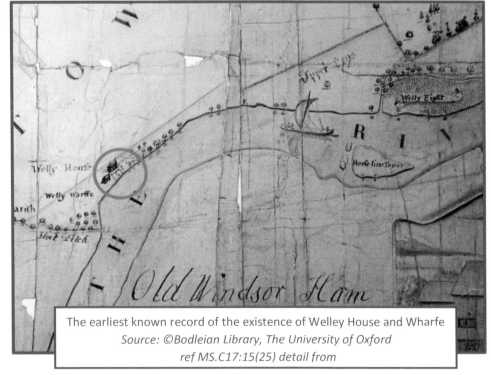

The earliest known record of the existence of Welley House and Wharfe
Source: ©Bodleian Library, The University of Oxford
ref MS.C17:15(25) detail from

A critical period in time came in1537, when the Priory at Ankerwycke was dissolved and the estate, valued at £132.0s.2d[1] was given to Bisham Abbey, which itself was dissolved in 1540 as one of the larger institutions. The lease of the land which had been granted to John Norris for 21 years, was transferred to Andrew, Lord Windsor, who is recorded as being a steward at the Priory in 1534. Lord Windsor was a Knight of the Bath, a Member of Parliament and was present at the Field of the Cloth of Gold when Henry VIII met Francis I. In addition to the land, he owned all the weirs and fisheries in the Thames from Ankerwycke Ferry to Old Windsor. Thanks to him, some of the land at Queensmead, subsequently known as the Bridge Lands Trust, became one of the larger charities in the gift of Wraysbury Parochial Charities.

In 1550, Sir Thomas Smith was granted the Ankerwycke Priory estate and started building the first Ankerwycke House. He had become a fellow of Queen's College, Cambridge at 17 and a Professor at 19. Under the Catholic Queen Mary I, who became Queen in 1553, his ownership was challenged unsuccessfully, but he lost office because he was a Protestant. He was possibly Wraysbury's most important resident, a statesman and a scholar, he moved in 'high circles' and became a courtier under Edward VI. In 1547 he was made Provost of Eton College where there is a portrait of him. He was knighted in 1549 and managed to remain a figure of influence in Henry VIII's reign and his succeeding children's reigns and religions!

Sir Thomas Smith
Source: © National Portrait
Gallery D25353 – R.W. Sievier
Poss. Early 19c

In Elizabeth I reign he served as a Member of Parliament and was twice ambassador to France. He was granted more land in Wraysbury which included the old Manor of Remenham and this thereafter followed the same manorial descent as Ankerwycke, the two now combined to form the Manor of Wraysbury.

In 1560 he was involved in a very nasty dispute with Edmund and Thomas Windsor, sons of Sir Andrew Windsor. They claimed that Henry VIII had granted Ankerwycke to their father for life and that Sir Thomas's claim was fraudulent as it had never been the Crown's to sell. Not content with trying to drag Sir Thomas through the courts, they raised a gang and marched on Ankerwycke, breaking into the property with swords and daggers drawn and evicted Smith's staff and took the keys. Sir Thomas being notified of this, raised his own men plus the local constable to recover the house. They were attacked again by the Windsor rebels with swords and bows and arrows. Smith was so outraged that he appealed to Star Chamber who found in his favour, he had no more trouble from the Windsor set.

He later moved away as he found 'it was obnoxious to rheums and colds as being cow and waspish'. However, he did not move until after Queen Elizabeth visited him in 1565, which must have involved vast expense and preparation. He surveyed Ankerwycke and Wraysbury, listing tenants, their holdings, acreage of the fields and their yields, but his tenure was not without difficulty as he accused his Bailiff of cheating and not producing enough crops. He had wanted the estate to go to his illegitimate son, also Thomas, but he was murdered by his

[1] Old money had £'s, shillings and pence. £1 = 20 shillings, 1 shilling = 5p and 2.4 pence = 1p. A Nobleman's income was £1,500 - £3,000 p.a.; A merchant £100 p.a.; A parson £20 p.a.; A carpenter £13 p.a. and a labourer £5 – 10 p.a.

own staff during an ill-conceived skirmish in Ireland. His nephew who he also greatly favoured, died also before Sir. Thomas and after his death in 1577, the estate passed to his brother.

It was the closing of the priory and the transfer of its Ankerwycke lands from ecclesiastic to secular hands that effectively changed the seat of manorial power from Remenham to Ankerwycke and there it remained until the Harcourt family sold Ankerwycke in the 1920s. Whereas Wraysbury was still Crown land, it could now be split into three different areas of ownership under the Crown. In the north-west, Remenham; the centre, Ankerwycke and finally, the south-east, Queensmead.

Queensmead had long been assigned by the King for his Queens as dower lands and this has been the case from the reign of Edward III in 1327 through Richard II, Henry IV, Edward IV, Henry VIII and finally to three of Henry VIII's Queens, Catherine of Aragon, Anne Boleyn and Jane Seymour. Queensmead went on to have rather a difficult period in more modern times with the compulsory purchase of The Church Lands[2] by the South-West Suburban Water Company, once freely roamed by residents and owned by Wraysbury Parochial Charities.

Other leading residents of Ankerwycke included Edward de Vere, Earl of Oxford who lodged with Sir Thomas Smith, Lady Elizabeth Hoby[*1], who was part of Henry VIII's sixth Queen Catherine Parr's circle, and her son Walter who moved into Remenham Manor.

Edward de Vere - 17th Earl of Oxford - *Source: © National Portrait Gallery-After Joseph Brown*

In 1627, Charles I started the break-up of the ownership of Wraysbury by selling Ankerwycke to the London merchant John Sharowe, for £617.16s.1¼d (old money-pre-decimal). It was not long after that the Remenham part was also sold off to the Smith family, then the Hale family whose last owner Dr. Richard Hale, bequeathed it to Thomas Tower, who was responsible for the map of the estate found in the Bodleian Library as mentioned earlier. Accordingly, Wraysbury ceased to be part of the dower lands of the Queens of England and ended the direct connection with the crown of England through its Royal ownership.

The Tower family sold off Remenham in 1785 and it came into the hands of the Gyll family, eventually coming down to Gordon Gyll in about 1865. On Gordon's death it went to his son Fleming who sold it to Captain Charles Hargreaves and it believed that he built Remenham House about 1885. Although the Gylls owned the Remenham Estate, they do not appear to have ever lived there, choosing to live instead at Wraysbury House, the former original rectory on the Glebe Lands owned by the church from whom the Gyll family leased it. There is not much information on this house except that Gyll states that it had not had a spiritual tenant since 1349, this was around the date that St. Andrew's church and lands were granted to

[*1]See also page ML2   [2]Now a Gravel Pit – Queensmead Lake

St. George's Chapel. It was later occupied by the Herring family. On its change from Rectory to Vicarage in 1348, the Vicarage in Vicarage Lane, Staines Road was used. This old house is still standing but set back from the road and not easily seen.

Subsequently, in about 1885, the then vicar Seymour Neville bought The Grange and made substantial alterations, and what we see today is predominantly the result of his changes. This then became the next vicarage. When the next vicar came, the Revd. John Hindson, who was vicar from 1880 to 1895, a new vicarage was built c.1890 in Station Road. There is more on these old houses on page ML10 and in Part 4 of this book.

William Pynchon
Source: City of Springfield 1888

Wraysbury had experienced religious changes arising from Henry VIII's break with the Church of Rome, which resulted in St Andrew's Church ceasing to be a Catholic church and becoming Anglican. However, there is also evidence of Puritanism in the village and William Pynchon of Wraysbury proved an outspoken preacher. He emigrated to America and founded the town of Springfield, Massachusetts. He returned to Wraysbury during the Commonwealth in 1652 and was buried in the churchyard.

In 1634 Communion silverware was presented to the church. Over the years bells were added to the church, the first in 1591. In 1657 two more bells were installed, followed after the Restoration of Charles II in 1664 by three more. An altarpiece made of leather and painted by Hassel was a feature of the church but this was taken out in the 19th century, a picture of it is shown here along with St. Andrew's wooden pulpit which dates from 1680. The Ankerwycke portion, having now assumed the

St. Andrew's leather Altarpiece
Source: Tony Kimber

St. Andrew's Pulpit - 1680
Source: Tony Kimber

manorship of Wraysbury from Remenham, passed into the hands of the Lee family in 1685 and eventually, through their female line, into the first of the Harcourt family, Philip in 1725. Philip lived in the house built by Sir Thomas Smith probably for some of the time. Property owners often leased out their properties and lived elsewhere. This can be quite confusing when trying to find out who actually lived where and when. However, Philip must have spent some time here as he was a Church Warden and attended Parish Vestry Meetings, also we have his signature on a Vestry Minutes Book of 1734. Registers exist from St Andrew's church dating from 1734 and marriage registers from 1754.

Philip died in 1759 without issue and was succeeded by his brother John, who upon his death in 1785, was succeeded by his son, John Simon Harcourt. It seems he was not as financially aware as his ancestors and the estate became run down and was sold off to John Blagrove in 1794, who held it until his death in 1829. John Blagrove built a new Ankerwycke House in 1805 and spent a lot of money in restoring the Ankerwycke Estate, which is believed to have been generated from his plantations in Jamaica, presumably of sugar cane and slave labour.

Glorious Ankerwycke House in its sad demise 1974
Source: Wraysbury Archives

This house was to become the new manor house and so it remained through many families and dire situations.

Open to wind, rain, vandals and the occasional visit by Wraysbury History Club, there were no tea and cakes at the Manor when this photo was taken! Note the cars of the era. Whatever happened to this lovely old house? Find out later in this book.

Wraysbury village was still largely an agricultural area but some industry existed. Henry Bulstrode of Horton owned both the paper mill and the Hythe End Mill. In 1722 the mills in Wraysbury were offered for sale in the Daily Courant and one was listed as an iron mill. Copper milling took place until 1820. Working at the mills could not have been a healthy occupation as arsenic was used in the production of paper. There is an advert for the sale of the Mill in 1842 on the next page.

At the beginning of the 19th century, the Enclosure Acts were implemented in Wraysbury and common land was coming under private ownership. The Lord of the Manor of Wraysbury presented a Bill to Parliament claiming what was then a lot of common land. A great number of villagers protested and presented a petition of their own to Parliament. For poor villagers, loss of common rights presented a threat to their livelihood, hardly enabling them to exist. To ensure passage of the Bill, a clause was added which awarded the 8 yards either side of the River Colne in perpetuity to the inhabitants of Wraysbury, to cut withies from the stream and throw mud from it upon the bank. Over the centuries in difficult times of bad weather and harvests, the amount of common land diminished, as smaller landholdings proved inadequate to support families. The Inclosure (Enclosure) Award map in the Wraysbury Archives details the provision of space for a Wraysbury Fair.

Sales by Auction.

WRAYSBURY COPPER MILLS, PLANT, AND MACHINERY, BUCKS.

MR. GADSDEN has received instructions from the Assignees of Messrs. Glascott, (and with consent of the Mortgagees), to SELL by AUCTION, at Garraway's Coffee House, London, on WEDNESDAY, August 10th, 1842, (instead of the 13th of July, as previously advertised), at 12 o'clock, an important and valuable property known as the WRAYSBURY COPPER MILLS, about five miles from the Slough and West Drayton Railway Stations, comprising extensive ranges of buildings completely fitted with powerful water wheels, several pairs of iron rolls, hammers, shears, lathes, drawing benches, furnaces, and every description of machinery of the best construction and ready for immediate working, possessing capability of manufacture to a very great extent. The water power is unlimited, and the situation of the property (on the banks of the Colne) is extremely convenient. There are also Two excellent Residences, suitable for the occupation of the partners, together with a superintendent's house, ten cottages, out buildings, gardens, and land, and an excellent wharf on the Thames, opposite Old Windsor, affording the greatest facility of water carriage. This extremely desirable property is admirably arranged, and the Plant and Machinery are of a superior order, and when, in addition to its present great advantages, the alteration in the tariff admitting foreign ore to be smelted for home consumption is considered, it may be fairly asserted that the opportunity of acquiring a rapid fortune afforded by this sale has been rarely equalled.

The premises may be viewed till the sale by order, to be obtained at Mr. Gadsden's offices, 18, Old Broad-street, where full particulars and inventories of the plant may be had ; particulars may also be obtained of Mr. P. Johnson, official assignee, Basinghall-street ; of Mr. Phillips, solicitor, 31, Lombard-street ; at the Castle Hotel, Windsor ; the White Hart, Slough ; and at Garraway's.

Wraysbury Copper Mill for sale
Source: Windsor & Eton Express
6th August 1842

In the first National Census of 1801 the population of Wraysbury was shown as 616 with 96 inhabited houses, 2 uninhabited dwellings and 103 families. In 1811, the numbers had fallen to 560. In 1821 the population was 520. From then on, the population steadily rose with the result that in the 1831 the population was shown as 682, with 62 families working in agriculture and 68 families involved in handicrafts, mills, basket making and glove making.

During the Canal Age, work was being done to make the River Thames navigable and in 1817 Bell Weir Lock opened, named after its first lock keeper, Charles Bell. New roads were being constructed and machinery, particularly steam engines were being added to mills to take advantage of the new technology available.

The fortunes of the Harcourt family now seemed to take a turn for the better, as in 1829 George Simon Harcourt repurchased Ankerwycke and once again the Harcourts resumed the title of Lord of the Manor. This quite spectacular turnaround is all the more intriguing for George Simon, the only son of John Simon, who had frittered away the estate, was orphaned at 4 years of age and yet at the age of 22 years, bought back the estate. George Simon Harcourt did a great deal for the village and was very active in village affairs helped by wife Jessy Rolls. Jessy took a great interest in the village school established in 1831 and provided the children with uniforms. There is a water colour painting of the children in their school uniforms by the artist Delamotte, which was in the possession of the great, great, grandson of the Harcourts, also George Simon Harcourt born 1957.

In the course of nine years of marriage to Jessy, the Harcourts had six children of whom four died in early childhood. Jessy herself died in childbirth in 1842. This event was thought to have been the reason why George Simon stepped back from village affairs but this was not the case. Certainly, there was a grieving period but the real reason was much more straightforward and that is explained further in this book. He married again in 1846 and produced another nine children.

Magna Charta (Carta) House c.1950
Source: Wraysbury Archives

George Simon was responsible for the building of the cottage on Magna Charta Island in 1834 and built, in addition, a special room called the Magna Charta Chapel. In this room he had placed the large stone set in an oak table on which he said the Great Charter was sealed. Villagers will remember The Queen visiting the house in 1974 and planting a commemorative Walnut Tree. Among the benefits that he gave to the village was the construction in 1842 of a new bridge over the stream at the top of Windsor Road which flooded regularly. He had built, a new higher-level suspension bridge known as Long Bridge, being 200 feet long and 17 feet wide. This was eventually replaced in 1874 by the present one. His greatest contribution however, was the construction in 1843 of the new road from Hythe End to the High Street. The old road being flooded to a great depth nearly every year and virtually isolated the village, causing great financial hardship. This new road was surveyed for him by William Buckland, the Baptist Minister of whom more is told later in this book. The old road used to run behind all the houses on the south side from Hythe End down to and along the Staines Road and came out at the rear of what is now Bennett's Estate Agents, crossed the road into the old Concorde Garage and came out the other end of the High Street. Parts of the old road can still be seen, for example at the entrance to Ankerwycke, where the original gate posts abut the old road and also, the site of the old Concorde garage, where the old road goes down between the two buildings, which are now destined to become a Co-op.

George Simon Harcourt gave the land, advanced the money and became the driving force behind this major enterprise, which enables villagers today to travel to Staines irrespective of the weather. George Simon Harcourt died in 1871 and Ankerwycke was inherited by his first and only surviving son, John Simon Chandos Harcourt, 1835 – 1890. On his death the inheritance passed to his only son Guy Elliott Harcourt, 1869 – 1936, and it was he who finally disposed of the Ankerwycke property in the 1920s. Thus bringing to an end, 200 years of ownership by the Harcourts.

However, the village went through one of the biggest changes experienced by its residents in 1847 with the arrival of the railways. This opened up the village to new and expanding markets and enabled farmers and villagers alike to move about as never before. With the coming of the railway the road through to Horton adopted the grand name of Station Road. The first Wraysbury Station was built for a line which came from Nine Elms to Datchet and then was extended to Eton and Windsor Riverside in 1849, at the request of Prince Albert and Queen Victoria. As the first station flooded regularly, a new station was constructed in 1861. It is now difficult to envisage the impact that this form of travel made with the provision of Parliamentary trains which charged 1d a mile.

Wraysbury Station Staff 1904
Station Master (sitting) Charles Holmes
Source: Wraysbury Archives

Station Road once had some of the finest houses in the village, namely:- 1) Wraysbury House, the home of the Gyll family and latterly the Herrings, now under a gravel pit; 2) The Vicarage built in c1890, demolished to become The Worple housing development; 3) Old Bowry House, home to the Mosley family and demolished in the 1990s to become the current Bowry House; 4) New Bowry House built on land once belonging to Old Bowry House, demolished to become Bowry Drive and 5) Chelston House, which became the first bank and then was demolished to become four houses. Continuing along Station Road over the railway bridge towards Horton, we reach the outskirts of the village and the place known as 'Whitehall', home to Mr. Francis Buckland at the end of the 19th century, later becoming home to Mr. White of R. White's Lemonade fame. The Beale family then purchased the house and Mrs. Betsy Beale MBE, became a great asset to the village as mentioned later in this book. Her husband the brilliant and renowned physicist, Professor Evie Beale, made significant discoveries in fibre optics. The house was later demolished and became a number of smaller houses. Lastly, is Wraysbury Mill, originally an iron mill then a copper mill in the early 1800s, thereafter producing paper for the de Buriatte family and latterly others until its closure in 1971. It was later demolished becoming a small residential development. Find out more about Mr. White and Wraysbury Mill later in this book.

Changes in transport were not the only changes experienced in Victoria's reign. The population of Wraysbury rose from 701 in 1851 to 779 in 1901. St Andrew's Church was remodelled by Raphael Brandon and the work was completed in 1862. The interior was substantially altered with new wooden pews being added. New bells were also added to make a peal of 8. The tower and spire were added in1871.

Social changes brought about by the railway had an impact upon Wraysbury. There was an old workhouse, which housed the poor in receipt of parochial charity. However very few paupers were to be found in Wraysbury and a comment is made that 'the condition of the poor is very creditable to the parish and equally so to the rich; the former looking to latter to redress the balance of their lot and they are not deceived'. Wages were low but rose from 8s.6d to 12s a week and work was available.

1875
Midnight fire
at Wraysbury

ON FRIDAY the annual Wraysbury Pleasure Fair was held on land adjoining "The George." As people were leaving the fair soon after midnight the alarm of fire was raised. Rose Cottage, near the fairground was alight and a number of children came running out of the building. Joseph Pusey and his wife Sarah, arrived from the fair and she said she had left two candles burning in the children's room. It was subsequently found that a four-year-old girl had been burnt to death. Mrs Pusey says she had had 27 children but only ten were in the cottage, to the best of her knowledge, at the time of the fire. — May 29, 1875.

Slough Express
Source: Wraysbury Archives

Large families were the norm then, the children being the 'parents' pension' and an investment for their future well-being. However, the news cutting here shows one Wraysbury family taking things a bit too far, although the circumstances of its broadcast to the general public are tragic.

The school previously set up by the Baptists moved into the old workhouse in 1851. A new purpose-built Wraysbury Board School opened on the High Street in 1874. This was set up as a result of the W.E. Foster Education Act of 1870 which ensured compulsory education for all children between the ages of 5 and 13.

As the village now moves into the beginning of the twentieth century and the start of a new chapter, we find a village that had been through significant changes, particularly in the Victorian period, when the railways came and the two churches took their current form. Wraysbury, as with all parts of the UK, had adapted to national requirements such as universal schooling and changes due to farming and industrial revolutions.

Wraysbury School 1904
Source: Wraysbury Archives

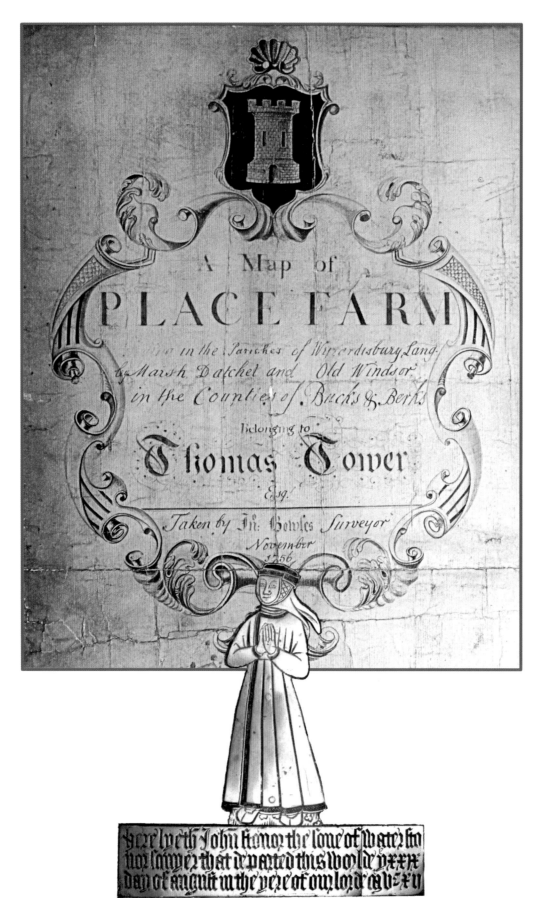

[1]Brass of John Stonor in St. Andrew's Church d. 12th August 1512
Also showing detail from a [2]Map of Place Farm House
by John Bowles for Thomas Tower 1756

Source: [1]Tony Kimber - [2]© Source: ©Bodleian Library, The University of Oxford
ref MS.C17:15(25) detail from

From WW1 to More Modern Times

A Village in our Time

Now I know you've had to wait to get here but it's been worth it. From the gloom of the First World War to the Queen's 90th birthday et al, there should be something to interest you all!

WW1 Post Cards – the two extremes!
Source: ancestralresearch.org.uk

I've thoroughly enjoyed writing this and met wonderful, friendly villagers along the way. I hope you enjoy reading it.

Graham Morley

Part 4
of
The Wraysbury History Project

gmi

Contents

Wraysbury High Street 1960s
Source: Wraysbury Archives

A Village in our Time - Events covered by this Section

Wraysbury's Independent Prep School – *Ormiston House c1928/34 – The Tiny Grange
Source: ancestralresearch.org.uk

Wraysbury's Independent Prep School – *Ormiston House c1934/70s – No.3 Welley Road
Source: ancestralresearch.org.uk

*See also page GM53

ib

What villagers often don't see – an early photo of volunteers bulb planting for the benefit of all
David Martin, Diana Hughes, Graham Sinclair, Dennis McDowell, Tony Morgan,
Christine Morgan, Tim O'Keeffe and son Chris O'Keeffe
Source: ancestralresearch.org.uk

'Let me help you with that' – Anthea Christie giving a helping hand - lunch at *The Grange 2012
Source: Wraysbury News

*See also page GM110/111

Festival of Britain Parade 1951

Wraysbury's Kings and Queens Parade – Festival of Britain, Summer 1951*
Source: Wraysbury Archives

Can anyone put a name to the faces?

*See also page 3 of Memory Lane Photos and the Bibliography

if

Rivernook later known as Wraysbury Hall built 1890, Hythe End
Source: Wraysbury Archives

The VILLAGER   3

Double Cup Wins at Wraysbury's Horticultural Summer Show

BLOOMS BLOOMING SUCCESS

• **Charlie Larcombe winner of the 'Pananza Cup'**

Six year old Charlie Larcombe's little green fingers successfully lifted the 'Pananza' Cup with his Octopus garden in a seed tray for the Under 8's at last month's Wraysbury Horticultural Society's 'Summer Show'.

Over 60 categories of flowers, vegetables and fruit provided strong competition for the awards.

Shelia Marshall and Dennis McDowall, both had double triumphs with their roses and sweet peas respectively.

Mrs Marshall received the 'Lister Challenge Cup' and 'Rose Vase' from the society's new President, Lady Craigton, and Mr McDowall with splendid displays in two sections of Sweet Peas won the 'Reg Spratley' and 'Grace Challenge' cups.

The children's class for Roses was won by Zara Dunster with Alex Linsay, second and Julie Croft, third.

The youngster's seed tray

gardens are always a popular section to view, showing great imagination and creativity.

Caroline Beck was presented with the 'Charles Sams Cup' for her success in the under 14 year old group.

Now it is back to the garden to prepare for the Autumn Show.

• **Dennis McDowall.**

• **Shelia Marshall's rosy triumph with two wins.**

CHILDREN'S RESULTS
Charles Sams Cup. C.Beck: **Children to 8 yrs:** Class 43. H.Croft: Class 44. R.Lindsay. C.Larcombe. H.Croft: Class 45. C.Larcombe. R.Lindsay. H.Croft: Class 46. A.Lindsay. C.Larcombe. H.Croft. **Children to 14 yrs.** Class 47. Z.Dunster. S.Patel. K.Sawgha: Class 48. Z.Dunster: Class 49. J.Bell. Z.Dunster. J.Croft: Class 50. C.Beck. J.Croft. J.Bell

FULL RESULTS
Reg Spratley Cup. D. McDowall: **Grace Challenge Cup.** D. McDowall **Lister Challenge Cup.** Mrs S. Marshall: **Rose Challenge Vase.** Mrs S Marshall: **Pananza Cup.** Charlie Larcombe. **Section A-Sweet Peas.** Class 1. A.Sleep. J.Froud: Class 2. D.McDowall. A. Sleep. J.Forud: Class 3. D.McDowall: **Section B-Roses.** Class 6. J.Hunt. S.Marshall: Class 7. S.Marshall. A.Elston. P.Bunn: Class 8. Lady Craigton. S.Marshall. K.Dunster: Class 9. Lady Craigton. J.Hunt. S.Marshall: Class 10. S.Marshall. Lady Craugton. P.Green: Class 11. K.Dunster: **Childrens Class.** Z.Dunster. A.Lindsay. J.Croft: **Section C-Flowers.** Class 15. T.Rooks. P.Bunn: Class 16. D.Webb. P.Green J.Hunt: Class 18. P.Bunn: Class 19. P.Bunn: Class 20. T.Dobson. T.Rooks. S.Turner: Class 21. P.Green. P.Bunn. T.Rooks: Class 22. P.Bunn. K.Dunster: **Section D-Pot Plants.** Class 23. P.Green. S.Turner. D.Webb: Class 24. P.Green. J.Froud. K.Dunster: Class 25. J.Forud. D.Certon. L.Pitt: Class 27. K.Dunster: Class 28. R.Elletson. A.Pearce. C.Beck: **Section E-Vegetables.** Class 29. B.Willatts: Class 30. A.Elston. B.Willatts. R.Marshall: Class 31. B.Willatts: Class 32. B.Willatts. T.Dobson: Class 33. T.Dobsobn. R.Marshall: Class 34. R.Marshall: Class36. B.Willatts: Class 37. T.Dobson. B.Willatts: **Fruit Section.** Class 38. T.Dobson: Class 41. D.Webb. R.Marshall. A.Elston: Class 42. D.Webb.

---

april 10, 2003   **WX NEWS**   Editorial/Advertising: 01753 825111

Daring duo fail to foil robbers

A COURAGEOUS couple in their 60s were injured as they fought to stop robbers raiding the small horticultural shop they were manning.

Robbers targeted the Wraysbury Gardeners Club and Horticultural Society trading hut in the High Street at 11.30 Saturday morning.

Two of the perpetrators stayed outside, while one went in and grabbed money from the

EXCLUSIVE by Francis Batt

till. The 66-year-old woman assistant tried to tackle the man.

She said: "I grabbed him and pulled him to the floor hurting my knee in the process, and he managed to fight free."

She shouted to a male colleague, also in his 60s, who

was helping sort flowers outside the hut. She said: "He chased the man into the car park and managed to rugby tackle him, but the second man was waiting there and pulled him off. A third man was waiting in a car and they escaped in it."

The quick-thinking Horticultural Society members who tackled the robbers have asked for their names not to be publicised.

The woman assistant gave police a description of the man she tackled, who was in his mid 20s, stocky and about 5ft 7ins to 5ft 8ins tall, dressed in black.

She believes the robbers may have been watching for some time. One came in and asked about compost just before his colleague robbed the till.

The assistant said: "He looked a bit young and I knew he wasn't a member of the

Horticultural Society. I thought to myself then he would have to pay his membership if he wanted to use the shop."

The hut was open for the first Saturday of the season and had had a particularly busy morning.

There were a lot of people about and anyone who saw anything of the incident can ring the police on 01753 835553 or Crimestoppers on 0800555111.

Daring Robbery at the Horticultural Hut – 10th April 2003

*See also pages GM12/13

ih

Chapter 1

The First War Years & The 1920s

In 1911 and those halcyon days before the world went mad and bucolic idleness was disturbed by marching feet, the number of souls in Wraysbury was under 1000. They consisted mainly of agricultural workers, railway workers or mill workers at the William Warwick de Buriatte's paper mill in Coppermill Road. There was a smattering of other jobs such as at the Lino Works in Staines or other manual labouring. The opportunities for young girls were limited to domestic duties for the wealthier inhabitants, or at the mills.

Scene of Mary Norris's death – Clark's Grocers Stores aka Budgen's Corner
Source: Wraysbury Archives

In the same year, the village experienced its only double murder[1] together with a suicide. The story was that Arthur Norris, a retired gardener, suspected that Bertram Woodward, a booking clerk at Wraysbury Station who lodged with the Norrises, was having an affair with Mary Norris, the wife of Arthur Norris. On the 6th October, Arthur Norris rushed into the house and into Woodward's room, shot him dead and then turned the gun on his wife and shot her in the chest. Mary managed to stagger to the shop next door (Clark's grocers, later to become Budgens, then Gems Stores and then Bennetts Estate Agents) where she died on the floor of the shop. A customer in the shop at the time was a young boy called Cyril Francis Brants, who became the village postman when he grew up.

Meanwhile back at the scene of the crime, No. 2 Alexandra Villas (later owned by the Willatts family and leased to the NatWest Bank, then eventually RK Leisure), Arthur Norris had turned the gun on himself and shot his brains out. A verdict of wilful murder was returned in the case of Mary and Bertram whilst *felo de se* (suicide) was recorded for the death of Arthur. According to Mrs. Barbara Board, the whole affair drew crowds of sightseers all anxious to see the murder scene. Mr. Clark's store did good business and the whole incident became a cause for gossip for some time.

---

[1] London Daily News 7th October 1911

Whilst this murder was still a hot topic of conversation, another resident was planning to open a plant nursery and this he did six months later in 1912. Called Wraysbury Nursery,[2] it was formed as a Limited Company and started trading at a site off Welley Road. The two principal shareholders were Mr. George L. Gray, a Wraysbury nurseryman and Mr. George Burch, a fruit merchant and businessman. Unfortunately, it didn't last long. The men filed for insolvency in June of the same year and officially finished trading as a company in 1916. However, Wraysbury Nursery was still shown on plans for the village as late as 1962 and eventually became Waylands, the small housing development built in the late 1990s. This was named after the house on that site that belonged to the Keighley-Peach family.

There were other plant nurseries in Wraysbury, in particular the one owned by the Brinkman Brothers, who purchased their first piece of land (four acres) from Raymond Reffell of Manor Farm in 1910 and it was known as 'The Nurseries'. The Brinkmans were Dutch and quite wealthy and Johan Brinkman, seemingly the more senior partner, became a naturalised British citizen in 1921. Johan lived in Nursery Cottage, which is now 52 Fairfield Approach, and the rest of the plot was used for cultivating roses, for which he had a sales office in the garden from where he did his trading. Johan bought some more land from Mr. Reffell in 1923, this time eight acres, which immediately adjoined his original plot. By this time, houses were more profitable than roses and the land was gradually sold off in plots, making Johan an even wealthier man. That is why, even today, the area of Fairfield Approach, Nursery Way and the immediate locale is known as the Brinkman Estate. The Brinkmans continued with roses and fruit growing but they eventually moved away to Walton Farm, Bosham, Hampshire.

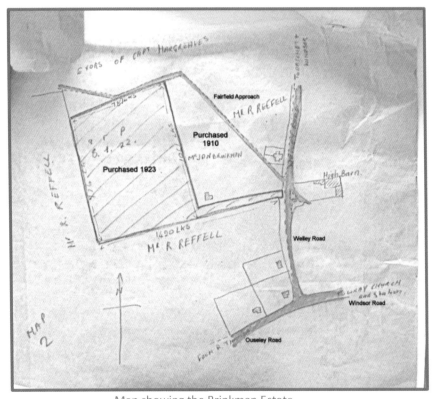

Map showing the Brinkman Estate
Source: Family Archives of Marcelle and Franco Cresto

---

[2] National Archives

Talking of nurseries, there wasn't much help for pregnant women in the early 1900s. They were expected, mainly, to do two things: firstly, to lay back and think of England and secondly, to grin and bear it! Wraysbury wasn't much different until some well-meaning ladies set up a small 'lying-in home' known as 'The School for Mothers'.[3] This was started in the Oast House* (previously Elmslea) and was the forerunner of government-led clinics for the care of babies and their nutrition. Started in 1913, it existed as a voluntary organisation helped by occasional donations from local residents, grateful parents and, from time to time, a £1 from the Wraysbury Parochial Charities** (which is still active today). It is an amalgamation of six ancient parish charities, entrusted to distribute income from its investments, according to its constitution, for the sole benefit of residents who live in Wraysbury.   **See Appendix 7.

In 1915, a further grant was made in the form of a Maternity Bag, provided it was used for parishioners whether or not they belonged to The School. A charge of 2 shillings was made for borrowing the bag and, providing it was returned in a clean condition, 1 shilling was refunded. Unfortunately, the School never made it to the end of 1918.

*It is worth noting that this beautiful Queen Anne house is linked to the Astronomer Royal – William Herschel, a resident of Datchet and Slough, who, it is reputed, used the tower for his planetary observations. It was also the home of Mr. James Doulton, the son of John Doulton one of the founders of the Lambeth Factory for Doulton Ware, where they specialised in pipes and sanitary ware which was big business in those early years. James ran the Baptist Chapel for 30 years until his death in 1900. Needless to say, the house had a grand assortment of Doulton tiles, which featured on floors and walls. The house, like so many others, has disappeared under the bulldozer, and Oast House Close is the result.

The Fabulous Oast House – winter 1963
Source: David Cater [ex-resident]

---

[3] The Archives of Margaret Rooks.

By 1913, the storm clouds were gathering and tongues were wagging but Wraysbury had its mind on other business: two local society weddings. The Hargreaves of Remenham House, one of the village's society families, saw the weddings of Capt. Hargreaves Snr's two daughters, Rhoda Violet and Norah Beatrice. Rhoda, known as Violet, married Basil Barrington-Kennet on the 8th January 1913, and Norah married Robert Pigot on the 28th August 1913, both army boys and members of the RFC. Violet and Nora both had their ears to the ground so would have known war was imminent but decided to grab happiness whilst they could, knowing it was possibly then or never. Robert ended his army life as a brigadier-general and was later to be elevated to the peerage but Basil was not so fortunate – he was killed in Flanders on 18th May 1915. See also The Scouts p.25.

| Basil H. Barrington-Kennet | The Two Loves of the Hargreaves Sisters | Robert Pigot |

Source: National Archives - Great Britain, Royal Aero Club Aviators' Certificates 1910-1950

The villagers turned out to both weddings and cheered the young couples on their way. Among the many wedding presents received by Violet and Basil were two of particular note as they were presented by Wraysbury villagers. Firstly, a silver tea-caddy and secondly, a table cloth, embroidered with all the village schoolchildren's names. Needlework was a part of the school curriculum in those days and well into the 1960s, with the girls being expected to sew just like mother!

Although both boys were in the Royal Flying Corp, and Basil married first, Robert caused the bigger stir when, after the ceremony, the military airship 'Beta' flew over their reception and dropped messages of congratulations. The excitement of the villagers and all the wedding guests, including the bride, is obvious in the picture (opposite) - although the village bobby looks rather perplexed!

MRS. ROBERT PIGOT (FORMERLY MISS NORA HARGREAVES) FOR HAVING AN ARMY AIRSHIP AS SKY-PILOT AT HER WEDDING.

The military airship "Beta" put in an unexpected appearance at the reception | Hargreaves at Wraysbury. It dropped messages of congratulation, and then descended
after the wedding of Captain Robert Pigot, of the Royal Flying Corps, and Miss Nora | in a neighbouring field. The bride (X) is seen walking beneath it.

Photograph by C.N.

The Cause of all the Excitement
The Army Airship dropping-in to the fields at Remenham House
Source: British Newspaper Archives – 28th August 1913

When war was declared on the 4th August 1914, mass employment of a different sort reared its ugly head as hysteria gripped the nation, young men flocking in their thousands to enlist and punch the Germans on the nose. A spirit of almost gaiety spread as the marching young men went to war: well it'll be all over by Christmas, won't it?!

Wraysbury's young men were no different from any others in the country and over the next year most - if not all - the young men in the village, enlisted in Kitchener's Army. These totalled at least 75, all who had direct connections to the village. Of these 75, there was a 43 per cent mortality rate with 34 either killed, missing in action or dying of wounds. Wraysbury was not, therefore, lucky enough to be called a 'Thankful Village'[4] although in other villages mortality rates of 100 per cent are known. The lives of these brave men deserve to be remembered, not just on memorial boards in draughty halls but here in our modern lives. Here we celebrate two in tribute to the rest:

Local Heroes

John Pinnock was born in the village in 1888 and the family lived in Goaters Cottages, The Green. The cottages are no longer there, being demolished for the development of the recreation ground and football pitches. John's tranquil life as a local gardener was shattered when he enlisted in the Royal Field Artillery in 1915. Given the number 106035 he was posted to 'B' Company, 56th Brigade as a driver/gunner. After initial training, on the 25th October 1915 he was sent overseas to the Balkans in readiness for the action in Mesopotamia (modern day Iraq). His brigade was attached initially to the 10th Irish Division and later, in 1916, the

---

[4] Thankful Village – one where all the men came back after the war.

13th Meerut Division. In November 1917, they were in action at Samarrah, 78 miles north of Baghdad on the east bank of the River Tigris. His company supported an infantry attack on the right bank and, on the 5th November, they sustained heavy casualties from the enemy's shelling. From 'B' company four were killed and 14 wounded. John was one of those missing in action presumed dead, leaving behind his beloved wife Mary and three-year-old daughter Nancy. He is remembered on the Basra War Memorial, the Village Hall Memorial Board and both church memorial plaques.

We also remember **Tom Lewis**, born in the village in 1895, his parents were George and Ellen Lewis. George was a builder and contractor and the family lived in the High Street near the Post Office. Tom was a paper machinist assistant at the paper mill in Coppermill Road. He enlisted in the King's Royal Rifle Corps at Egham on the 2nd June 1915 and was given the number R/14002 in the 11th Service Battalion. After training, on the 4th September 1915, he embarked for France and joined the battalion on the 21st October 1915. The battalion took part in the defence of Ypres and was based at Poperinge on the banks of the Ypres-IJzer Canal where the trench system was just a sea of mud. He was admitted to a field hospital on the 8th April 1916, suffering from gunshot wounds to the chest and abdomen, and he died on the 11th April 1916. He is buried in Lijssenthoek Military Cemetery between Ypres and Poperinge and is remembered on the Village Hall Memorial Board and both church memorial plaques.

The civilians weren't left out either, being called to work all hours in the local factories on war work. The loss of life and stalemate situation some two years into the war, caused the British generals to blame this on the lack of artillery shells and questions were asked in House of Commons as to how this was going to be rectified. This caused local factories such as the Lino Works and the Lagonda car factory at Egham Hythe to be put to making artillery shells.
(*This pressure also caused the government to take risks and, despite warnings, they pressed ahead with the development at Silvertown,[5] south-east London to purify TNT. This is a process more dangerous than manufacture itself and the factory was sited in a highly-populated area! The resultant explosion on the 19th January 1917 killed seventy-three people and more than 400 were injured. Up to 70,000 properties were damaged, with 900 nearby homes destroyed by fire or beyond repair; the cost was put at £250,000 then or £2.5 million in today's terms.*)

Fire! Fire!
Fire in any community is a dreadful affair and when in 1915 the beautiful Georgian residence Ankerwycke House, one of Wraysbury's leading buildings, caught fire, it was a disaster. A house where it is said Henry Vlll wooed Anne Boleyn, Ankerwycke was steeped in history and it was subsequently successfully rebuilt. (As an aside, the wealthy Benson family had lived at Ankerwycke since at least 1900 and Mr. Benson, a jeweller, wasn't removed from the odd piece of drama. Already known in the village as a bit of rogue, he was to court the whiff of scandal when in 1923 he came unstuck over fiddling his tax returns. Summoned before The Bench to answer to fraud, he obtained a 'sick-note' from no less a person than Lord Dawson of Penn, the king's physician! Nevertheless, he had to repay £20,300 in underpayments and a fine of £40,000. Despite this heavy outlay, on his death in 1934, Mr. Arthur Henry Benson left his brother and nephews just over £300,000 – a huge sum then and not insignificant now!)

---

[5] The Silvertown Explosion – The Newham Story

Source: Wraysbury Archives

Source: Illustrated Police News
8th February 1923

It is unclear whether before 1916 the village had any proper fire protection, relying rather on buckets and neighbours plus Staines and Windsor Brigades to render assistance. Therefore, from 1919, to cope with the dreadful prospect of fires, the village had its own fire cart/appliance which was kept initially at the school, under the guidance of the Chief Fire Officer from Windsor. Fire appliance is a better term for the early engine as it was a pump unit mounted on a Lewis gun carriage, redundant from the First World War. Mr. Cox, the local butcher, wrote to the Chief Fire Officer at Windsor, suggesting the setting up of a village fire service and between them they made it happen. However, Mr. Hall of Windsor Brigade was unhappy about the appliance being locked up in a shed at the school. He didn't want to take the chance that, if and when wanted, no one would have access to the school or the key! Subsequently, George Darling of Station Road, the local plumber and general builder, was asked to supply an estimate and later build a shed for the appliance. While doing this, he also made it big enough to accommodate the village's Bath chair, which had lain for years mouldering away at the school. This he did for sum of £22 and made sure the appliance was always available by the key being in a glass case fitted to the shed. The Bath chair was bought in 1922 for £42, and last seen in 1952 when it was restored and handed over to the Nursing Association.

The Fire Brigade made do over the years with odd pieces of equipment until 1928 when the Parish Council and the Parochial Charities contributed to the purchase of a secondhand Merryweather 'Planet' motor fire engine for £150 6s 1d. This they bought on favourable terms and by May 1930 it was fully paid for: the extra funds coming from public subscription and village fetes. They also had a new garage for the engine at the Old Forge by The Splash (later to become a motor repair garage). By this time, they were more of a professional outfit, although still all volunteers. They all had a uniform, with Capt. File as the leading fireman helped by the Hammond brothers and few others.

Under Capt. File's leadership they attended a number of fires in the village and numerous stories abound of scrapes the fire crew found themselves in. One in particular was at

Greenshadows, the Riverside home of Mr. John Greatrix.[6] On Tuesday the 25th June 1935, Berkshire and Buckinghamshire experienced the worst electric storm in years and a petrol mower in Mr. Greatrix's shed was struck by a thunderbolt, which set the house alight. Wraysbury Fire Brigade duly attended and parked the engine on the slipway at Butcher's Ferry to pump additional water from the river. With the hoses and the suction pumps going like mad, the engine rolled back down the slope into the Thames. In all the rush and bother the driver hadn't put on the handbrake!

Sadly, Mr. Greatrix's bungalow burned to the ground. It wasn't only the engine that was red that day! However, they did rescue Miss Jones the maid, Mrs. Bayford the chauffeur's wife, a monkey, two dogs and a cat. Mr. and Mrs. Greatrix also happened to be away in Brighton, so it wasn't all bad news.

Merryweather Fire Engine – of the type at Wraysbury
Source: ©Bonhams Auction House 2014

The fire engine was changed in 1940 to a 'Dennis' and subsequently, in 1946, that engine was given up to the National Fire Service. Since then Wraysbury has not had its own brigade and is now protected by engines coming from Staines and other larger towns.

Food Shortages

Life in the village had to go on despite the sadness and shortage of men but it was difficult to adapt. At the start of the war Britain produced approximately 35 per cent of its food and the bulk of the rest was imported. Germany knew this and in 1915, in an attempt to starve the nation into submission, successfully mounted blockades using block ships and submarines to prevent supplies reaching our shores. This made the country very much more aware of its food production and a great effort was put into making the country's methods more efficient.

[6] Hartlepool Northern Daily Mail – 26th June 1935

Farmers in Wraysbury attempted to turn all waste ground and odd field corners into food production. However, with the men being away and most farm horses taken and sent to The Front, there was little progress. Therefore, the Board of Agriculture set up the Women's Land Army to try to get things back on track. By the end of 1917 some 250,000 girls had joined up.

In the meantime, the Navy had introduced the convoy system and this was instrumental in ensuring the continued import of food. This was very lucky as in 1917 the nation's harvest failed and the country had only reserve supplies left. The convoys between Britain and Holland were sometimes called the 'Beef Trip' as so much food was passing between them.

The Government was reluctant to introduce food rationing as it thought it would affect the morale of the people, but by 1918 it had no choice and in January rationing was introduced, starting with sugar and followed by butchers' meat and most other food stuffs.

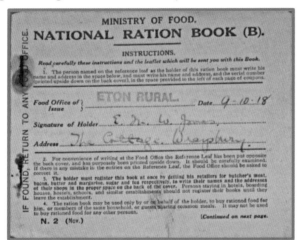

1918 Ration Book
Source: Wraysbury Archives

One of the larger farms involved was Manor Farm owned by the Reffell family, with interests in brewing as well as agriculture. The Reffell family had farmed in Wraysbury since about 1850, before which the farm formed part of the Duke of Devonshire's large estate in the area. The original house, which was constructed of oak framing and wattle and daub, was rebuilt in 1725. Parts of the original oak framing still remain. During 1956, the magazine *Homes and Gardens* visited the farm, which was then nearing the end of its working life. The photograph below is taken from that issue. The building and interior at the time was reported to be 'in an excellent state of preservation' and the furnishings were considered to be 'of good quality'.

Manor Farm, Wraysbury
Source: Homes and Gardens 1956
Wraysbury Archives

Another of the well-known local farms was Tithe Farm, owned by the Willatts family,[7] not far from Wraysbury Station. Tithe Farm covered a large acreage and, again, employed local men and women plus itinerant workers during harvest. They had the first tractor in Wraysbury (1916) and it was soon put to work with the Land Army girls ploughing up forgotten field corners. The farm delivered cream, eggs, butter and milk. Initially there were very few cars so the farm also ran a parcel delivery service from the station for local residents. It also supplied horse cabs for trips to Windsor or Burnham Beeches. However, the increase in motorised transport in the 1920s soon meant that these services were no longer required.

The supplies and deliveries from the farms were in addition to the few local village shops and pubs, which were dotted along the High Street and local area during the Great War. The village had two general stores, Clarks, later to become Budgens in the 1930s, which was opposite the school, and Lovell's, which was near The Perseverance pub. Mr. Cox the butcher, arrived about 1917 and Butler's Bakery delivered the daily bread. James and Christie Willatts clearly remember knocking up the baker in 1916 to order some extra bread and noticing to their horror his awfully black toe nails and feet! It turned out that he kneaded the bread with his feet and the encrusted dough went black!

There was George Watson a local builder, based near The George pub, who also doubled-up as an undertaker. Whilst up at Hythe End there was a carriage and cab maker called George Pendry, whose family later ran the Feathers pub at Hythe End. Supplies of 'Bully Beef' for the troops were a major concern and Hythe End Mill was converted to a canning plant for the duration of the war, afterwards becoming a slightly seedy, run-down industrial area.

The Government at this time also tried to introduce school meals for all. It was very concerned with the lack of good nutrition in children due to food shortages and the parents being either at The Front or working long hours in factories so struggling to provide for them. Luckily, being a farming village, the families in Wraysbury, more often than not, either had enough food or were able to get help from others in the community.

Getting By

In addition to the shops, the village had five pubs: The George, believed to date from the early 17th century, The Perseverance, The Green Man (Stags Head), the Railway Arms (now a private house, The Barleymow) and The Feathers at Hythe End. The Railway Arms, known previously as the Papermakers' Beer House[8], was originally built as near as possible to the railway station. The platform then was down the entrance to where Wraysbury Dive Centre is now. However, as the platform was susceptible to flooding, it was moved in 1861 to its present and more suitable position.

Life for the average villager wasn't easy, water had to be pumped up from a borehole or well in the garden and lighting was by candle or paraffin lamps, as electricity did not arrive until 1924/5. Most of the cottages and farms had outdoor toilets or 'privies' with the waste being collected on a regular basis. Even in 2017, there are properties in the village that have cesspit drainage and to whom the 'Violet/Lavender Tanker'[9] is a regular visitor.

---

[7] The Memoirs of Christie Willatts
[8] Gyll's History of Wraysbury 1862
[9] Lavender Tanker – waste collection vehicle

Most villagers walked everywhere, some every day as far as Staines or Windsor, or they cycled, as cycling was by far the most common form of general transport. In addition, at this time, the village had a very clear divide between the rich and the poor with many villagers that were agricultural workers or labourers of one sort or another living in real hardship.

For the poor, existing in such close proximity made it easy for infections such as TB to spread and in 1915 it became a notifiable disease. The doctor attending had to notify the local Sanitary Inspector and the Wraysbury Nursing Association would arrange for the house of the sick person to be disinfected.

Redevelopment

At the time of the Great War, the village was much more open with fields stretching from Coppermill Road down to Sunnymeads, broken only by Welley Road with no gravel pits or housing estates to spoil the view. Floods were a problem for Wraysbury even then: the houses situated near the Thames being flooded from the 1800s through the 1920s and the more recent floods of 1947 to the present day. This openness was itself the passport to expansion and enterprising farmers sold off land for redevelopment at Hythe End and Sunnymeads between 1911 and 1921. Due to the building and development work the population increased still further and to cater for this, in the 1930s a small council estate was built in Mud Lane. It was renamed Douglas Lane on the suggestion of Mr. Willatts Snr., after the adjacent Douglas Field, on what was previously farm land on the edge of the village. In early years, Pelham's annual fair was held in a field in Douglas Lane, just past where the Medical Clinic is now. It was on land thought to be owned by the Willatts family. WW1 put an end to this, as it did so many things where young men were involved.

The village also suffered from the General Strike of 1926, having no trains running. Mr. Robert White, son of the founder of R. White's Lemonade, know colloquially as 'Ginger Beer White', who lived at Whitehall, just over the bridge at Wraysbury Station, decided he wasn't going to allow this to continue. He promptly commandeered the train at Windsor and set off. He was met at Wraysbury Station by one of his staff in full uniform carrying a tray and a glass of sherry! Unfortunately, his train driving wasn't up to much and at Richmond Station he applied the brakes so fiercely that they jammed on for half an hour, much to his chagrin. This simply couldn't happen today - how the power of the gentry has fallen!

The years between the wars saw an influx of newcomers looking for weekend retreats. They built riverside bungalows mainly of timber and asbestos but old railway carriages and buses were also used. This practice is not unique to Wraysbury, as all along the south coast are a number of enclaves of these long-forgotten carriage conversions, slowly deteriorating in the salt air.

As part of this population surge, Mr. Balgarnie-Wyld an architect of some repute, moved to the village in 1924 and lived at Walnut Tree Cottage, Matthew's Lane (now The Green). He designed and had built numerous bungalows and houses in the village. He recalled two of his more colourful clients for a talk with the History Club in 1972.[10]

One was built on the island off Riverside, for a chap who was suspected of being the jewel

---

[10] 10th April 1972 History Club Talk – Margaret Rooks

thief who stole the Duke of Windsor's jewels from Lord Dudley's house in Sunningdale. The police tramped all over the Riverside site digging up the ground but never found anything. Mr. Balgarnie-Wyld remembers being paid for his design work and the police remarking, 'Well he could afford to!'

The other house was The Thatches, at 92 Staines Road, built on the ruins of another house, The Hollies, owned by Mr. Francis Samuel Blackwell of Crosse & Blackwell fame. It was destroyed by fire on the 18th September 1915. The previous owner of The Hollies, was Mr. J.P. Taylor in 1891, a private Estate Agent who assisted with the sale of Ankerwycke in 1885.

Mr. Balgarnie-Wyld built The Thatches for Wing Commander Lionel Cohen, known as 'Sausage', a famous airman who served in both the First World War and the Second. He was the oldest airman and rear-gunner in WW2 and received the DFC in 1944 at the age of 70. He died in 1960 aged 86. Unfortunately, when the thatched roof caught fire in 1974 it could not be saved and was replaced by a tiled one.

Wing Commander 'SOS' Cohen
From his biography *The Crowded Hours*
by Anthony Richardson

Horticultural Society*

There were some clubs and sporting activities in the village, in particular, the Horticultural Society. It was believed to have been founded in September 1897, but the late Len Pearce recalled there being some earlier records from 1880![11] Len brought the club 'back to life' in 1960 and set up the Trading Hut with Denys Webb in the High Street car park in 1970, reflecting the growing demand for plant cuttings and seeds. In these early years, the club held four shows a year on the village green, with entries from all over, not just Wraysbury! The hut, manned by members every Sunday morning, continued into the early 1980s, when the garden centres started to make their presence felt and sales dropped in line with membership. Len recalled it was hard work collecting all the subs, walking around the village and knocking on doors.

Now under the care of Pam and Ray Alletson since about 1990, the Society celebrated its centenary in 1997 and now offers travel services such as day trips and short breaks that focus on gardens or horticultural establishments, with occasional travels abroad to interesting

*See also page **ih** of the Timeline

_____

[11] Silver Jubilee Program 1977.

places with a horticultural theme. Whilst far removed from the club's beginnings, it reflects the move away from gardeners growing their own seeds and plants to 'instant gardening' provided by garden centres with which the Horticultural Society couldn't compete. It also shows, though, how the love of plants and gardens thrives nonetheless.

Pam Alletson
Source: ancestralresearch.org.uk

Remembering the Late Len Pearce
Source: Royal Bor.Observer-20th July 2017

Ray Alletson
Source: ancestralresearch.org.uk

Cricket Club

Cricket was another well-established sports club in the village, thought to have been started in 1860 by the Rev. Seymour Neville. The matches were played on the Church Meadows behind St. Andrews Church. It lapsed certainly throughout the First World War at this difficult period of village life, with the men going to The Front.

Wraysbury Cricket Team on Church Meadows – date unknown
Source: Wraysbury Cricket Club

In its early years, The Rev. Hake of St. Andrews insisted that no cricket be played after 6.30pm on Sunday in Church Meadows, as it would interfere with worshippers attending church.

After WW1 the club was re-formed around 1926, with members later creating their pitch from scratch on the village green. Originally divided by a central hedge, this all had to be grubbed up and grass re-laid, not an easy task by any means. Initially offered the land for £110, it was beyond the club's means at that time and so it became the property of the Parish Council and the village. The last season played before the Second World War was in 1939, and the next playing season was 1946.

Source:
Wraysbury
Cricket Club

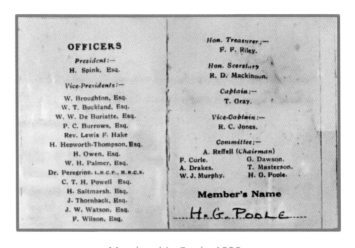

First Xi Fixture List – 1929

Membership Card c 1930s

The cricket club is still going strong and is a well-respected member of the Morrant's Chilterns League and Berkshire Cricket Board. The late Tom Rooks, a parish councillor for twenty years, was the club's long-term chairman whose love of cricket was legendary. A member of the M.C.C. he was a major force in raising the money to build the new pavilion.

Tom Rooks
Source: The Observer

Cricket Pavilion
Source: Wraysbury Cricket Club

Long term president the late Richard 'Dickie' Dean was also a stalwart of the cricket club, living at Ankerwycke since about the 1940s, he and his family were the last occupiers of Ankerwycke House before its sad demise in yet another fire in 1962. Wraysbury Cricket Week is still held in his honour. The club has had some memorable matches and amongst the most popular have been the President's XI, for which the Dickie Dean Trophy or Rose Bowl is presented.

Dickie Dean Trophy
Source: Wraysbury Cricket Club

Richard 'Dickie' Dean
Source: Wraysbury Cricket Club

Two of Wraysbury's players from the early years of 1946-1959, were David Dailey and Bill Perkins. Both went on to play county cricket for Buckinghamshire and Berkshire respectively. David made over a 1000 runs and took over 100 wickets on three occasions and 179 wickets in one season, and Bill made over 1011 runs and won the batting and bowling award for 1955. Other members from the past of note were Gerry Hollis and Evan 'Jimmy' Jones, both villagers for many years. Gerry scored over 12000 runs in his playing career and along with Fred Cherry

Fantastic Fred

HEARTY CONGRATULA-TIONS to my old friend Fred Cherry of Wraysbury who scored 569 runs in August for an average of 81. This mammoth run-getting spree was accomplished in ten innings and included three centuries and a 90 not out. I should think this performance wants a lot of beating in club cricket re-cords. No wonder they call him "Fantastic Fred."

achieved the club's highest opening partnership of 210 runs, which stood until the year 2000. Evan, known as Jimmy, was First XI team scorer and travelled all over Berkshire and the Home Counties, score book in hand. On one occasion, missing the team transport, he cycled the 15 miles to Binfield so as not to let the team down. Related to the Buckland family, he was founder member of the Wraysbury History Club and edited and distributed the Wraysbury News for over twenty years.

Now with a new pavilion built in 1991, with bar and full facilities, the club runs a First and Second XI, plus a Colts junior programme under the care of Andy Freeman. Secretary is Tom Dibley who would like nothing more than to see you down at the green cheering the team on.

Winners of the 2017 Chilterns League Knockout Cup – 21st July 2017
Source: Wraysbury Cricket Club

The club produces good cricket and still enjoys great success: on a lazy summer weekend, there's nowhere better to be than watching cricket on the village green.

Rifle Club

There was also a small-bore rifle club on the village green, started before WW1, it was well supported initially with both a men's and women's team. They were certainly among the best shots as the following illustration shows. It was an expensive sport and the members of the women's team, in particular, were from the more affluent of Wraysbury society.

REIGATE LADIES v. WRAYSBURY LADIES.

A post match was shot on Friday at Reigate. Conditions: 10 shots on a double or 2 bull target; possible 100. There was some very good shooting in both teams, the Wraysbury Ladies winning by 11 points. Scores:—

Reigate Ladies.—Miss Colson 98, Mrs. Nicholson 97, Mrs. Fearon 96, Miss Watney 96, Miss Benton 95, Miss Morris 94, Miss Merriman 93, Miss Aston 92; total, 761.

Wraysbury Ladies.—Miss Benson 98, Miss E. Benson 98, Mrs. Brinkman 98, Miss Buckland 97, Mrs. Heseltine 97, Miss A. Hewitt 95, Mrs. Pearson 95, Miss E. Pratt 94; total, 772.

Source: Dorking and Leatherhead Adv – 31st January 1914

The club ceased to be used during the Great War in favour of the local rifle ranges. Whilst these were thought of as two ranges, they were, in fact, one large range with two entrances: one at Staines Moor and the other further down Coppermill Road. A very high wall was built towards the end of Coppermill Road to protect the local inhabitants from flying bullets or 'overs' as they were called.

The Guards from Windsor Barracks journeyed by train to Wraysbury and then marched to the ranges for target practice. Mrs. Board remembers the teacher Mrs. Dowd, allowing the children out of class to wave to the soldiers as they marched to the ranges. Although there was a simple railway 'halt' built for the Staines part of the range, known variously as Runnymede Range or Yeoveney, it fell into disuse closing in 1962.

Tennis Club

The redevelopment and influx of new blood in the community encouraged the growth of even more recreational facilities. As a result, a tennis club was started early in 1922 in the field that used to belong to the now defunct rifle club, by a small nucleus of villagers and the Rev. Lewis Hake (vicar of Wraysbury from 1895 till about 1932). Mr. Reffell of Manor Farm, the new tenant of the field, agreed to sub-let to the tennis club and the club was formed.

The club officially opened on the 20th May 1922 with what was called an American Tournament. This was a round robin mixed doubles competition in which participants were initially paired at random, and anyone could play irrespective of their playing standard.

c1989/90s – Peggy Willatts*
Source: Roger Willatts

1925 – Men's Team
Source: Wraysbury Tennis Club

Needless to say, the club thrived despite the odd sheep or cow grazing on the courts! The land changed hands in the 1930s with the lease then being held by the Revd. Shorrocks, who offered to sell the land to the club, spread over a two-year period. This was done and the land is now held by the club's Trustees in perpetuity.

Knowing the club was now here to stay, many improvements were made to the grounds. Play was also allowed on Sundays and, as a consequence of both, membership increased.

*See page GM19

The club became affiliated to the Bucks County Lawn Tennis Association in 1936 and men's, ladies' and mixed teams entered league fixtures. Unfortunately, war came along in 1939 and, in October, it was agreed to suspend the club until the end of the war. The club re-opened in 1946.

After the war things took time to get back to normal but in 1958 a new pavilion was built and here is a lovely photograph of that event. Mrs. Reffell, a lifelong supporter of the club was presented with a bouquet. The club progressed through grass courts to en-tous-cas (clay) and, in 1978, to the latest all-weather hard courts.

1925 - Love the hats and long dresses
Source: Wraysbury Tennis Club

Front Row	Rear Row L- R	OPENING OF PAVILION	
Dennis Wood-Dow	Frank Burr	SATURDAY MAY 3rd. 1958	Mike Wordham
Wynne Wood-Dow	John Spencer		Maureen Burr
Jackie Roper	Marjorie Hale		Mrs. Reffell (President)
Jane Evans	Peter Foster		
Diana Hammond	Hilary Wordham		
Jean Bell	Toni Dain		

Source: Wraysbury Tennis Club

OPENING OF THE ALL WEATHER COURT BY MRS P. WILLATTS
30th April 1978

Doug Evans   Peggy Willatts   Jackie Roper   Frank Burr

Source: Wraysbury Tennis Club

Wraysbury LTC continued to expand, offering coaching at all levels and match-play as well as plenty of just-for-fun tennis in club sessions and privately-arranged games. In 2001, thanks to rigorous fundraising and grants from the Parochial Charities, The Prince Philip Trust fund and Windsor and Maidenhead Borough Council, the clubhouse was extended and rebuilt by Glyn Larcombe. The new facility provided changing rooms and showers, a new kitchen, a big picture window overlooking the bowling green, and the extended size meant there was plenty of room in the main clubhouse for social gatherings or even to play table tennis! It was formally unveiled by the Mayor of Windsor and Maidenhead, Councillor John Webb on Saturday 7th April. The courts were also refurbished and repainted that year and nets repaired, which encouraged more new membership and play potential.

Ladies', men's, mixed teams and juniors all compete in league matches with varying amounts of success. The members also have annual club tournaments, including the Maureen Burr (pictured on page GM21), the Peggy Willatt's Rose Bowl (see page GM17) and highly competitive summer championships.

The Australian Grand Slam winner, the great Ken Fletcher visited the club in 1985 and opened the new hard courts. This was a terrific coup for the club and aroused great interest.

The great Ken Fletcher – Australian mixed doubles and Grand Slam winner
Source: Wraysbury Tennis Club

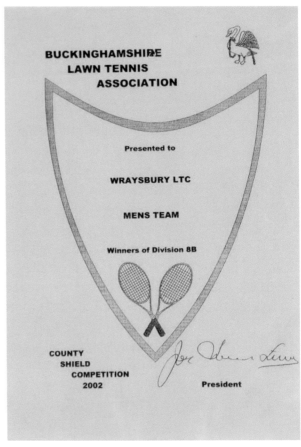

1993 Men's Team   2002 Men's Team
Source: Wraysbury Tennis Club

Aegon Team Tennis Buckinghamshire	Aegon Team Tennis Buckinghamshire	Aegon Team Tennis Buckinghamshire
Wraysbury Tennis Club	CONGRATULATIONS Wraysbury Tennis Club	CONGRATULATIONS Wraysbury Tennis Club
12&U Girls Division 2A WINNERS 2017	14&U Boys Division 1 WINNERS 2017	18&U Boys Division 2B WINNERS 2017
LTA BRITISH TENNIS	LTA BRITISH TENNIS	LTA BRITISH TENNIS

Hot Shot Juniors!
Source: Wraysbury Tennis Club

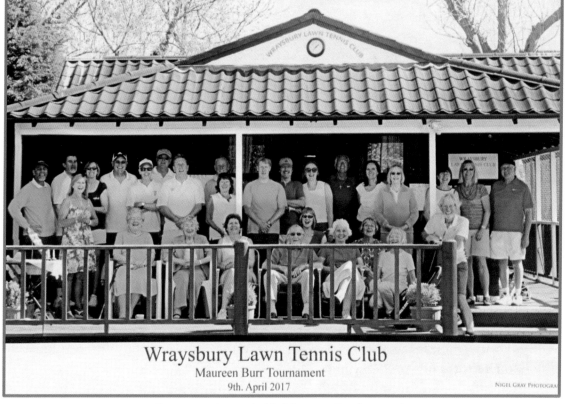

Wraysbury Lawn Tennis Club
Maureen Burr Tournament
9th. April 2017

Tournament awarded in Maureen Burr's name in
recognition of her long service to the club as Secretary
Source: Wraysbury Tennis Club

Wraysbury LTC has an enthusiastic coach in Doug Robinson. He offers junior coaching three times a week, starting with Teddy Tennis on a Saturday for children aged two upwards. Adult coaching is on Tuesday evening or private sessions by appointment and all abilities are catered for.

It's fair to say that the club has moved with the times over the years and now has all the attributes of a modern sports club: all-weather courts, floodlights, a pleasant clubhouse with kitchen, changing rooms, loos and showers, a friendly atmosphere and a good social life. The current President is Anthea Christie who with her committee, look forward to welcoming you.

Football Club

WRAYSBURY FOOTBALL CLUB
Winners—Windsor, Slough & District Junior League, Division I.   Season 1933-34.

Standing: W. Barratt (Sec.), W. Foster (Trainer), N. Shaw, H. Cordery, S. Hammond, W. Woods, A. Gillard (Chairman), F. Wolfe.
Seated: T. Moore, L. Hodge, A. Eavis, F. Hammond (Capt.), G. Newman, R. Clarke, J. Hughes.

Wraysbury Village Football Team – 1934
Source: Linda Colegate

Tennis was not the only sport doing well in the between war years: Wraysbury Football team won the Windsor Slough and District Junior League Cup for season 1933-4. This was an exciting thing for a club that was thought by many to have been in existence since 1902. However, evidence proves that the team was playing long before that and certainly in 1893 (see the excerpt from the local newspaper below). It may have been in existence even since 1877 but under the name of Runnymede.

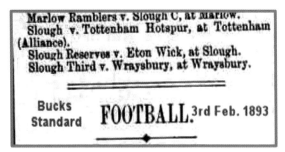

Marlow Ramblers v. Slough C, at Marlow.
Slough v. Tottenham Hotspur, at Tottenham (Alliance).
Slough Reserves v. Eton Wick, at Slough.
Slough Third v. Wraysbury, at Wraysbury.

Bucks Standard   FOOTBALL.3rd Feb. 1893

The club must have ceased playing and reformed in 1902: it certainly stopped for the first war and was reformed in 1922[12] with £5 borrowed from the Wraysbury Village Association, with Tom Hammond as secretary, and they played a good game of football.

---

[12] Silver Jubilee Program 1977 – Margery Ashton

1910-11 Wraysbury Football Team
H. Lewis, G. Shanks, W. Bell, J. Cousins
Fred Ing, G. Pinnock, W. Your
Bill Shanks, A. Cousins, S. Bradford, H. Manley, A. Herrett

The club closed again throughout the Second World War but was later resurrected by Basil and Ronald Masterson, Percy Nicholls and Bob Jewson as secretary. Looking at the club's Minutes for the early 50s makes interesting reading, such as cattle grazing on the pitch when wanting to cut the grass and from 26th September 1950, "It was generally agreed that provision for visiting teams to wash after a game should be made. The secretary was given permission to purchase two buckets"!

Teas for half time were provided by Mrs. Lidsdale of the Cake Shop and numerous dances were held in the George Hall which helped keep the club's cash flow going. Eventually they managed to amass funds to purchase a new 5-gallon boiler and the half time tea problem was solved for a while.

Trips also to the London Palladium were provided at competitive prices, all with the one idea of keeping a happy club. The team then, after some time, managed to re-join the Windsor, Slough and District League.

Since those early days, it has had mixed fortunes, with various sites for the pitch over the years from near Douglas Lane, which also doubled as the Hockey pitch, to the rear of the excellent Village Club (opened in 1894), the village green and now to the Memorial Ground. Supported over the early years by the Parish Council and a backbone of villagers and local residents such as the Beadles, Hammonds, Mastersons and Burrs. A later generation of stalwarts such as Gordon Coates, John Stevenson, Ron Watson and John Rice also put in their all and have made Wraysbury one of the top teams in the league. John Rice has been rewarded for his loyalty with the Vice-Presidency, having marked out the pitch for nearly 30 years. They between them all, have produced remarkable results.

The club merged with the Slough factory team, Cooper Payen in 1990, which was helpful to both clubs at the time but Wraysbury Coopers was too much of a stretch and Wraysbury was by far the better team so the name Coopers was dropped after about a year. From the early days till about 1992/3 they played in the Slough, Windsor and District League and in that period won the Premier Division Championship and Slough Town Cup several times. Later competing in the Chiltonian League and the Middlesex League brought other wins and overall, in the last 100 or so years they have also won the Berks & Bucks Cup, Slough Town Senior Cup and the Maidenhead Norfolkian Cup.

They have had financial and administrative problems over the recent years but now with a new committee in place, headed by President John Meller, they can look forward with confidence and resume their winning ways. With new equipment and renovated changing rooms, they now play in the Thames Valley Saturday and Sunday Leagues. Let us celebrate their success and wish the club well for the future. Mark Foster, the new chairman is full of optimism because, helped by a major fundraising effort in the village, all debts are cleared.

WINDSOR SLOUGH & DISTRICT LEAGUE CHAMPIONS 1972-73

J.McGOWAN. J.HANSON. M.DAVIS. R.BUTLER.
B.WARD.(Capt). R.SHRIMPTON. T.SEARLE.
J.PERRY. P.SHAW. T.MELLIS. G.STOBBART. K.PAINE.

1972/3 Winning Team
Source: Wraysbury Football Club

The Scouts

Mr. F. Sibbons – 1st Scout Master
Source: unknown

These middle years saw the rise of the Scouting movement, initially set-up by Mrs. Rhoda Violet Barrington-Kennet (Hargreaves).[13] In 1922 she purchased a war surplus hut and had it carted to Wraysbury and re-erected, the walls re-lined and new floor joists fitted at a cost of £150. Violet and her brother each donated £10 and the boys set to and raised the balance of the money by collecting jam jars, old paper and other salvageable items. She recruited and cajoled Mr. Sibbons to become the Scoutmaster in 1922 and this he did until his retirement in 1927. Mrs. Barrington-Kennet* left the village in 1925 and moved to Fulmer. It is believed the Scouts then disbanded until reformed in 1935 by Reginald Milton-Cottam, a civil servant who lived in Glergavin in Coppice Drive.

*Mrs. Rhoda Barrington-Kennet, known as Violet, was the daughter of Charles Reginald Hargreaves of Remenham House. She married Basil Barrington-Kennet on the 8th January 1913; he was a major in the 2nd Battalion Grenadier Guards and also in the RFC. He was killed on the 18th May 1915 in the battle of Festubert. He is remembered on the village Memorial Plaques. Rhoda was born in Wraysbury in 1888 and died in 1977.

The Parish Council took responsibility for the Scout Hut c. 1929 and it was then known as the Village Hall. Scout numbers were never high and with the rise in population in the 1930s, Mr. Watson, headmaster at the school, held a recruitment drive to increase the troop. This it did and the Scouts managed to keep going until the Second World War, when the hut was requisitioned as a school room for evacuee children.

The old Scout hut and Village Hall
Source: Wraysbury Archives

After the war, the Scouts re-started under the leadership of Mr. Head and Mr. Corke, and they met in the rear hall of the Baptist Chapel. Numbers increased in 1956 with the addition of Cub Scouts led by Jennie Francis. Also Venture Scouts were started at this time. However, in 1959 the Scouts almost ceased to exist, with no one to run the troop. Thankfully, Peggy and James Willatts worked tirelessly to keep it afloat and

Early 1950s photo of Scouts' Church Parade – Roger Willatts in front also showing Mr. Wood's Cycle Shop – the shed next to the church!
Source: Roger Willatts

---

[13] The notes of Joan Dick – Wraysbury History Group 1992

were given the Chief Scout's Commendation by the District Commissioner in 1966 for their almost individual efforts in saving the group.

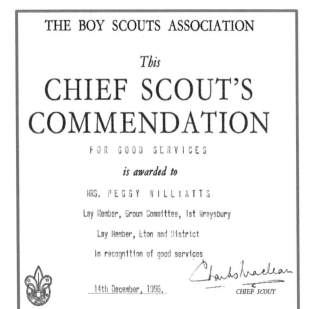

Bucks County Commissioner Mr. T. G. Martin presented the Chief Scout's Commendation, for the first time, to a married couple, Mr. James Willatts, and his wife, Peggy, at the Wraysbury Village Hall last Friday.

Couple saved Scout Troop from extinction

In front of the Scout Troop they saved from extinction eight years ago, Mr. & Mrs. James Willatts, of Wraysbury, were honoured for their efforts on Friday. For more than ten years they have worked behind the scenes for the 1st Wraysbury Scouts, and at the Village Hall they were brought into the limelight to receive their Chief Scout's Commendations, from County Commissioner Mr. T.G. Martin.

Those present agreed that it was the first time that two such awards had been given together to two lay members of the movement.

The new Scoutmaster expressed his thanks to Mr. and Mrs. Willatts who live at Churston House for the help given to him in 1959, when he took over the troop, which now has 60 members. Mrs. Willatts was almost solely responsible for the resuscitation and reformation of the troop in 1959 by obtaining the services of the new Scoutmaster.

Source: Windsor & Eton Express 1967 - Roger Willatts

HM The Queen opening the
Village Hall in 1974
Source: Diana Hughes

In 1974 the new Village Hall* was opened by HRH Queen Elizabeth. The Scouts, who in the 1960s had moved to the Old School Hall so their hut could be used as the Village Hall, were then able to move back to their original hut. At this time, they were led by Mr. Hughes then subsequently Mr. Sumner, Dave Morris and Mrs. Stocker. Under these new leaders, the Scouts went on a number of camping expeditions around the local area and succeeded in winning football and swimming competitions.

*See page 86

Wraysbury Scouts Dragon Boat
Source: Peter Knott

In 1984, Peter Knott became Group Scout Leader and introduced new activities and, in the 1990s, new young blood with the Beaver Scouts and girls being able to join the previously boys-only groups. Around this time Jenny Fraser became Beaver leader in Wraysbury for about 7 years, becoming ADC (Assistant District Commissioner) for Beaver Scouts for the Windsor and Eton District in 1998. She retired in 2008. The new activities included family camps, a Christmas postal service, running the Village Bonfire where 2000 villagers were and still are catered for and also Dragon Boat Racing, in which, over the years, they won the Dragon Trophy, Ou Yuan Trophy and the Glass Dragon Boat Trophy. Some of the team later went on to represent England in Prague and Wales. Peter Knott retired in 2000 after 25 years' Service to the Scouting movement (In 2012 he was awarded the Silver Acorn Medal in recognition of Specially Distinguished Service to Scouting).

In 2003, the Scout Hut flooded so severely that the Scouts were able to canoe inside! The hut was left in a poor state but still continued to be used. Thanks to the Parochial Charities and various other donations, the necessary finance was raised to enable the Parish Council to arrange for it to be rebuilt as a new brick building.

Flooded Scout Hut 2003
Source: Peter Knott

On the 25th October 2008, it was opened by the Duke of Edinburgh as a new Community Centre for the benefit of all the youth groups and pre-school children. Displays were provided for the His Royal Highness, which included the Climbing Tower, First Aid, Camping, and Canoeing amongst many others. Local photographer Tony Britton recorded the event and a copy of his work in book form is held in the Wraysbury Archives.

The Duke of Edinburgh
at the opening of the
new Community Centre
2008
Source: Peter Knott

The Parochial Charities again supported the Scouts in 2010, to enable them to purchase the old swimming area on No. 1 Pit to provide canoe training facilities.

The Scouts have moved with the times and is now under the chairmanship of Andy Clemance and organised and led by Group Scout Leader Andy Bouche with his strong leadership team, they have plans to include orienteering weekends for up to 60 young people and other exciting group activities. Go to www.wraysburyscouts.org for more information.

The Guides
The girls weren't forgotten either, with the Guides being formed in 1919 and officially recognised in January 1920. Under the leadership of Rhoda Violet Barrington-Kennet they represented the village at the Empire Day Guide Rally on the 24th May 1920 in Slough, and at many other events. The Guides then disbanded in November 1923 and reformed in April 1933, thanks to the energy and drive of the Stump sisters Marcelle, Andrée and Gladys. They moved to Wraysbury with their parents from France in 1923 and lived in Johan Brinkman's old house known as Nursery Cottage (latterly The Nest), in Fairfield Approach. These are photos of the Stump girls in 1928 aged 17 and 15 respectively, as Guides, but with the Ashford Troop, which confirms there wasn't a Wraysbury Troop to join.

Stump sisters at Ashford 1928
Source: Cresto/Stump Family Archives

1st Wraysbury Guides - 1935
'The Nest', Fairfield Approach

The Stump girls thought the Guides, "A jolly good thing for young girls" and the 1st Wraysbury Guides was re-established on the 5th April 1933. Rita Brutnell certainly remembers joining the Guides with Marcelle Stump as Captain and Andrée Stump her Lieutenant, assisted by the younger sister Gladys. The terms Captain and Lieutenant, which reflect their Service origin, are not used now, Badger, Dolphin or other animal names being preferred.

At the outbreak of the Second World War, Dorothy Simpson became Captain. Dorothy was also County Commissioner for the Guides and the daughter of Roy Simpson ex-RFC pilot, who was shot down in WW1 and suffered brain damage from which he never fully recovered. The Simpsons lived at the Oast House, at which the Guides meetings were held throughout the war. Brownies and Guides were active in Wraysbury during the WW2 and both attended an open-air meeting at the George on Sunday, 14th June 1942[14] at 5.45pm. This was the first United Nations Day and it celebrated the coming together of the free 26 nations to fight against tyranny and war and to pursue peace for the benefit of all. Mr. Alfred Reffell, leader of the Parish Council, led the singing and gave a short speech on behalf of Mr. Churchill, the Prime Minister.

Unfortunately, the Guides have had a chequered existence[15] and they disbanded in 1953 and reformed in 1957 thanks to Mrs. Margaret Monsell-Davis who was also Captain. They disbanded again in 1963 and reformed in 1966 with Mrs. Margaret Auton at the head. Disbanded in 1983, the re-formed again in 1987 with Mrs. Susan Perkins as Chief, then Sandra Woods became Acting Chief Guider. They closed briefly once more in the mid-90s, joining forces with the Datchet group but then reopened in 1997 with Alex Wood at the helm.

Gladys and Andrée Stump c. 1928
Source: Cresto/Stump Family Archives

District Commissioner for the Guides, Brownies and Rainbows at that time was Carolyn Humphries, who served a total of ten years combined service. After another short closure in 2006, Giovanna Cochrane took over the Guides in 2007.

The Brownies also play an important part in the village for girls between the ages of seven and 10. The earliest records show the organisation to have been formed in 1939 under Miss Pauline Notting and they have a better survival rate than the Guides, thanks to long stints at the helm by willing villagers Mrs. J. North, June Lucas and Judy Lewis.

A Rainbow pack for five to seven-year-olds started up in the late 1990s with many local mums helping to run the unit. Towards the end of the 1990s

---

[14] Middlesex Chronicle 20th June 1942
[15] Guiding Association Archives – Mr. Peter Knott

some young leaders, former Brownies, Guides and Venture Scouts themselves, came in to train and help, particularly with the Rainbows and Brownies. Today, our Rainbows, Brownies and Guides are all in the seemingly untiring, and very capable hands of Giovanna Cochrane.

Wraysbury Guides' Camp Hurley
1937/8 – Bisham Church in
background.
Lieutenant Andrée Stump with dog
Source: Cresto/Stump Family Archives

The Death of Dr. Whitla*

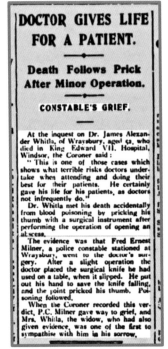

DOCTOR GIVES LIFE FOR A PATIENT.

———

Death Follows Prick After Minor Operation.

———

CONSTABLE'S GRIEF.

———

At the inquest on Dr. James Alexander Whitla, of Wraysbury, aged 42, who died in King Edward VII. Hospital, Windsor, the Coroner said :

" This is one of those cases which shows what terrible risks doctors undertake when attending and doing their best for their patients. He certainly gave his life for his patients, as doctors not infrequently do."

Dr. Whitla met his death accidentally from blood poisoning by pricking his thumb with a surgical instrument after performing the operation of opening an abscess.

The evidence was that Fred Ernest Milner, a police constable stationed at Wraysbury, went to the doctor's surgery. After a slight operation the doctor placed the surgical knife he had used on a table, when it slipped. He put out his hand to save the knife falling, and the joint pricked his thumb. Poisoning followed.

When the Coroner recorded this verdict, P.C. Milner gave way to grief, and Mrs. Whitla, the widow, who had also given evidence, was one of the first to sympathise with him in his sorrow.

One of Wraysbury's most popular doctors in the 1920s was James Alexander Whitla (Witla), he lived at Remenham Park after moving to the village from Hammersmith in about 1925. He was an eminent physician and surgeon and author of a number of important medical text books. His death in December 1928 was a sad loss to the village and a memorial seat was erected on the corner of St. Andrew's Close and Windsor Road. It was a lovely seat complete with pitched roof and was there for many years.

What happened was this, Fred Milner the village policeman, went to see Dr. Whitla as he had a serious abscess that needed lancing. Dr. Whitla lanced the abscess and went to put the scalpel back on the table when it rolled off. In trying to catch it, the scalpel cut Dr. Whitla's thumb and infection set in. It wasn't realised at the time just how serious it was. The infection turned to Septicaemia and despite a number of operations, Dr. Whitla could not be saved and he died on the 16th December 1928 at King Edward VII Hospital in Windsor.

*Daily Echo 21st December 1928 and Mrs. Jacqueline Wherlock

Chapter 2

The 1930s

The burgeoning population of the years between the wars, made the village attractive for new business and Frederick Sibbons, Wraysbury's first Scout Master, had not long retired and taken over the newsagent's and tobacconist in Blandford House, High Street near the Baptist Chapel. This was sold after the war to Charles and Mary Burr, helped by Charles's sister, who worked in the haberdashery shop next door. Up until his death in 1928, Walter Sleep had the ironmonger's, glazier's and carpenter's shop down at The Splash, which then became the Fire Station, and later the fish and chip shop and the garage buildings.

Source: Roger Willatts

The Jewson family started their pharmacy in the village in 1933 and remained here until they retired in 1985. They lived at Vine House, and the pharmacy adjoined it as can be seen in the photo, although the shop completely fronted Windsor Road then. The shop and house have since been rebuilt to allow a double aspect frontage onto both Windsor Road and the High Street. With the pharmacy came Dr. Howard who, until he moved into the village, had his surgery at the back of the shop. He was followed by Dr. Janney and Dr. Roper, although he had his surgery on the opposite side of the High Street next to Percy Powell's Garden Shop.

Entertainment!

Celebrities from the stage, film and music-hall were also attracted by the village's beautiful riverside location and to cater for this a number of diversions, such as greyhound racing and various nightclubs, were opened. This soon gave the village a risqué name and brought with it an air of notoriety and excitement. Len Pearce remembered a saying he still heard in the 1960s which reflected this Thirties and Forties image, 'are you married or do you live in Wraysbury?'!

The Staines Greyhound Track[16] opened in 1928 at Queensmead and although affiliated to the governing body, it remained as an independent. In 1937, it was one of three tracks chosen to attempt the short-lived Cheetah racing (using cheetahs instead of greyhounds); and in 1938 a motorcycle rodeo took place with tricks and skills. Various other events were tried in an attempt to increase its popularity and British cycling sprint star Reg Harris[17] rode here against

---

[16] www. greyhoundracinghistory. co. uk

[17] Warwick University modern records re. MSS. 328/N7/4/16

Arie van Vliet the Dutch champion, on the 15th April 1950. In addition, grass track cycle racing and stock car racing events, also popular in the Fifties, were also run.

So popular were they that they attracted top sports commentators of the day, such as Eamonn Andrews*, Peter West and Kenneth Wolstenholme. The track's owner, Jack Walsh, was in partnership with bookmaker William Hill and they won the English Derby with 'Lone Keel' in 1938. The track held a maximum of 5000 spectators and whilst not a great number, Frank Burr recalls they were generous in their donations when collections were taken for local charities. The track closed in 1960 and was finally dismantled in 1965 to make way for the Staines By-Pass and the M25 motorway.
*See page 74

1931 WRAYSBURY NIGHT CLUB RAIDED

On Saturday, the Bell Weir Night Club, at Wraysbury, was raided by the Slough Police, and the names of everyone in the club at the time taken.

The police, under the direction of Supt Tucker, crossed from the Bucks bank to the Island in boats and a complete cordon thrown round the premises.

The raid took place just after midnight and people tried to escape by getting out into the grounds through the French windows fell straight into the arms of waiting police officers.

It was over two hours before anyone was allowed to leave the club, as every name and address was taken.

The band continued to play for the dancing and the bar remained open. — April 18, 1931.

Source: Winsor & Eton Express 18th April 1931

Clubs like the Bell Weir Night Club[18] that opened in the Thirties, were magnets for those looking for a good time. It was raided by the police in April 1931 and, as in all the good stories, the band continued to play and the bar remained open, whilst all names were taken. Some tried to escape through the French windows but fell straight into the arms of the police! The club was struck off that same month by order of the magistrates for illegal gambling (fruit machines) and serving alcohol outside the permitted hours.

The Santa Monica Club was another riverside club, opened in 1935 at Ankerwycke House - a Georgian manor house - after the death of its previous tenant, Arthur Benson. The swimming pool was enclosed on three sides by Spanish-style lodges and it has been said, that there was a pink Rolls Royce with a black driver in a yellow suit at the Santa Monica Club, on hand in case anyone had one too many, but it all seems just a bit too colourful! With its slightly risqué reputation, the club was to attract

Santa Monica Club Advert
Source: The Bystander 15th July 1936

most of the glitterati - even Winston Churchill is alleged to have attended! It was meant to be similar to Cliveden, Lady Astor's place, which attracted its own notoriety in later years with the Profumo affair, involving another Wraysbury resident Christine Keeler.

---

[18] Windsor Express 18th April 1931 and 15th May 1931 and Lancashire Evening Post 13th May 1931

Jazz was all the rage at this time and the Santa Monica Club did its best to showcase the best bands in the country. The star attraction was Sid Millward and his quintet. An ex-Jack Payne alto sax player, his band was allegedly formed, clothed and engaged in 16 hours![19]

Sid was famous in the mid-thirties and despite the Santa Monica closing in 1938, he and his band went on to even greater fame and fortune in the 1940s. He was bandleader at London's Café Anglais and he formed a new style of band with great jazz and comedy. Known as Sid Millward and The Nitwits, they were still going in the early 70s as some of our more senior readers will remember. They appeared on Sunday Night at the London Palladium, Comedy Bandbox and in the film Juke Box Rhythm, to name but a few.

Despite all his fame and popularity, Sid died alone in a hotel room in Puerto Rico and was buried in an un-marked grave.

Sid Millward and later with The Nitwits
Source: ©The Daily Telegraph & Ronnie Genarder Biography

However, the Santa Monica Club petitioned for bankruptcy c. 1936 and a 'winding up' order was issued on the 5th May 1938.

WRAYSBURY, Bucks, 18 miles from London on the Great West Road or by electric train from Waterloo. Situate opposite Runny-mede, surrounded by Green Belt Property, a lovely Georgian Mansion known as THE COURT ROYAL HOTEL AND SWIMMING CLUB. 24 bed-rooms, all with h. and c., etc. Delightful recep-tion rooms. Hard tennis court, swimming pool, rough shooting, fishing, boating, golf (two miles). Historical surroundings. Moderate terms.

It is believed that the owners of the Santa Monica Club, Agar-Stevens Estates Ltd., fancied one more go at recouping their losses, for no sooner had the Santa Monica Club shut its doors, than another club and hotel was opened in Ankerwycke, under the name of The Court Royal Hotel and Swimming Club.[20] It again seemed to attract mostly the louche set, its advertising being mainly in the Illustrated Sporting and Dramatic News. It didn't last long, being struck off in August 1939 for illicit gambling and serving alcohol without a licence. When the club was raided by the police, of the 71 people there, only nine were found to be bona fide members!

---

[19] Dance Band Diaries Vol 7 1936
[20] 6th May 1938 – Ill. Sporting and Dramatic News

The main shareholder and owner of Agar-Stevens Estates was Marquis Stevens, by all accounts a bit of a rogue. He owed money left right and centre and in particular to Ivor Sinclair, who ran the haulage and general transport business* at Hythe End. His son Graham, remembers, with some mirth, the day his father had a set-to with Mr. Stevens in The Green Man pub, which, at that time, was opposite Douglas Lane. Now, like a lot of pubs, two modern houses have been built in its place. Graham recalls his father tackling Mr. Stevens for the money he was owed, and Mr. Stevens ended up being knocked to the floor. Needless to say, Ivor was charged with 'The chinning of Marquis Stevens' as it was then put but the Judge threw it out and asked both parties to go outside and have a cigarette and sort it out! So Ivor ended like all the others, with no money but he had given Marquis a thump! Other villagers weren't as lucky as Ivor, at least he'd had a go. They were left to scrabble around in the ruins of the club trying to salvage what they had supplied but it was all just too late: the proverbial horse had long since bolted and was never seen again.   ***See Appendix 3**

Getting Around

In the 30s, the village had a couple of river ferries, one being in Ouseley Road, which made life so much easier when going to Runnymede or Englefield Green, being dropped off at the Bells of Ouseley landing stage. Owned from the early Twenties, by Mr. Frank Butcher, it was sold to Mr. Foreman who sold it to Peter and Joy Norton in 1956. The Nortons sold it again in 1961 to the Farndens and it eventually ceased operating in 1963. Valerie Farnden, who ran the ferry, blamed lack of business and the state of the river for its ultimate demise. Looking back on it she was right but at the time its closure caused a great up-swell of attachment. However, no one was prepared to take it on so it remains closed to this day.

Old Windsor Ferry
Source: Wraysbury Archives

The other ferry - the Old Windsor Ferry - was a more localised affair, known in the early 1900s as Glaves Ferry and or Manor Ferry.   It was just a punt to take villagers to the landing stage near the church at Old Windsor or the island for picnics and maybe a trip down to the lock. The punts were quite wide and flat bottomed to enable the carriage of cattle and other commercial goods. The ferryman at one time was old 'Brusher' Grant who had a long grey beard down to his waist. What his real name was nobody can remember, but he was one of the local characters and is fondly remembered. He lived at the old barn, long since pulled down, opposite Fairfield Approach. He seemed to be always at the ferry no matter what time it was! The ferryman's wages in c. 1925 were eight shillings per week and the hours he was expected to work were: summer – 7am to 9pm and winter 8am to 6pm.

There has been a regular bus service to Staines since about 1925, when the fare was one (old) penny and Wraysbury railway station, built in 1847, ran steam trains to London and Windsor. An additional station was built at Sunnymeads in c. 1927, and by c. 1930, the first electric service was operating. During the 1947 flood, the steam trains were run for a short while again as the electricity was cut off to the railway.

One of the first villagers to have a motor car was Mr. Arthur Benson of Ankerwycke but some diehards, like the Hargreaves and the Herring families, held onto their 'coach and four' as long as they could.

A lot of villagers had motorcycles and those with families, a motorcycle and sidecar. Cheap to run and insure, they were the answer to early mobility for the masses.

c. 1936 at Horton View, Station Road
Margaret Willatts, Margaret Willatts (Worth), Christie Willatts and
Edna Willatts (Green) in the sidecar.
Source: Roger Willatts

With the coming of motorised transport, petrol stops were frequent and this brought numerous opportunities to the village in the way of garage services. Being only 19 miles or so from Hyde Park Corner, near Windsor, and in the country, Wraysbury was soon identified as the place to visit and a number of garages opened to cater for this new craze. For such a small village, there were at least four garages and each made a living as the petrol and diesel engine made inroads into villagers' lives. Even today, within the village there at least four garage and repair facilities, albeit no petrol facilities! Having such good road connections to the main motorways and airports makes Wraysbury an ideal location for garage services.

In the early 30s, flying for pleasure was beginning to become a popular pastime and more and more light aircraft took to the skies. Nevertheless, imagine Edward Gasking's surprise when in 1936 a lost pilot thought he would 'drop-in' and ask the way to Heston Aerodrome! The disorientated pilot landed in the field near Friary Road and spoke to Edward who can just be seen standing to the left of the aircraft by the wing.

The lost pilot dropping in
Source: Wraysbury Archives – Ray Gasking

Heston Aerodrome was a 1930s airfield located to the west of London, operational between 1929 and 1947. It was situated on the border of the Heston and Cranford areas of Hounslow, Middlesex. In September 1938, the British Prime Minister, Neville Chamberlain, flew from Heston to Germany three times in two weeks for talks with Adolf Hitler, and returned to Heston from the Munich Conference with the paper referred to in his later *Peace for our time* speech from 10 Downing Street.

A Village Character

In the years before WW2, during harvest time in particular, Wraysbury welcomed numerous wandering or itinerant workers, hoping to find employment on the many farms in the village. They knew that if they managed to procure work, a decent meal and somewhere warm to kip would be the reward. The village was lucky enough to have a number of such men but John Montgomery Mackinney stands out from the rest.

John (Jack) Montgomery Mackinney

Born in Richmond in 1870, the son of Thames lighterman, Thomas John Mackinney and Sarah Ann Woods, John was the youngest child of three. He had an elder brother, Thomas, and a sister, Elizabeth. Elizabeth went on to marry Thomas Cole, the great grandfather of villager Elsie Joan Cole of Nursery Way. John's father was a strong rower, as well as a lighterman, and won the Doggett's Coat and Badge in 1871. This was a rowing race between London Bridge and Cadogan Pier for watermen/lightermen only. John's grandfather was Thomas Snelling Mackinney, Waterman to HRH Edward, Prince of Wales and his great uncle was a Queen's Waterman, who rowed in a four which won at Henley Regatta in 1859 with the famous Harry Kelly. John Mackinney first gained his early livelihood as a Waterman on the Thames at Staines and Old Windsor.

John (Jack) Mackinney
Source: Wraysbury Archives

He married Anna Jackman in 1892 and they had two daughters, Amy Elizabeth and Annie Louisa. Unfortunately, his wife Anna died in 1900, leaving him with the two young girls to bring up. Her death affected John very much and he disappeared. His daughters ended up being cared for by his father and mother, Thomas and Sarah Mackinney in Staines. On the girls' subsequent marriage certificates, their father is listed as dead, when in fact he was living in the village just three miles from them.

He first appeared in the village in the early 1900s and lived in later life, in a shepherd's hut at the end of Garson Lane backing onto Church Meadows.

Ever a 'rolling stone', come 1911, John had left the village and gone to work on a farm at Lullington, in Sussex and later joined Kitchener's Army. Given number 38842 Royal Engineers, he was sent to Salonika in February 1916 as part of the Salonika Campaign against Bulgarian forces in Egypt and Palestine. He was discharged in September 1919. He reappeared in the village and picked up where he'd left off. He was proposed to the Salonika Campaign Society by a Mr. Bennett, himself a veteran and villager, who also lived in Garson Lane.

Jack was entitled to the British War Medal and Victory Medal but the military medals that he is wearing in the previous picture do not appear to be these. One of them depicts Edward VII, whereas George V was used for the British War Medal and none of the other WW1 medals, such as the Victory Medal, had Edward's head either! No separate medals were issued by the government for the Salonika campaign so the ones he is decorated with are bit of a mystery. However, he was always seen in the scruffy tail jacket he is pictured in, wearing a small lapel badge with crossed oars. This, it turned out, was the 'Doggett's coat and badge' his father had won forty years before so, maybe, the medals he is wearing, belonged to his father too!

Jack remained in the village for many years, surviving on odd jobs for Mr. Reffell at Manor Farm and any other job that came his way. Extraordinarily, although he lived in filthy conditions, his handwriting was beautiful.

How Jack's hut could have looked

© White Peak Shepherd Huts

But in all probability looked like this!

© Historic Shepherd Huts

Source: ancestralresearch. org. uk; Recollections of an Octogenarian, Wraysbury Archives and 'The Mosquito' – Salonika Ass

Anne Blake recalls that she was told that when her parents married, John gave them a wedding present of a scruffy old pot wrapped up in newspaper. After it had been washed it turned out to be a beautiful Lalique vase. Unfortunately, in the big freeze of 1947, it froze on the windowsill and cracked. There was no central heating in those days!

He was also a very proud man, refusing to take charity or even a pension. There was a great commotion one day, when his life savings of £500 were allegedly stolen by the village 'tart'. (Some people may still remember who this was as many had enjoyed her favours!). Alas his money was never recovered. Jack became very ill one day and he was put up in a warm shed and eventually carted off in an immaculate limousine and taken to a nursing home where they soaked and washed his body in disinfectant for a number of hours.

After his recovery, he came back to the village and it was amazing to see how his once wizened and calloused hands were now as soft as a baby's. He died on the 6th March 1958 and is buried in Old Windsor Churchyard.

Tragedies that befell the village

At this time, the village also had its share of tragedy and local disasters, firstly in April 1933 young Thomas Henry Blake, eldest son of George William Blake of DCL Cottages, shot himself.[21] Thomas was a butcher's assistant and had been fiddling the books to pay off £3 he had lost on betting at Staines Greyhound Track. He knew the police were coming for him and he couldn't face his mother for the shame. He left her a note explaining everything.

Here is a brief extract:

'...You'll find me down in the back field. If you do not want poor old Bob (his dog), sell him. Give my love to all the family.'

Of course, £3 in 1933 was a lot for a young man, today's value would be £199 and £3 will only buy a cup of coffee now. He must have been in a desperate state to feel there was no way out other than to kill himself. His mother died the following year, grief stricken.

In late 1934, an outbreak of Foot and Mouth[22] disease at the pig farm in Hythe End caused a blanket area curfew on livestock movement and subsequent severe losses for the farmer as his animals were destroyed. The lovely old manor house that was on this site dated 1626 was bulldozed and it is now a waste and fertilizer site run by the firm Fowles.

Also in 1934, one of the villages more well-known residents died, this was Alice Pleasance Hargreaves (Liddell) who married into the Hargreaves family of Remenham House, bought by Capt. Charles Hargreaves in 1886. It is not well known but Alice was the inspiration for the Alice in Wonderland of Lewis Carroll fame. When Alice was a young child c. 1859 to 1863, her father was the Dean of Christ Church College, Oxford and Charles Dodgson, better known as Lewis Carroll, went up to Oxford in 1851 and the two became friends.

Dodgson took Holy Orders in 1861 and spent a lot of time at Christ Church, especially in the garden, where he took many photos of Alice and was captivated by her beguiling innocence. The rest, of course, is history. After Alice was married to Reginald Gervis Hargreaves in 1880, they and Lewis Carroll stayed occasionally at Remenham as guests of Reginald's brother, Capt. Charles Hargreaves and his nephew, Captain Reginald Cornwallis Hargreaves.

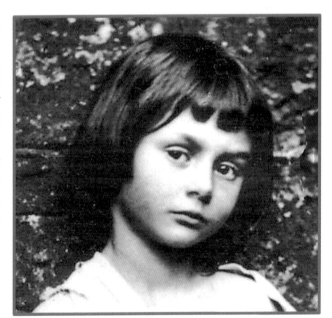

Alice Liddell 1859 as the 'Beggar Maid'
Believed to be by Lewis Carroll
Source: Wraysbury History Group Archives

---

[21] Daily Telegraph – 11th April 1933
[22] National Archives re. MEPO 2/4042

The Hargreaves were good to the village children, especially in the summer, when the schoolchildren were allowed to have their Sports Day in the park in front of Remenham House. Also at Christmas time, they were all invited to Remenham House to see the large Christmas Tree and each of them would receive a present. The Coach House was used as the venue for the children's tea and they all received a mug of tea, a piece of cake or bun, an orange and some sweets.

MARRIAGES.

CRUICKSHANK—HERRING.—On the 21st July, at St. Andrew's, Wraysbury, by the Rev. L. F. Hake, Captain A. H. P. Cruickshank, 32nd Sikh Pioneers, second son of Mr. A. Cruickshank, C.S.I., and Mrs. Cruickshank, of Brooklands, Crowborough, to Helena Marsden, eldest daughter of Mr. and Mrs. Herring, of Wraysbury House, Wraysbury.

The marriage of Helena Herring
Source: Sussex Agri. Express 30th July 1914

The Herring family at Wraysbury House also did many acts of kindness for the village and it is sad to relate that Helena Herring, one of the daughters, was widowed early in WW1. She married Capt. Arthur Cruickshank in April 1914 and he died of wounds received in the 2nd Battle of Ypres on the 28th April 1915. He is commemorated in the Hazebrouk Military Cemetery and on the village Memorial Plaques. Like many others in the village, the Herring household were plunged into depths of despair and widow's weeds (black mourning clothes) were worn. Helena was still living in the village in 1940 and never remarried.

Bertha Herring, the eldest sister, was involved in a murder incident in 1940[23] at a meeting of the East India Association in London, where Sir. Michael O'Dwyer was shot dead. Bertha threw herself forward to stop the assassin's escape. What a strong and determined woman!

WRAYSBURY

CAXTON HALL TRAGEDY

Wraysbury Woman's Gallantry

Reports in the national Press of the tragic occurrence at Caxton Hall, Westminster, on Wednesday afternoon, when Sir Michael O'Dwyer (former Lieutenant-Governor of the Punjab) was shot dead at the close of a joint meeting of the East India Association and the Royal Central Asian Society, give prominence to the courage and presence of mind displayed by Miss Bertha Herring, of Wraysbury House, Wraysbury.

Miss Herring was seated at the front of the hall, near the gangway. It is reported that in interviews with Press representatives she stated that as the meeting finished and she was bending down to pick up her umbrella she heard a shot; that there was then another shot, and she saw a man waving a revolver. She said that she rushed towards the man, who was attempting to leave the hall, and placed herself between him and the door, and that other people then closed on him.

On Thursday an Indian engineer appeared at Bow Street on a charge of murdering Sir Michael O'Dwyer.

Bertha Herring makes a stand!
Source: Middlesex Chronicle 16th May 1940

Arthur H. P. Cruickshank – died 28th April 1915
Source: Kent Courier 7th May 1915

[23] See **Appendix 2** for the background story.

The Grange

In about 1933, Mrs. W. F. Sams purchased The Grange, one of the larger houses still left in the village. The previous owner was Major H.E. Meade ex- Royal Fusiliers and a staunch conservative. It may be convenient at this point to give a little of its history to illustrate the part it has played in village life over the years.

The building now known as The Grange was in existence before 1828 but in a much simpler form. Owned by George Simon Harcourt of Ankerwycke, then Lord of the Manor, who let two of its rooms or an attached cottage to St. Andrew's Church and the Rev. George Hopkins for the village day and Sunday school. The property's initial construction is lost in time but it could have been of Elizabethan origin. Looking at the Tithe Map of 1845, it was then a much smaller property, with the addition of another dwelling nearby which was setback from the road and is possibly today's No.28 Windsor Road.

In 1855, it became the home of Mr. Seymour Neville, vicar of St. Andrews and he began a programme of improvement and enlargement that was to continue until at least 1862, when the house was mentioned in Gyll's History of Wraysbury as the Vicarage. It was thought that the last vicar to live at The Grange was John Hutchinson Hindson but that was not the case. He could not have lived there as it was in possession of the Bankes family, who purchased the much-improved property in 1876 and who lived there until c.1895. It is at that time that first mention of The Grange is made. Mr. Hindson received the living of Wraysbury in November 1880 and lived at Vine House[24], a large house on the corner of the High Street and Windsor Road, certainly from 1883[25] until at least 1891[26] when the new vicarage was built in Station Road. His mother, Ann Hindson, is shown as living at the new vicarage in the 1891 Census.

In 1897, the Bankes family sold to Mr. George Mellowes Freeman Q.C who remained in ownership until 1926. A founder member of the Parish Council, he employed landscape architect T.H. Mawson from the Lake District to create beautiful Italianate gardens at The Grange. The Gardens were somewhat ahead of their time being softened by different settings using mellow paving and roses, a wild garden, formal yews and a tennis court. The use of water was also featured, with lily pond and fountains.

Mawson was of international repute and from 1910 to 1924 he lectured frequently at Liverpool University. He also contributed articles on garden design to The Studio magazine and The Studio Year Book of Decorative Art. In 1923, he became president of the Town Planning Institute, and in 1929, the first president of the Institute of Landscape Architects. There is also an article/lecture by T.H. Mawson in The Builders Journal & Architectural Record of the 13th March 1901, featuring amongst others, the gardens of The Grange.

It is through the generosity of Mr. Freeman that the village has the village green today. One third of it belonged to The Grange by right, so Mr. Freeman bought the other two thirds for £254 and let it out as grazing for cattle. In c. 1929, he sold it to the village for £150, which was raised by public subscription.

---

[24] Possibly known as Ivy House in Gyll's History of Wraysbury
[25] Kellys Directory 1883
[26] Kellys Directory 1891

Whilst Mr. Freeman retained ownership, he let The Grange in 1916 to Lady Hanson (widow of Lord Francis Hanson, a wealthy London merchant) who lived there until at least 1924. It does seem strange, however, for Mr. Freeman to invest so much money in the gardens when Lady Pearl Norcott Hanson was in residence. One can only assume that Lady Hanson lived in a separate part, maybe the Coach House, although she was quite specific as to her address being The Grange!

The Freeman family c.1920 in their new rose garden – part of a
major scheme by renowned landscape architect T.H. Mawson.
Source: ancestralresearch.org – *Cumbria Archives, Kendal*

Now Lady Hanson was a bit of tarter and used to live at Easterly End, Thorpe where, in 1911, she was successfully sued by her housekeeper for slander. It seemed that Lady Hanson took objection to her staff having a social life, frequenting pubs and smoking, and she publicly harangued this woman for being a drunkard. Lady Hanson's only daughter, Violet, was engaged to William Bullivant but after their marriage she divorced him in 1922 for non-performance! She later married Donald Gregson, in Bombay in 1924. I presume he must have been up to the mark as no further rumblings of discontent were heard.

Eventually Mr. Freeman sold The Grange in 1926 to Major H.E. Meade (Royal Fusiliers) and moved back to Winchester where he had another property, The Priors. Major Meade lived at The Grange until about 1933 when the property was sold to the Sams family.

By direction of D. Borden-Turner, Esq.
"THE GRANGE," WRAYSBURY,
Under one mile from Wraysbury Station.
Messrs. CHANCELLOR & SONS

HAVING let the property, will sell by auction on the premises on Thursday and Friday, 3rd and 4th August, 1916, commencing at one o'clock each day, the surplus FURNITURE, including carpets, Indian and Persian rugs, bedsteads and bedding, bedroom furniture, ash bedroom suite, mahogany tallboy and wardrobe, toilet ware, silk brocade, velvet and other curtains, a large quantity of nearly new linen, oak dining room appointments, Louis XVI. gilt frame settee, very fine carved Japanese cabinet, oil paintings and engravings, kashmir tables, pair of ormolu and crystal candelabra, full-sized billiard table (by Cox and Yeman) with all accessories, Chesterfield and other settees, china, table services and contents of offices, stove and greenhouse plants, quantity of garden tools, rubber hose, lawn mowers, roller, garden seats, pure-bred black minorca poultry, punt, etc., several sets of valuable furs.

On view Wednesday, 2nd August, from 10 till 4. Catalogues can be obtained on the premises or from the Auctioneers, Staines, Ascot and Sunningdale.

Sale of surplus furniture after the house was let.
Source: ancestralresearch.org – Middx. Chronicle 19th July 1916

ENGAGED TO MR. WILLIAM BULLIVANT: MISS VIOLET S. HANSON.
Miss Hanson is a daughter of Lady Stanhope Hanson, of The Grange, Wraysbury. Mr. Bullivant, of The Mill House, Burghfield, and Ryder Street, is the son of the late Mr. W. Pelham Bullivant, of New Mills Court, Stroud, and Bayswater Hill.
Photograph by Bassano.

Engagement of Violet Hanson to William Bullivant
Source: ancestralresearch.org – The Sketch 29th Jan 1919

Getting back to the 1930s, the Sams family thoroughly enjoyed their time at The Grange, in particular Daphne Sams. She had a gift for training and schooling Shetland or miniature ponies for theatre and pantomime work. So well regarded was this that even Pathé News came down and made a short black and white film to show at the cinemas.

PONIES FOR PANTO: Miss Daphne Sams, of the Grange, Wraysbury, near Staines, Middlesex, with four of the thirty-five white Shetlands she has trained herself. They are in great demand for Christmas shows in London and the provinces

Daphne Sams and Team
Source: ancestralresearch.org-The Sphere 19th Dec 1937

The Sams also advertised on a regular basis in The Stage[27], the magazine for the theatrical profession, and from this came most of their stage and pantomime work.

WANTED Known, White also Coloured Cinderella Ponies for Hire, and Coach.—The Grange, Wraysbury. Wraysbury, 149.

Elsie Joan Cole, another village resident, recalls the Grange very well, as she was given her first job there aged 14 years as librarian, plus she had the opportunity to work with the ponies, which she loved.

Thanks to the largesse of the Sams family, The Grange was always a focal point for villagers, with special days: whist drives, musical concerts and fairs being held in the grounds.

---

[27] The Stage – 28th October 1937

It was very helpful with the St. Andrew's Church Restoration Fund and put on special garden fetes with celebrity attendees. The first event was in 1973[28] when the gardens were open for the first time since 1931. The Wraysbury Conservative Association had organised a Garden Party and it attracted over 300 people to The Grange for tea and cakes and to part with their hard-earned cash.

Today it still plays an important part in village society by its very being here and thanks now to the Larcombe family, there is still an annual garden party to fund raise for St. Andrews Church. It would be a sorry day indeed if The Grange ever went the way of The Oast House, Wraysbury House et al.

Meanwhile, in 1938 as the country was awash with rumours of impending trouble in the Balkans, the village was dealing with its own more serious matter. The Paper Mill, also known as Culvett or Coltnett Mill, in Coppermill Road was ablaze. This was a major fire, which threatened to destroy the works. Although it was saved, many workers were put on short time or lost their jobs until it was restored to working order. Originally built in the early 1600s to produce paper, it was converted in the 1800s to mill copper ore. This ore was delivered by river to the landing stage at the end of Wharf Road, then taken by cart to the mill. An interesting fact is that when the mill was producing copper c. 1824, it produced the copper for the Copper Horse statue by Sir Richard Westmacott, which is on the Long Walk, Windsor.

Isaac Warwick initially owned the mill, but around 1919 The Bell Punch and Ticket Company also occupied the premises, the site having been developed over the years from a simple mill area to becoming a small industrial complex. At some stage two modern hydro turbines coupled to a generator were installed to supply electric power to the factory. The Mill continued to supply paper and card up to at least 1969, finally closing in 1971.

> THE Wraysbury Paper Mills, near Windsor, were severely damaged by fire on Saturday, the flames spreading so rapidly that the majority of the buildings were involved. It is feared that several hundred employees will be thrown out of work.

The Scotsman – 21st March 1938
Source: British Newspaper Archive

The two sons of William W. de-Buriatte Paper Mill Owner

John Philip de-Buriatte d.1915 aged 27
Source: WW1 dead

Warwick H. de-Buriatte d.1918 aged 32.
Source: Cranleigh School

[28] Windsor & Eton Gazette 14th September 1973

Chapter 3

World War Two and the 1940s

On the outbreak of World War II, the gravel pit on the Staines road was enlarged by the excavation of a 14-acre barley field for the sand that lay underneath. This was to fill sandbags for the defence of London's properties. Our riverside weekend bungalows became occupied on a permanent basis by evacuee families from London too. A reception area was set up in the village under the watchful eye of Miss Eunice Jones as Billeting Officer. It was her job to persuade and cajole residents to make room for the evacuated families. It was not unusual for two or more families to share a bungalow. The evacuee children were billeted on relations or willing families who were paid accordingly by the government.

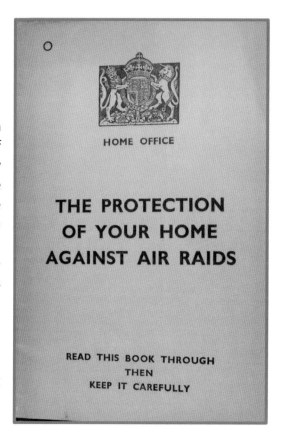

Each family received 10s. 6d. from the government for taking in a child. For each additional child they billeted, a further modest 8s. 6d was paid.

For mothers and infants, the receiving family provided lodging only at a cost of 5s. per adult and 3s. per child. Wraysbury School could not take the evacuated children at first and the old Scout hut on the village green was used as a temporary schoolroom until the 1950s.

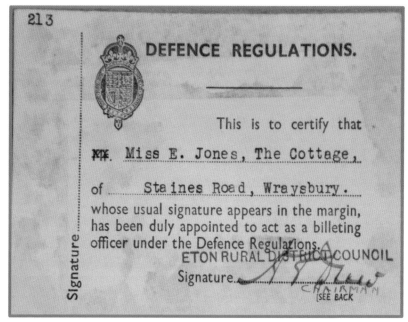

Source -Wraysbury Archives

Maureen Burr, an evacuee, came to the village aged 9 years in 1941 and stayed to this day. She lived with her aunt opposite King John's Hunting Lodge in Old Ferry Drive and clearly remembers her schooling in the Scout Hut, with the little ones on the stage area and older ones gathered around in the main body of the hut. Mr. Hanefey, the head of the school, came down from London to teach, supported by Mrs. Board, who Maureen remembers as being very strict.

Wraysbury School

Girl's Boxwork Team
Source: Wraysbury Archives

Whilst evacuee children were being taught in the Scout Hut, most village children went to school in the High Street but this was not the original site.

Wraysbury Day & Sunday School was originally, certainly in 1845, opposite the George where The Grange/Grange Cottage now stands. According to Gyll's History of Wraysbury, the school was founded in 1828 by St. Andrews Church and the Rev. George Hopkins. However, I suggest that this date is wrong and that the school that opened in 1828, was in fact, the Baptist Sunday School. The reasons for this are twofold, firstly the fact that both establishments should open in the same year is an odd coincidence and secondly and more pointedly, there is editorial space given in the local press to the Wraysbury Day & Sunday School grand opening in 1836, with *"Established Anno Dom 1836"* stated. Why, if it was opened in 1828 would they say 1836?

TO FARMERS, TRADESMEN AND OTHERS.

WRAYSBURY DAY & SUNDAY SCHOOL,
Established Anno Dom. 1836.

THIS School, as a DAY and SUNDAY SCHOOL, will be OPENED for the reception of the Children of those residing in Wraysbury and the neighbouring parishes on SATURDAY, the 23rd of April, 1836, being St. George's Day. It will consist of a Day and Sunday School ; there will be a resident Master and Mistress fully competent to manage and instruct Children of all classes. The principles of the Master and Mistress are those of the Established Church, but the children of Dissenters will be allowed, at the request of the Parents, to attend Chapel, provided that such be open in this parish, between the hours of sun-rise and sun-set, and they produce if required a certificate to that effect ; it being indispensably necessary that the Children instructed at this School should attend regularly some place of public Worship. The Children will be required to meet every Sunday morning at the School, at nine o'clock, and Parishioners will be requested to assist if necessary in the instruction on that morning. There will be one whole Holiday every week ; two Vacations, viz., one at Christmas of one fortnight, and one during Harvest of one month.

Children paying One Penny per week will be instructed to Spell and Read correctly ; those paying Two Pence per week, to Read, Write, and Cipher as far as Practice ; those paying Ninepence per week, or if more, then one from the same family Sixpence each, may be instructed in Reading, Writing, Arithmetic, Mensuration of Land, &c., &c., &c., as available for the business of Farming or useful in Trade, combined with such requisite fundamental information as will be found generally useful.

Instruction in Plain Needlework will be afforded to the Girls, and for this purpose work will be taken in at the School—the Books in general use will be—the Old and New Testament—the Psalter or Psalms of David—an approved Spelling Book—Crossman's introduction to the Knowledge of the Scriptures.

Those with Slates and Pencils will be supplied by the School. Extras beyond these will be supplied at the School at the wholesale price, and must be paid for by the Parents.

In order to meet the extra expenses of this School Voluntary Contributions will be thankfully accepted.

Ankerwycke House, April 10th, 1836,

WRAYSBURY DAY & SUNDAY SCHOOL.

THE PARENTS of CHILDREN admitted into this SCHOOL are required to conform to the following RULES :

I.—To send their Children regularly at nine o'clock in the morning, and at two o'clock in the afternoon, Saturday's excepted, and to see that their hands and faces are clean and their hair combed and kept properly cut.

II.—On no occasion to keep them from School without leave of the Master. An unsanctioned absence of three days will subject them to a fine or punishment, and of a longer period to expulsion from the School.

III.—To cause them to attend regularly on the Sabbath-day either place of Worship in the Parish they may prefer, and to use every means in their power to instruct them in the first principles of their religion.

IV.—To encourage a strict obedience to the Rules and Orders of the School, and particularly to allow their Children to act in such situations as the Master may think most useful either for them or the good of the School.

V.—Each Child is required to bring, on every Monday morning, One Penny or upwards, according to the terms and rate of their education.

N.B.—Rewards, consisting of Articles of Wearing Apparel, &c. &c., will be given to those Children who obtain Tickets for their good behaviour or improvement.

Applications for Admission are received at the School on Saturday mornings, at nine o'clock ; or any morning before one o'clock, at Ankerwycke House.

N.B.—No Child will be allowed to continue as a pupil who shall have neglected for three following weeks to pay two or three weekly subscriptions.   (Signed)

Ankerwycke House,   GEORGE SIMON HARCOURT,
9th April, 1836.   Director.

Confirmation of School Opening in 1836
Source: Windsor & Eton Express 16th April 1836

In addition to the press coverage, there exist also hand bills or flyers reinforcing the 1836 date. Furthermore, when the school moved in 1851 to the old workhouse*, they issued press coverage about the school *re-opening*. Therefore, ipso facto, had the school originally opened in 1828, I would have expected the 1836 press release to say *re-opening* and not *"Established Anno Dom 1836"*. Knowing how much value the Victorians gave to longevity for adding quality, they would surely have put 1828 if the school had indeed opened in that year.

* Francis Buckland, brother of William Thomas Buckland, was Trustee of Church Property from as early as 1828 and, as such, was responsible for the workhouse. He agreed, in 1851, to rent to the Wraysbury School Committee half of the old workhouse for £5 p.a. In doing so however, they booted out the existing tenant and gave him 10s (50p in today's money) for any inconvenience! The workhouse foundation stone was saved from the developers by Nelly Goodman and was built into the front wall of 7 The Green when the new houses were built on the site.

were sent from Horton. This leads us to allude to the absence of G. S. Harcourt, Esq., of Ankerwycke House—a circumstance that must have struck every one present, but which, with a considerate feeling, was never even distantly alluded to. Mr. Harcourt, up to the present year, had been the president, treasurer, and secretary of the association, doing the whole of the work with a scrupulous attention to the most minute details, and, certainly, in the best and most benevolent spirit. An unfortunate dispute arose, within the last twelve months, respecting the management of the Wraysbury School, and has ended in Mr. Harcourt withdrawing his name as a subscriber from every local institution. To prove, however, the deep root which the association had taken in the affections of the landowners and farmers of the district, it is only necessary to state that it survived the defection of Mr. Harcourt, and closes its anniversary with a heavier subscription list and brighter

Source: Windsor & Eton Express
15th September 1851

In early 1851, there was also a falling out with Mr. George Simon Harcourt, the provider of the original school premises, over matters of administration of the school and he withdrew his support for all clubs and activities to do with the village. As a result, the school closed for a number of months. This I believe was the cause of the move to the workhouse. With the school now unable to use The Grange, it closed until Francis Buckland, trustee of church property, was persuaded to rent out the workhouse to the new school committee, consisting of the Rev. George Hopkins, Francis Buckland and other notable worthies and the school reopened in the September of 1851. See below.

REPORT OF THE COMMITTEE OF MANAGEMENT.

The subscribers to the Wyrardisbury Day and Sunday School met July 30th, 1851, at the Vestry Room, for the purpose of adopting and carrying out the best possible method of conducting and managing the affairs of the same, and as every subscriber is considered a member of the general Committee, it was agreed that a Committee of management should be elected for the purpose of superintending all things belonging to the said School—the undermentioned willingly undertook the office, viz :—B. H. Gyll, Esq., G. W. Gyll, Esq., R. Ibotson, Esq., Mr. Pullin, Mr. Roumieu, Mr. Jordan, and Rev. Geo. Adol. Hopkins, M.A.

It was unanimously resolved that the Rev. G. A. Hopkins should continue Honorary Secretary, and that he also take the office of Treasurer.

The Committee having agreed with Mr. F. Buckland—trustee to the Church property—to rent of him half of the old workhouse for the sum of £5 per annum, and that they might have immediate possession of the premises, agreed to pay the rent from Midsummer day last, and to recompence the then tenant, by paying him 10s at Michaelmas next for any inconvenience he might be put to in removing upon so short a notice ; and he is also allowed to take his crops off the ground when the proper period arrives.

The Committee of management, anxious that no time should be lost, forthwith sent for Mr. Clark to prepare an estimate for the thorough repairing and painting the premises, as well as the fitting up of the two lower rooms for the schools ; his estimate having been laid before the Committee, and having had their serious attention, it was agreed between the parties that the sum of £13 should be paid for the same, and Mr. Clark undertook to fulfil his agreement by the 13th of September, provided two new grates were found by the Committee, which has been done.

The Committee then took into consideration the appointment of a Master and Mistress ; it was resolved that the Secretary should advertise and obtain the most eligible parties he possibly could, and their joint emolument should be £20 per annum from the Treasurer—the children's pence (according to the rules laid down by the Committee)—apartments over the school-rooms—and any profit that may accrue from their providing the scholars with copy and ciphering books, pencils, or any article that may not be found by the subscribers.

The Committee of management then called upon the inhabitants of the parish, soliciting their kind aid to support that which must be acknowledged so desirable an object, and it is with grateful thanks they have to report that their exertions were met in the most liberal manner ; yet they would wish to impress most respectfully upon all not to relax in any way from obtaining donations and subscriptions.

The Committee have elected, through the Secretary, Mr. and Mrs. Ellis, as School-master and School-mistress, and sincerely do they trust, under Divine Providence, that there will be Christian charity amongst all, and that their endeavours to carry out the wishes of the subscribers may prove beneficial to the families of the labouring classes of the parish of Wyrardisbury.

The Committee announce that all subscriptions are due on the 29th of September, and will be collected on that day or within one week afterwards.

By order of the Committee,   GEO. ADOL. HOPKINS, Hon. Secretary and Treasurer.
September, 1851.

The following notice was issued previous to the re-opening of the School in 1851.

"This School as a Day and Sunday School, will be re-opened for the reception of the Children of those residing in Wyrardisbury, on Monday, September 29th, 1851.

It consists of a Day and Sunday School. There will be a resident Master and Mistress, fully competent to manage and instruct the Children.

The principles of the Master and Mistress are those of the Established Church, but the Children of Dissenters will be allowed—at the request of their parents—to attend Chapel, provided such be open in the parish, and they produce, if required, a certificate to that effect; it being indispensably necessary that the children instructed at this School should attend regularly some place of Public Worship.

The Children will be required to meet every Sunday morning at the school, at half-past nine o'clock, and parishioners will be requested, if necessary, to assist in the instruction on that morning.

There will be one whole holiday every week; two vacations, viz. one fortnight at Christmas, and one month during harvest.

Children paying one penny per week will be instructed to spell and read correctly.

Those paying twopence per week, to read, write, and cipher as far as practice.

Practical instruction in plain needlework will be afforded to the girls, and for this purpose work will be taken in at the school.

The books in general use will be the Old and New Testament, secular reading books, an approved Spelling Book, and Crossman's Introduction to the Knowledge of the Christian Religion; these, with slates, will be supplied by the Committee; all beyond these will be supplied at the school by the master, and must be paid for by the parents.

In order to meet the great extra expenses of this school, voluntary contributions will be thankfully received by the Committee of Management: B. H. Gyll, Esq., G. W. Gyll, Esq., R. Ibotson, Esq., Mr. Pullin, Mr. Roumieu, Mr. Jordan. Rev. G. A. Hopkins, Hon. Secretary. Wyrardisbury, September, 1851.

Source: Gyll's History of Wraysbury 1862

Wraysbury School c. 1950s??
Source: Wraysbury Archives

In 1874, a new school was built in the High Street and it was enlarged in 1907. Originally boys and girls were taught separately, there being separate entrances for each. They were later taught by age group and the pupils allowed to mix.

Rosalind Willatts remembers her infant school days[29] with affection and recalls a clear divide of pupils from middle class and working class families. The lack of underwear on some of the boys being noticeable through rents and holes in their trousers, and the bucket sanitation being quite vivid memories!

---

[29] Memories of Wraysbury School – Rosalind Willatts

School's two sets of twins c. 1954/6
Gerald and Flossie Young (Head Prefects) and Billy
and Dorothy Taylor (Head Boy and Girl)

By 1952 the main school was an all-age school of 250 pupils and by the end of April 1954, work had at last begun on replacing the bucket sanitation!

Mrs. Barbara Board retired in 1968 and ended a long association with the main school, which started with her grandparents (Samuel and Elizabeth Worth) when they opened the school in 1874. Mr. Watson, who was headmaster throughout the war years, retired in 1953 after 25 years' service. Mr. Robson became the next headmaster and at the time there was also a teacher Mr. Dunn, notorious for knuckle rapping with a three-foot ruler! Mr. Robson retired a well loved and respected head in 1978.

Later in the 1970s a new school was built in Welley Road and the first admission was in October 1974,[30] thereafter a staged admissions process was used to absorb pupils from the old school. In 1987, the old school was converted into houses and is now known as Old School Court, which was opened by Beryl Reid. The school has a good reputation both with OFSTED and parents, many seeing their children blossom and develop, gaining a foothold on the ladder to university, thanks to the dedication of various heads and teachers throughout the years.

Class from the Past
Source: Wraysbury Archives

---

[30] Wraysbury School by J. L. Robson

1955-6 School Football Team
Source: Wraysbury Village Archives

Girls Pottery Class
Source: Wraysbury Village Archives

Baptist Chapel and Sunday School

At this point in our look back at school life, the Baptist Chapel and Sunday School should be acknowledged for the part they played, and that the church continues to play, in village life. During the Second World War the Rev. Thomas Black was the minister and much loved by his congregation for his devotion to the sick. He discontinued the afternoon services and moved the evening service to 6pm due to the numerous air raid warnings.

From the start of the war, the school room extension fund was active and finally in 1956 enough had been raised to complete the renovations. A milestone agreement by the church in 1946 allowed ladies to become deacons and Gladys Jones, a missionary who served in India became the first.

Sadly, on the 28th August 1942, Stuart Cecil Holden, son of church deacon Cecil Holden was killed. Stuart was a Sergeant (Wireless Op./Air Gunner No. 1261903) in the RAF and is commemorated at Reichswald Forest War Cemetery, Germany and Ashford County School, Church Road, Ashford now Spelthorne College.

On a historical note, it was thought that Mr. William Thomas Buckland first opened the Sunday School for Baptists (or Dissenters, as they were known) on the 1st May 1827. But, having now had the opportunity to examine his personal diary[31] for that time, I can confirm that it did not open until March 2nd 1828 (the same year as allegedly, the Wraysbury Day and Sunday School with which, I believe, it has been confused as stated earlier). The Baptist Sunday School was indeed the first to open.

William Thomas Buckland was born at Rectory Farm (later known as Tithe Farm) in 1798, the youngest of six children. He went to school in Camberwell and afterwards was apprenticed to a company in Reading, of which he spoke with little affection, having found it a very difficult period in his life. He later started his own bakery in Hammersmith, west London, and was made a Freeman of the City of London. He married in 1826 and moved back to Wraysbury, becoming the farm manager and establishing the then well-known firm of Buckland Surveyors and Auctioneers. Both he and Mary, his wife, were very devout and were somewhat taken aback by what they considered to be the lack of morals and spiritual condition among the villagers. A passage from Mr. Buckland's diary states, 'Like sheep without a shepherd, the people wandered far from God, and no man seemed to care for their souls.' As such he was determined to do something about it.

According to his writings, on the 1st May 1827 he 'took two cottages to convert into a meeting room and signed the licence for it.' (The exact whereabouts are unconfirmed see * and **).

It is possible that this was the workhouse, also collectively known later as Church Cottages, 5/6 attached cottages. According to again the North Surrey & Middlesex Mission, 26th January 1831, 'The new meeting house has been opened but prayer meetings are held at several houses in the village, including the workhouse and are crowded to excess.' Therefore, can it be concluded that despite the new chapel being opened, the original meeting room was still kept on, to which eventually, the Wraysbury day and Sunday school moved to in 1851?

---

[31] Courtesy - The Baptist Magazine 1871.

**It is also recorded that two cottages were leased from a Mr. Howlett but the Tithe Map only records a Mrs. Howlett living in the High Street near where Vine House is now. He did later buy property in the High Street but this was from Mr. Leno to build the chapel. It is clear from Gyll's History that Francis Buckland, brother of William Thomas Buckland, was Trustee of Church Property from as early as 1828 and was responsible for the workhouse. With the workhouse 'in the family' so to speak, William Thomas Buckland would have been able to have ready access to it. So, it may be that the original meeting room and Sunday school, were at the old workhouse.

On the 20th May 1827, the first meeting was held and thereafter on every other Sunday. From September of the same year, evening preaching once a fortnight began with, ultimately, on 6th January 1828, the meeting house being enlarged still further to accommodate two hundred souls. With the parents now attending in numbers, William now thought it right to introduce the Sunday School and, on the 2nd March 1828, the meeting room had its first session. This is confirmed by published correspondence of the North Surrey and Middlesex Mission, which was charged with the spread of the Gospel to so-called 'destitute' villages, of whom the secretary was the Rev. J. H. Hindson, who, in 1880, became vicar of St. Andrews. (There is perhaps another clue to the meeting room/school's location and that is from another diary entry dated the 23rd January 1829, where William remarks that the 'meeting house bible and hymn book have been robbed – but found 6 months later when the corn was cut in the field opposite.')

With the Baptists' growing popularity, William decided that a new place of worship was required and in 1830, for £45, he purchased a plot of land in the High Street, from the Leno family, and it is this plot of land that the chapel stands on today. Within four months, the new chapel, named Providence Chapel, was finished and it was later extended at the rear.

In 1862, with the help of a generous donation of £100 from John Doulton of Doulton Pottery fame, a new and much larger chapel was built. William Buckland died on the 1st November 1870 and was buried in the village churchyard on the 7th November. In 1880, William's son, Virgo Buckland, had the clock tower built and the chapel enlarged in honour of his late father. The Doulton family was also involved in the design of the tower and Mr. James Doulton became Sunday School Superintendent and deacon. He died after thirty years' service to the Baptist Chapel.

Baptist Chapel in 1862 with William Buckland
Source: Baptist Chapel

The Sunday school thrived in the 20th Century, largely thanks to a wonderful treasure of the village, Daisy Darling, who was adored for many years by the young pupils in her care. The Chapel, or Church as it is now called, still plays an important part in many villagers' lives and, in addition to its services, holds weekly coffee mornings, various larger events and organises support for local charities for the hungry and homeless. Much effort is put into collecting food for the Slough Foodbank and clothes and bedding for Slough Homeless Our Concern. The emphasis of the church being to make a difference to people's lives and the life of the village. The church, its history and its congregation are now in the care of the Revd. Carolyn Urwin whose dedication and hard work are known and seen by all.

Then and Now

William Thomas Buckland
Source: Baptist Chapel

Revd. Carolyn Urwin
Source: Urwin Family Archives

Ormiston House Preparatory School

Wraysbury also had a small private school called Ormiston Preparatory School, founded c. 1928 at The Tiny Grange in Hill View Road. In 1934, it then moved to No. 3 Welley Road where it remained for the duration of WW2 and shortly thereafter. The Principal was Miss Dorothy Jane Ormiston Lundie, assisted by her sister Evaline Mary Taske Lundie and their mother Mrs. Elizabeth Lawson Lundie. It was in existence up until c. 1950 when the Lundies moved to Worthing. It then became Ormiston Nursery for infants and lasted until about the late 70s when it reverted to a private house.

*Ormiston Prep. School c. 1948
Source: Joan Mitchell Family

*See also page **ib** of the Timeline

Country Life – getting back to business

More shops were opened in the village by the 1940s, of which two were cycle shops, Price's next door to the present Sai News and Post Office, and a cycle repair shop run by Mr. Frederick Woods, next to the Baptist Chapel. There were also two men's barber shops, one owned by Alfred Head in what is now the Sai News and Post Office, and also one in Welley Road run by Arthur Davis. Arthur had a club foot and was an epileptic, so it was always a bit of risk having a neck trim or shave when he had the cut-throat razor out!

There was a credit drapers shop on the corner of Windsor and Welley Road and next door a confectioners and general store. There were two butchers, Reeves (previously Jordans) and Gilletts, plus, as mentioned earlier, a haberdasher next to the paper shop in the High Street near the Baptist Chapel. Also, round the back of The Green was a greengrocer's and general store called The Handy Store, owned and run by the Catchpole family. Jennie Francis remembers hearing that they had some bananas and running there with the ration books and being given one banana per book! It later became a Co-op.

Where RK Leisure's office is now, in Staines Road, used to be Eavis's Dairy from Manor Farm, later owned by the Willatts family. There was also another dairy, this was in the farm at Wraysbury House owned by the Herrings. Bertha Herring had a prize herd of Guernsey cows and their farm sold eggs, milk, butter and buttermilk. Buttermilk was a favourite of Mrs. Powell, who was convinced it helped her rheumatism! The Herrings also bred rabbits and specialised in Angora ones, which they brushed daily. The cottage from the farm was called Greenwood Cottage (now Greenwood by the Lake) and is still in existence at the beginning of the lower entrance road to Wraysbury station.

Mr. Tilbury the shoe repairer, who was initially next to Budgens, on land that was originally Longbridge Farm, was lucky enough to be able to move from his old shed into one of the shops on the new parade, and we also had Mr. Balthazzar, who made shoes by hand in the house near to the Baptist Church. Opposite Mr. Tilbury was Kemp's the general grocer's (later known as Stonells), whilst next to Mr. Tilbury was Mr and Mrs. Henry's tea and cake shop followed by Phyllis Fleming's ladies' hairdressers and finally Percy Powell's The Garden Shop.

The village also had a number of garages. Concorde Garage, originally run by Lesley Bayford and later by Mr. Horace Saltmarsh, another one by the Splash run by Reg Spratt a bit of a character, and one that is now Reeds in Welley Road. According to Rosalind Willatts, when Princess Elizabeth, then in the ATS, was driving her vehicle through the village, it broke down and was fixed by Mr. Saltmarsh. This was all hushed up of course and never made the papers.

Wraysbury, like every other part of Britain, was on rations, both during the war and up to the 4th July 1954, when meat and bacon were finally declared free from rationing. Through the war years, those families with children were generally better off*, as extra rations over and above the standard amount were allowed for each child.

*The Government was good to children in World War Two in spite of the severity of rationing. Children had their own ration books, which were more generous than those of adults. Pre-school children had allowances of cod-liver oil and orange juice, which were collected from the local clinic. This continued well after the war and the clinics became, in effect, a local health centre for the community.

A thrifty housewife could make her limited provisions stretch but certain items were to remain impossible to obtain or else the housewife was persuaded to give them up for the 'war effort'. Wedding cakes are a classic case where most couples had to 'make do' using a fancy wedding cake cardboard cover over a simple sponge cake or suet pudding; dried fruit and glacé cherries being almost impossible to find! Friends and family would come together and save up their coupons for that special cake or occasion.

Elsie Cole's father bred rabbits and others did too, a healthy and cheap addition to weekly meals, rabbit was very popular with both stews and casseroles being firm favourites. It fell out of favour as other meats became available after rationing ended. Being a rural farming community, there was always someone who could supply that little extra. There were, in addition, numerous allotments throughout the village and every spare piece of ground was turned over to vegetable growing in the 'Dig for Victory' campaign, which supplemented many a household's rations.

Jennie Francis, or Jennie Head as she was then aged about 14 years old, worked at The Garden Shop owned by the Powells where she learned to make wreaths from individual hand-wired flower stems, not the foam blocks as are used now! She then moved on to Sunnymeads Stores with Mr. White where she learned the grocery trade. By this time, Wilf Newington had had enough of the Fish Shop by the Splash and fancied buying Mr. Lovell's grocer's shop called Wraysbury General Stores. This he did and he and his wife, Nancy, engaged Jennie to 'teach them the ropes'. Here Jennie put her experience into practice and, in return, was taught every aspect of the catering trade and, in particular, how to dress a pig from head to tail so that none was wasted. This was very important to know when working in the shop as bacon and other cuts had to be prepared. Mr. Lewington used to take her in his car to Amersham where the pigs were processed and she was 'thrown in at the deep end' so to speak, witnessing the whole operation from start to finish. Quite something for a young teenage girl to take in! In the meanwhile, Mr. Lewington went off to socialise with his pals at the Grocers' Association.

Jennie remembers Mr. Lewington was always on the phone to the suppliers, trying to increase his quotas to keep up with the ever-increasing demand of the swelling wartime population. There was never enough. Cheese was a particularly difficult item. Supplied in blocks, it had to be cut with a cheese wire for each person's ration and not every piece could be exactly two ounces! Consequently, customers who didn't have enough felt short changed, whereas others felt they had got a good deal! And the ration coupons - well that was a job and a half, she recalls. She would be upstairs on the floor counting out hundreds of those little square coupons, all of which had to be accounted for against what was supplied, so you needed to be on the ball!

Jennie loved her work and was soon poached by the grocer in Eton High Street for an extra £1:10s (£1:50p) a week, a well-deserved increase which went a long way then.

Wraysbury had its own Home Guard troop or LDV (Local Defence Volunteers), some would say, 'Look, Duck and Vanish', made up from the men in reserved occupations or more senior citizens, not able to go into the Services. Under the leadership of Mr. Tim Haines of Elm Lodge, men like Sid Andrews, postmaster, and Benjamin Willatts, dairy farmer, met on Sundays at

The George and were issued with armbands and sworn in, the minimum age being 18 years - the same as for the armed forces. Although, rumour has it that a lot of younger boys 'joined up' and became irregulars for the LDV, passing them bits of information and generally keeping their ears and eyes open. The job of the LDV was patrolling the railways, rivers, reservoirs and factory sites, and keeping their 'ears to the ground' for anything that sounded suspicious. Ultimately, they would have had to harass the enemy had it reached Wraysbury and generally conduct a guerrilla war until such times as help or further instructions were received. Initially they had no uniforms or rifles but these were supplied gradually as they became available. They seemed to have had a good time nonetheless, if their invitations to the Railway Arms and reunions after the war were anything to go by!

Wraysbury LDV Reunion Card
Source: Hattie Shinkle (nee Haines)
Wraysbury Archives

HOME GUARD

No. 3 Platoon, "B" Company, of the 10th Bucks Battalion, Home Guard, is open for a few volunteers in Wraysbury willing to become members of mobile units.

Source: Middlesex Chronicle 10th Jan. 1942

THE VILLAGE AMBULANCE

The ambulance for which a great many of the residents of Wraysbury have subscribed was delivered last week. On arrival it was driven round the district by the chairman of the fund, Mr. Guy Baron, who was accompanied by the treasurer, Mrs. Reffell, and a nurse attendant, Mrs. Mason. It is a Chrysler chassis with accommodation for four patients, and is complete with blankets and hot water bottles.

Source: Middlesex Chronicle 26th October 1940

Welcome Home Scroll
Source: Wraysbury Archives

Whilst the servicemen and women of Wraysbury were away in the war, the residents arranged to send them all a Christmas card with a £1 note inside every year.[32] Bill Warner, an ex-RAF man and old resident who returned for the War Memorial dedication in 2000, remembers the card had the greeting 'We wish you a merry Christmas from the residents of Wraysbury', a token from home that was much appreciated. Later, when the war ended and our village servicemen come home, they were presented with a Certificate of Thanks by Alfred Reffell, chairman of the Welcome Home Committee on behalf of the villagers. This was a wonderful gesture as many servicemen had felt forgotten sometimes, especially those who served in Burma long after VE Day.

Not all of our Wraysbury boys came back from the war as our war memorials sadly confirm. Let's look at three of them who died, so that future generations could remain free. We'll take two that have their graves in St. Andrews Churchyard and one whose grave is the Mediterranean Sea.

Pilot Officer 1169534 Anthony Hugh Denison Reffell, Royal Air Force Volunteer Reserve died on Active Service on the 6th February 1942 aged 21 years. Anthony Roberts (Reffell) was the son of Hugh Denison Roberts and of Hilda Frances Buckenham. When Hilda later married Alfred Reffell of Manor Farm, Wraysbury, Anthony took the Reffell surname. He volunteered for the RAF at the outbreak of hostilities.

On 6 February 1942, PO Reffell and two others, prepared for night flying training[33] in a Bristol Beaufort Mk I. Their flight took off from RAF Chivenor just after 6pm when the aircraft suffered an engine failure in the initial stages of the flight. Engine failure on the Beaufort was a major problem in 1940 and all Beauforts were grounded for a while. After modification they resumed service but the Taurus engine was never fully sorted out until the Beaufort Mk.11 was produced using Taurus Mk.XII engines. In the resultant crash, all three on board were killed. PO Reffell is buried in St. Andrews to the right of the Lytchgate on the way in.

Private 6091271 John Hazel Fulton, 1/5th Battalion Queen's (Royal West Surrey Regiment), was killed on Active Service on the 5th July 1940. The son of George and Mary Jane Fulton of Roseland, Ouseley Road, Wraysbury. He enlisted in 1939 and the 1/5th Regiment were part

---

[32] Staines and Egham News 7th March 1975

[33] Reffell family archives.

of the 131st (Queen's) Infantry Brigade (44th [Home Counties] Division), a 1st Line Territorial division. They were sent to join the British Expeditionary Force in 1940. They quickly became involved in what was later to be called the Battle for France and later, between 26 May and 4 June 1940, the Dunkirk evacuation. He is listed as being accidentally killed but how is not recorded on the Casualty List. John's Regiment is the oldest English line Infantry Regiment in the British Army as it was first raised in 1661 as The Earl of Peterborough's Regiment of Foot, by Henry Mordaunt 2nd Earl of Peterborough. John is buried in St. Andrew's churchyard alongside the railings of Church Meadow. John's parents both died in 1941, within a month of each other and are also buried in the churchyard.

Seaman C/JX398741 Geoffrey Kenneth Grenville Bilton, Royal Navy rating on HMT Rohna, previously the S.S. Rohna, died on Active Service 26th November 1943, aged 19 years. He was the son of William and Mary Bilton of St. Helena, Staines Road, Wraysbury. HMT Rohna was a British India Steam Navigation Company passenger and cargo liner that was built on Tyneside in 1926 as the SS Rohna and requisitioned as a troopship in 1940. She was part of convoy KMF-26 travelling from Oran to Alexandria when the convoy was attacked by Heinkel 177 bombers and sunk by a radio-controlled glide bomb. 1138 men were lost of whom 1015 were American, plus 5 ship's officers and 117 naval ratings and 1 gunner.

This is still the largest loss of American lives at sea in a single incident. The US Government released sketchy details over the years but it was not until 1967 and the passing of the Freedom of Information Act that the full story came out. Geoffrey Bilton lies with his ship off the coast of Algeria and is commemorated on our church and village hall Memorial Boards, he is also listed on the Chatham Naval Memorial, for those who lost their lives at sea.

In an interview with me, one of Wraysbury's WW2 veterans, Mr. John Sleep of Hythe End, recalled his army life with humour and no regrets. John volunteered into the Royal Berkshires and was sent to North Africa, where he took part in the chase with Eisenhower's forces to trap Rommel at Tunis. Hoping that with Montgomery coming up from Tobruk, Rommel would be caught in the pincer movement. Unfortunately, he got away but the whole of the Africa Corps was routed and that really was the beginning of the end or 'the end of the beginning' as Churchill said.

John volunteered for parachute training and became one of the first in what was called 1st Airborne. Along with the Commandos, these were to be the first troops landed by air to establish surprise bridgeheads in occupied Europe and Italy. However, when John was sent to take part in the invasion of Italy, the 1st Airborne were sent in by boat, not plane! At that time, amphibious landings were in their infancy and one of their boats hit a mine, causing a large number of casualties.

He later took part in Operation Market Garden and on D-day +4, found himself alone except for an officer of the Norfolk Regiment. They joined forces and John became a de facto member of the Norfolks. Whilst making their way through Holland, chasing the Germans, John surprised a Panzer tank by the Molenbeek near Venray and, luckily for John, the tank fired in such haste that the shell penetrated the soft river bank. However, some of the resultant shrapnel fragments badly wounded him in the hand, elbow and backside.

After being invalided out to hospital, John remembers his mate sending him a letter to say their Commanding Officer had received the M.C. for the action but all John had received was 'two arseholes', referring to him being wounded in the backside! Such was the humour and life of the British soldier.

It wasn't only Service men and women that did their bit in the war, civilians played their part too. In addition to the villagers on war work making bombers, guns, ammunition and flame throwers at places like Lagonda Cars and Vickers, two of our residents come to mind. Firstly, the late Kay Walters, wife of one of the village archivists the late Arthur Walters, was recruited to Bletchley Park, the code-breaking centre, in 1944 (she may have felt driven as both of her brothers were killed in the war). Churchill had a saying that the staff there were like 'the geese that laid the golden eggs but never cackled.' After the war, Kay, a talented singer and actress, performed at various theatres including the former La Scala theatre in the West End.

Secondly, we are indebted to Christie Willatts, cartographer par excellence, whose parents lived at Horton View, Station Road. He was recruited by the wartime government to run a geographic information system in the days before the term itself was invented.

He had been the organising force behind Britain's first land utilisation survey and from his knowledge was able to advise on what land throughout Britain was suitable for food production. From the London School of Economics, he took all his paperwork to the government's printers, which were then promptly blitzed! He started over again from a drawing office in his home at Horton. The Royal Geographical Society awarded him the Gill Memorial Award in 1950 for research and he was appointed an OBE in 1958. He helped to found, and later became, an honorary member of the British Cartographic Society.

Another resident worthy of note was Cyril Long of 23 Staines Road, father of Audrey, better known to older Wraysbury residents as Betty. Cyril worked for the Ministry of Fuel and Power and is believed to have been involved with PLUTO, the pipeline under the ocean, crucial to the nation's success on D-Day.

'Come Friendly Bombs and Fall on Slough'
Bomb damage and munition accidents in Wraysbury were relatively small compared to other more industrialised places but nonetheless were still devastating to those it affected.

To deal with four that wrecked families in Wraysbury, we must first look at the flying bomb, or Doodlebug as it was nicknamed, that landed in Ouseley Road. These Doodlebugs were the forerunner of today's rockets and were simply a high explosive charge on the end of a rocket motor, filled with a predetermined amount of fuel. Once the fuel ran out, the engine stopped and the rocket fell to earth. They emitted a weird noise in flight and those under their flight path would listen intently hoping that the motor wouldn't cut out above them!

The one in Ouseley Road arrived in the early hours of the 17th June 1944 and landed on the bungalow called Lyndhurst, belonging to Mr. and Mrs. Essling, a retired master baker and his wife. Both were killed and their bungalow was destroyed. Mr. and Mrs. Essling are buried in St. Andrew's cemetery. Sadly, they are not remembered on the village Memorial Board.

Further extensive damage was done to other surrounding property in particular the bungalow next door. An evacuee boy was billeted there and he slept in the loft and was alone in the house that night. The explosion blew the outer wall off and left him trapped upstairs by his arm. He was rescued by the ARPs and volunteers but his arm was so badly damaged it had to be amputated. In later life, he re-visited Wraysbury and called in at the Archives to tell the tale of that dreadful night to archivist Anne Blake.

The V-1 Flying Bomb or Rocket (Doodlebug)
Source: Tony Kimber

Secondly, there was a bomb at The Feathers Pub at Hythe End in October 1940, where again casualties and deaths occurred. It was rumoured to be a doodlebug but it is not supported by official evidence and in any event, doodlebugs (V1's) were not used until 1944.

Thirdly, a dreadful accident occurred on the 18th March 1942 to three young boys, Lawrence and Lewis Hatcher, twins aged 13 years, and Reginald Jacobs, an evacuee, also aged 13. They were all playing in The Spinney, an area of woodland that ran down the end of Riverside, towards and along the embankment. In all it was about 300 yards long and was then also used for exercises by the army. The boys discovered boxes of a type of mortar bomb and took some to their hideout hidden further in the woods. Whilst playing around, one went off killing all three of them. At the inquest, Mr. Duthie, Counsel for the parents, tried to pursue the army for negligence for leaving the bombs unguarded but it was ruled against. The boys are buried in St. Andrew's cemetery. They too, are not remembered on the village Memorial Board.

Lastly, William and Evelyn Powney of 1 Somerset Villas, Hythe End lost their newly married daughter, Evelyn Elsie Bishop. She was killed in the Blitz in the early hours of the 17th April 1941 when Paddington station received direct hits. She was 20 years old and is buried in St. Andrew's cemetery. She *is* remembered on the Memorial Board in the Village Hall.

The Death of Elsie Bishop (Powney)
Paddington Station Departure Road 17th April 1941 after a direct hit with a Landmine
Source: ©Swindon Steam Museum – Museums & Heritage

Air Raids	28/29th September 1940	Sand and Gravel Company	No damage. Occurred overnight 28/29th September
Air Raids	30th Sep/1st October 1940	Wraysbury	Damage to private rail line and Wraysbury Tithe farm.
Air Raids	9/10th October 1940	King John's Hunting lodge	No damage. Occurred overnight 9th to 10th October.
Air Raids	19/21st October 1940	Hythe End The Feathers pub	Casualties. Occurred between 19th and 21st October.
Air Raids	26/28th October 1940	Wraysbury Gravel pits	No damage. Occurred between 26th and 28th October.
Air Raids	15/16th November 1940	Wraysbury	House damaged overnight 15th to 16th November
Air Raids	23/24th February 1941	Wraysbury	Fire caused. Occurred overnight 23rd to 24th February.
Air Raids	23rd February 1944	Douglas lane	Hayrick burnt.
Air Raids	23rd February 1944	Riverside, Wraysbury	Houses splashed with phosphorous.
Air Raids	23rd February 1944	Staines Road	No damage.
Air Raids	25th May 1944	Old Ferry	Boats and riverbank damaged.
Air Raids	16th June 1944	'Bells of Ouseley' public house.	Many houses damaged.
Flying Bombs	16th June 1944	Wraysbury	'Bells of Ouseley' public house.
Flying Bombs	17th June 1944	Wraysbury	Ouseley Road, casualties and houses damaged.

Officially recorded bomb and Doodlebug damage on Wraysbury in WW2
Source: Bucks.gov.uk-culture services[34]

---

[34] Bucks C C.gov.uk – The Blitz

Another related tragedy that had a profound effect on the lives of a number of residents was the bombing of Vickers aircraft factory. The town of Weybridge was home to the Vickers and Hawker factories during the war and Vickers was heavily bombed on Wednesday 4th September 1940[35] at 1.30 in the afternoon. Despite trees planted in barrels around the perimeter and acres of camouflage netting, the constant stream of cyclists and workers going to and fro didn't leave much to the imagination that something was there: It was a secret hive of industry where Vickers made the Wellington bomber and the factory worked around the clock in a series of shifts. This day was no different when German bombers came and bombed the factory complex. No warning had been given, they were used to aircraft noise anyway and nobody thought much about it until the bombs started to fall. 83 workers were killed and 419 were wounded.

One of those wounded was James Blake, Anne Blake's father. He was an engineer working in one of the hangars when the bombs fell. He was blown off his feet by the blast and all his clothes were shredded, in particular his trousers! Anne remembers very well, her mother telling her, of the day her father came home with shrapnel debris embedded in his face and jaw, and no part of his body left untouched, with his trousers all gathered around his legs with bandages and pins. Feeling shocked, vulnerable and exposed, James slept for many months under the bed rather than on it.

In addition to her father, a number of other members of Anne Blake's family worked at Vickers. It also employed a number of other Wraysbury residents but despite the bombing and the injuries, it was back to work if you were able: the country needed bombers and they were going to get them!

There were no Barrage Balloons fitted at Vickers but after this incident they were installed within a week! The Vickers site is now under Brooklands Museum and other modern offices, but it is remembered in the road and site names around the complex. After the war, it still employed village residents and Graham Sinclair completed his toolmaker's apprenticeship there, for which he was always grateful. It gave him the opportunity to supervise Jupiter missile installation in Turkey and later the ability to look after his own race cars.

Air Crashes

Wraysbury and its environs had a few air crashes as well, in particular an American Air Force B17E-Flying Fortress[36] crash-landed at Runnymede in autumn 1944, after running out of fuel. The pilot made a good wheels-up landing and finished opposite Magna Carta Island. (In addition, something not readily known is that Runnymede was an emergency landing strip and at least two Spitfires were known to have landed and taken off from there.)

A German Dornier bomber[37] also crashed into the Runnymede fields opposite Magna Carta Island and Mr. Butcher, who ran the ferry, made a lot of money from inquisitive Wraysbury residents anxious to see the crashed plane!

---

[35] All About Weybridge. co. uk

[36] Staines and Egham News 31st Mar 1983

[37] Peter Norton's WW2 memories.

On the 27th November 1945 Flight Lt. John Collinette Evans was killed when his Fairy Firefly crashed[38] at Hythe End. The aircraft took off from Heston and was soon in trouble. It was determined afterwards that the cockpit hood had become detached and stunned the pilot, leaving the plane to nosedive into the ground.

There were other reports of a crashed Spitfire and a Hurricane in 1942/44 in the Wraysbury area but these cannot be substantiated with documentation or records of any kind. This does not mean, however, that they never happened. Depending on the circumstances of the flight, they may not have been listed as missing for official/security reasons.

Another interesting local fact concerns the RAF Memorial at Egham. It is said that it was positioned at the top of Coopers Hill, because this was the spot the bombers circled before forming up and heading off across the Channel, many never to return. It celebrates the lives of servicemen like John Collinette-Evans and it is one of the most moving places to visit. If you were to stand there at dusk, looking up to the sky, it wouldn't take too much imagination to see them all, the night air filling with the heavy drone of bombers. *Per Ardua Ad Astra - Through Adversity To The Stars.*

Keeping up Appearances

The Wraysbury WI or Women's Institute played its role in the war. Formed in 1929, its first president was Mrs. E. Henry (of cake shop fame!). It had numerous other village figures as president and during the war years and just after, the president was Mrs. Sherriff and, under her guidance, the institute was responsible for various initiatives such as, in 1942, they set to with a canning machine and made 151 tins of vegetables and fruit. This was followed in 1943 by the writing to Prisoners of War with home news, and knitting garments for the Russians, who were then, of course, our allies.

WRAYSBURY W.I. PRESIDENTS			
1929 – 1935	Mrs. E. Henry	1960 – 1961	Mrs. M. Bicknell
1935 – 1936	Mrs. Reffell	1961 – 1962	Mrs. V. Goodfellow
1936 – 1938	Mrs. J.E. Willatts	1962 – 1964	Mrs. E. Richmond
1938 – 1940	-----	1964 – 1965	Mrs. V. Benney
1940 – 1948	Mrs. D. Sherriff	1965 – 1968	Mrs. B. Hannay
1948 – 1953	Mrs. D. Badham	1968 – 1971	Mrs. O. Satterthwaite
1953 – 1956	Mrs. C. Hope	1971 – 1976	Mrs. I. Smith
1956 – 1960	Mrs. D. Badham	1976 –	Mrs. P. Willatts

Presidents of Wraysbury WI
Source: Wraysbury WI by Peggy Willatts

They had their fingers in all sorts of village activities but Mr. Lewington of the Fish Shop by The Splash was one that was grateful for their assistance.

Petrol was rationed during the war and his shop was in danger of closing as he hadn't enough fuel to travel to Billingsgate to replenish his stocks. Representation was made to the Petroleum Officer for the Borough by the secretary of the WI and, as a result, enough petrol was granted to visit Billingsgate three times a week. Just after the war, in July 1946, when things were beginning to get back to normal, the WI ladies retired after their meeting to Mrs. Cook's house and watched a play on television. Afterwards members went home either by car or motor launch! So, it wasn't all Jam and Jerusalem at Wraysbury WI, *Television* in *1946*, how the other half lived!

---

[38] thunder-and-lightning.co.uk

In December 1969, a sister organisation called Magna Carta WI was started with its meetings held in the evenings and for this inaugural meeting, Wraysbury WI provided the tea and coffee. Wraysbury WI continued for about another ten years with Peggy Willatts as its last president in 1979.

Magna Carta Women's Institute, held its first monthly meeting on the 5th January 1970 at the Scout hut, which at that time was the official village hall and they did much good work for others less fortunate in society during their 32 years of operation. In particular, raising money for the Ken Thomas Scanner Appeal, and the annual tea given in aid of Westminster Age Concern at The Grange, courtesy of Vivienne Sams.

Magna Carta WI Inaugural meeting – 5th Jan 1970
Source: Wraysbury Archives

A pictorial look at their history shows what was achieved by the women of Wraysbury.

MAGNA CARTA W.I. OFF TO GOOD START

WRAYSBURY'S new Magna Carta Women's Institute got off to a good start on Monday night when more than 40 women braved one of the coldest nights of the winter to discuss the work of W.I.s and plans for 1970.

Members (many are seen on the left) decided that one of their first fund-raising efforts would be a jumble sale. They'll fix the date later.

The new institute is led by president Mrs. A. Keating, who was elected at the inaugural meeting held early in December. The Magna Carta group will meet in the George Hall on the first Monday evening of each month. It is an organisation separate from the existing Wraysbury Women's Institute.

"We're not specifically a club for the working woman, but we'll probably attract basically those women with small children or others who work during the day, because our meetings are at night," said committee member Mrs. Pamela Bunn.

She said that village pride in the history of Wraysbury helped to decide the name for the new institute. Many historians believed that Magna Carta could have been signed at Wraysbury and not at Rannymede.

Ist. Meeting in the Scout Hut
5th January 1970
Source: Wraysbury Archives

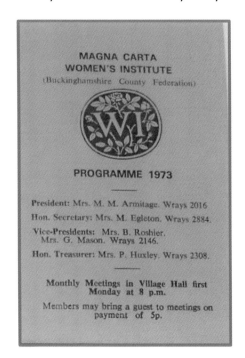

MAGNA CARTA
WOMEN'S INSTITUTE
(Buckinghamshire County Federation)

PROGRAMME 1973

President: Mrs. M. M. Armitage. Wrays 2016

Hon. Secretary: Mrs. M. Egleton. Wrays 2884.

Vice-Presidents: Mrs. B. Roshier.
Mrs. G. Mason. Wrays 2146.

Hon. Treasurer: Mrs. P. Huxley. Wrays 2308.

Monthly Meetings in Village Hall first
Monday at 8 p.m.

Members may bring a guest to meetings on
payment of 5p.

23rd June 1979 - Tea at Jill Hopkin's
house - the Oast Barn.
Magna Carta host Cranford WI
Source: Wraysbury Archives

1985 - 15th Anniversary Tea at The Grange
Magna Carta WI
Source: Wraysbury Archives

ALL GOOD WISHES TO THE
MAGNA CARTA W.I.
Thelma Barlow (MAVIS)

Mavis from Coronation Street – actress
Thelma Barlow was guest of honour at the
1983 Magna Carta annual tea at the Grange.
Source: Wraysbury Archives

1984 Christmas meeting
l – r Mrs. Ottoway,
Miss Donaldson, Mrs. Stephenson, Mrs. Grey, Mrs. Rogers, Mrs. Francis
Mrs. Sams, Mrs. Baker
Source: Wraysbury Archives

c.1990 – Beryl Reid at The Grange
Source: Wraysbury Archives

2000 – 14th August meeting
Source: Wraysbury Archives

2002 – Christmas meeting
Festive socks knitted by Jennie Francis
Source: Wraysbury Archives

WRAYSBURY
ALL FOR ONE-AND ONE FOR ALL
1922

The last presidents of Magna Carta WI were Jo Hook, 1993 - 4; Jennie Francis, 1994 – 2001 and Rita Brutnell, 2001 – 2002.

So, there you have it, 74 years of the WI in Wraysbury, all gone. All that remain are faded memories and equally faded photos of the good work done. The nearest WI now is Datchet, unless YOU, dear Wraysbury ladies, bring jam and Jerusalem back to the village! What about it then, are there any volunteers?

The Magna Carta WI banner is waiting to be unfurled. and is in the safe keeping of Rita Brutnell, whilst the original Wraysbury WI banner, handmade by Miss. K. Burke in 1930 with the embroidered motto, "One for all and all for one", is sadly missing. This motto, the testament to friendship, loyalty and the caring for others, is what has made the WI what it is over the years.

It is hoped that by the time this book is published, Wraysbury WI will have been re-formed thanks to the efforts of Barbara Hearne.

Ankerwycke Again!

Wedding of Patricia Dean
Source: The Tatler – 20th Oct 1943

FINED FOR MAKING HOUSE EXPENSIONS

The difficulty of correctly interpreting Government Orders because of the "obscurity of the language" was referred to by Mr. Glanville Hall, counsel (M.P. for Colne Valley), when defending a Wraysbury man who was summoned at Slough last week for a breach of the Defence Regulations by carrying out extensions to his house between November 1st, 1942, and May 19th, 1943. The defendant, Ralph S. Dean, of Ankerwycke Priory, Wraysbury, pleaded guilty on technical grounds and was fined £5.
Mr. Glanville Hall stated that, after reading a memorandum on the provisions of the Order that came into force in January 1942, Mr. Dean was under the impression that he did not need a licence and that the law did not apply in his case as the extensions to his house were begun two years previously.

Understanding the rules!
Middlesex Chronicle – 13th Nov 1943

A local 'society' wedding also occurred during 1943, that of Patricia Dean of Ankerwycke House. Patricia's brother, Ralph, had also upset the local magistrates by completing the extension to Ankerwycke Priory whilst the war was on. Building materials etc., were the preserve of the War Effort, and woe betide anyone who abused the system!

With regard to the Dean family, it is sad to relate that in 1962, Ankerwycke House, owned by them since c. 1940, experienced another dreadful fire. At that time, the house was subdivided into three flats and let to various families. One of the families, the Somervilles[39], had a small son and he knocked over an electric fire, which set the place ablaze.

---

[39] Memories of Andrea Watson

'The Death of Ankerwycke'

OUGH AND ETON EXPRESS, FRIDAY, 28th DECEMBER, 1962

SS PHOTOVIEW

● *This dramatic picture was taken by an Express photographer at the height of the blaze which practically destroyed the Wraysbury Mansion, Ankerwycke Priory, in March. Firemen from five brigades—Slough, Windsor, Staines, Uxbridge and Datchet—fought the flames which, fanned by a strong breeze, swept through the house, built early in the last century to replace one which had stood on the site since the thirteenth century.*

Although this article is captioned 28th December 1962 – the fire was actually 23rd March 1962. The article is a review of the Windsor, Slough and Eton Express photographs of the year. It is such a dramatic photo that it is understandable why it had been included in the paper's review of the year.

Source: Windsor, Slough and Eton Express
23rd March 1962-Wraysbury Archives

This fire, in conjunction with the death of one of Richard Dean's sisters, cast a pall over the house and it was never lived in again. Richard Dean moved back to his other farm estate and other members of the Dean family moved into the estate cottages. The house ruins were subsequently demolished in the 1990s.

Having fun

During the war, to keep the spirits up, dancing became a favourite pastime everywhere and in the immediate years after, most of the hops were called Victory dances or similar. In Wraysbury, dances were held in the hall at The George pub and also at the Scout Hut with the Tennis Club. Harold Hutt and his wife, Barbara, were exceptional dancers, winning Gold medals at various competitions. Another twinkle-toed couple were Frank and Maureen Burr, taking Bronze in one of the same events. Both couples fondly remember taking to the floor and demonstrating their skills at these village dances.

In all this high kicking and celebration, the youngsters weren't forgotten and in the late 40s a youth club known as the Oaks Club was formed at the Church Rooms. This was the house known as High Trees in Welley Road and was 'attached' to St. Andrew's church. The club later transferred to the Scout Hut. This was followed, in the 60s, by the 1325 Club, which held dances and BBQs on Wayward Island in Wraysbury 1 lake, reached by a floating pontoon bridge. Wraysbury Youth Club was started on the 13th January 1977 based in the canteen of the school whilst it tried to find a permanent site. Various sites in the village were put forward but faced with many villagers' objections, the club fizzled out in the late 70s or early 80s. St. Andrew's church also ran a Youth Club from the early 1980s until it is believed, about 1987.

A children's playground was created in 1949, in a corner of the village green and has provided endless hours of fun for youngsters. Come 1974, thanks to the generosity and help of Staines Metal Products, Gordon Cullen (Architect), Ready Mixed Concrete, and the Fair Committee, a new playground was established that set high standards in safety and landscaping.

The Floods - 1947

The rain in the year of 1946 seemed to be relentless, and come the winter things looked even worse with heavy snowfalls and severe frost. Going into 1947, it still hadn't let up, with February bringing with yet more heavy snowfalls, blizzards and bitter cold. So, when March finally arrived with yet more snow, the die was cast and the rivers rose with a vengeance. On the 10th March 1947, tremendous rainfall occurred and over the next two days, even heavier rain fell onto the frozen earth with nowhere to go. Drastic fuel cuts affected both home and industry alike, the country grinding slowly to a halt, shivering in the gloom.

On Friday 14th March, the River Thames burst its banks and the flood began, assisted by the Colne Brook which had overflowed into Colnebrook High Street. Now Wraysbury was caught between these two rapidly rising bodies of water. Come Saturday, the general thaw had begun and millions of gallons of water that had previously been trapped as ice began their rush down the hills and water courses spilling into the Thames and its tributaries. Slowly but surely the village began to flood, swallowing up Riverside and Ouseley Road, and appearing ominously in Welley Road.

Mr. Watson (headmaster) turned the school into an Emergency Relief Centre[40] and co-ordinated evacuation, hot meals and transport, with the aid of the appropriate agencies. The science room and hall were both taken up with emergency staff from the police, local councils and ever-willing volunteers. Many of the flooded-out residents moved in with kindly strangers or were taken to Slough Social Centre. For example, Mr. and Mrs. Jewson, at the chemist, had 14 extra people staying with them. They pooled their money and ate communally. The villagers had all been issued with extra ration books during this time, so between the Jewsons and their guests they had 32 books, including their own. Despite the close living arrangements, everyone behaved decently and made the best of bad job.

Ouseley Road 1947
Source: Wraysbury Archives

During the move to Slough Social Centre, one of the lorries carrying evacuees ran off the road at Welley Corner into water so deep it came above the bonnet. A child started to cry and general panic started to set in. Police Constable Mayden, who was travelling with them, waded away to fetch help and found someone with a wireless transmitter. A message for help was sent out and remarkably this was picked up in Italy! The message was re-transmitted to London and given to Scotland Yard who in turn phoned Slough Police Station. By this time more local assistance had been found and the evacuees transferred to another lorry and continued to Slough. The state of the village made headlines around the world and food parcels were received from as far away as Australia.

Even during these awful times, the doctor, Dr. Howard, did his rounds by 'Duck' or any other form of boat he could get his hands on. As returning home was difficult, he stayed overnight on his examination couch in his surgery at the back of the chemist shop.

The flood was slowly drowning the village, with water as high as 3ft in some places, now, with extra strong winds and more rain, telephone wires and trees were brought crashing down adding to the general chaos.

---

[40] 'And The Waters Prevailed' – Eton Rural Council 1947

The train service was cancelled as the water had now become almost level with the top of the platforms and the electricity supply had to be cut off: it was said that the view between the platforms resembled the Grand Canal in Venice! Mr. Basil Masterson, the railway signalman, was trapped at the station over the weekend, giving two hourly reports of the rising water to Woking, the then head office. The water was getting ever nearer the previous high flood mark. He was eventually rescued by 'Duck' and then assisted with other duties. There remained only a few unaffected areas, such as the school and parts of the High Street and Staines Road.

And so the village waited in those grey days, amidst swirling water and human detritus for the waters to subside. This they did on the 20th March with an almost imperceptible decrease but an instantly noticeable and welcome tidemark on walls and wallpaper. By the 24th March most of the water had gone. The flood was over and the clean-up begun but the devastation left behind took months for the people of the village to come to terms with.

Scenes all too familiar to Wraysbury residents
Source: Wraysbury Archives

Courtesy of Bucks County Council
WRAYSBURY

The floods return year after year, despite promises of this and that and grandstanding by prominent politicians as was seen in the latest floods 2013/14, that made TV stars of Wraysbury residents Su Burrows and Dave Francis (Flood Warden). A few f words 'thrown' at the Environment Agency by desperate and be-wellied residents now reduced to living in attics, possibly didn't deserve to be said but, they certainly got the attention of the media.

Wraysbury became for a number of weeks the place to be, certainly for politicians even though they would rather have been anywhere else! They were forced to appear some in totally unsuitable attire, for the interview and inevitable tongue lashing by visibly upset residents at the lack of action by the authorities. Next was the visit to the Flood Relief Centre at the school. There they met the wonderful Wraysbury Volunteer Team, all residents come together in common cause for the good of all, showing the spirit that had kept Wraysbury going, lots of tea, coffee, sandwiches, hugs, blankets and all sorts of practical help was available, in some cases 'round the clock'.

The authorities despatched the Army to help and the call went out for sand, lots and lots of sand to fill thousands of sand bags. How ironic that all this sand should come back to Wraysbury after being plundered from Wraysbury during WW2 and shipped to London for sand bags!

After the floods were over and a little later in the year, the village made a presentation to Cllr. Colin Rayner of the Arthur Walters Community Award for his efforts on behalf of the village to raise help and assistance in its time of dire need. His 'string-pulling' was greatly appreciated. He accepted the award graciously, 'On behalf of all those who helped'.

Also to receive the same award in 2014 was Graham Sinclair, his services to the village over30/40 years as Senior Flood Warden and his falling into the Weir being at last recognised! This was followed by Dave Francis being awarded the Thames Valley Police Commanders Award, itself a great accolade and also an invitation to No.10 along with Graham Sinclair and Oliver Francis, to discuss flooding. The village has much to thank these great people for and all the many village volunteers who took part.

Meanwhile the village awaits the completion of the Flood Relief Scheme!!

2014 Keep smiling through – Dave Francis in the lead
Source: Facebook-Wraysbury News

1960 - End of an Era and to Graham's car park charges pocket money!
Source: Thanks to Graham Sinclair

Stock Car racing - Those were the days, at Staines (more correctly Wraysbury!) track, the height of its fame and glory, and egg head crash hats were all the rage!

1958 and the floods had been left far behind in years but not perhaps in memory. Here we see Eamonn Andrews* congratulating Alec Lecroissette on winning. Alec however, was more famous for his number of **3½** than for his racing consistency, the Tow Truck being a regular companion! *See also page 32

Chapter 4

The 1950s and 60s plus a bit later!

May 1955 saw the arrival of the first Catholic Church, St. Monica's, built in Station Road, on ground given to the church by the Willatts family in 1923. It was not a very inspiring building, being made mainly of wood, the construction of which is believed to have been raised by public subscription. It became unfit for purpose over the years and was eventually closed in December 1990. The church was demolished and a new doctors' surgery opened in 1992. Owned by Drs. Hassan and El Sayed, it replaced the cramped consulting rooms at the Village Hall. This new surgery didn't last long either (Sept. 2006) before it was turned into a private clinic and left the village without their own surgery, which is still the case in 2017. Wraysbury's patients were transferred to Datchet Health Centre.

There were, by this time, lots of shops and small businesses in the village, all wanting to bank money, and a growing population that also wanted to avoid the trudge to Staines or Windsor for banking services. Despite writing to all the big banks (another initiative put forward by the WI after the war) none could be persuaded to open a branch in Wraysbury until 1951,[41] when National Provincial opened an office in one room in Chelston House (now four houses, opposite the Baptist Church) for two hours per day.

The bank in 1955 – Beautiful Chelston House
Source: ©NatWest Archives

The Bank in 1974 now RK Leisure
Source: ©NatWest Archives

The National Provincial Bank was subsumed by the National Westminster Bank and began trading as the NatWest group in 1970. They then leased from the Willatts family in about 1971, the old dairy, scene of the double murder in 1911 and what is now RK Leisure's office. NatWest continued as the village bank until the late 80s/early 90s, when it closed due to re-organisation. The village is now back to where it was in those dark days after the war, with no bank representation at all but at least money can be drawn out using the Post Office facilities!

---

[41] WI Notes – Peggy Willatts

With all the extra shops and increase in bus, rail and road transport, the village was becoming more important locally and, in the 1950s, it was decided by the Council to install electric street lighting. Well, this caused a great uproar and split the village into two opposing camps. In the end, a public vote was agreed upon to settle the matter and the 'yes camp' won.

After George VI died on the 15th February 1952, the country was getting ready for our present Queen's coronation and television saw a great boost in popularity. Families with reasonable income could either buy or rent this new and wonderful box of tricks that later would come to dominate family life. Rosalind Willatts recalls her first viewing of television was to see the funeral of George VI on the TV in the parlour of S. R. Jewson the chemist.

Wraysbury Young Bloods

350cc A. J. S. 7R - 'The Boy Racer'

In the 1950s and 60s motorcycles were popular amongst the village youths. None more so than the Willatts boys, Graham Sinclair, Rex Norman, and Ray and Reg Watmore. These were the days when Wraysbury had its own policeman and police house, and a clip round the ear and 'I'll tell your mother' seemed to work.

The lads were all keen on motor sport, achieving various successes in both motorcycle and cars. Robert Willatts went to compete in the Isle of Man GP races in 1961 and 1962. He owned a number of motorcycles and, in particular, a 350cc AJS 7R and a 250cc Adler water-cooled twin. The AJS was the racers' machine and both Robert and Graham Sinclair owned one of these, known as the 'Boy Racer'. It had it all: looks, speed and handling.

Early 60s Photo
Graham & his lovely Triumph P 500cc

Graham grew up with motorcycles and had his first motorcycle race in 1956 and has since competed on most of the National Circuits, winning the 1962 vintage distance TT and the ACU National Rally on his vintage Triumph P500cc. He inherited his passion from his father, Ivor, the same Ivor who was involved in the fracas with the fraudster Marquis Stevens. Ivor was a major force in setting up Speedway riding in the early 1920s and the first event was held at the old Greenford trotting track on the 7th April 1928, for which Ivor held the lap record of

73mph. With his reputation and knowledge, Ivor went to sunny Barcelona in 1929 and set up the first Speedway meeting in the bullring, the wine flowed freely and cash rolled in - happy days indeed!

Graham progressed on to four wheels and Formula Vee before moving up to larger cars using Formula Ford engines. He won a number of trophies over the years, including the Rex Norman Memorial Cup. This was of particular interest as it was in honour of another Wraysbury

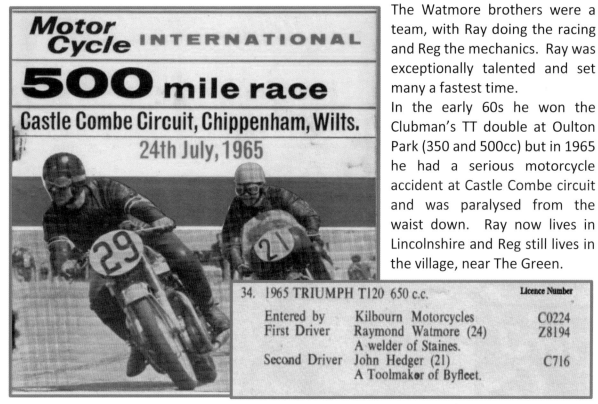

OCEANAIR CLUBMANS SPORTS CHAMPI

EVE

This is the first qualifying round of the 1976 Oceanair Clubmans Championship. A race for clubmans sports cars as defined by the RAC, engines are identical to those used in Formula Ford, thereby limiting costs.

ENTRIES

No.	Driver	Entrant	Town	Car
1	Nick Scott	—	London	Mallock U2 Mk.16B ADA
2	Ron Morgans	—	Longfield	Mallock U2 Mk.14/16 Minister
3	Keith Money	—	Abingdon	Mallock Mk.16 Davron Ford
4	Alex Ferrada	Team ACE Plant	Olney	Mallock Mk.16B Davron
5	Ian McCullough	—	Doncaster	U2 Mk.16 Rowland Ford
6	Robin Henderson	—	Yateley	Mallock U2 Mk.16 Minister
7	N. Linney	—	Nottingham	Mallock U2 Mk.14/16 Minister Ford
	Graham Sinclair	ShellSport	Wraysbury	Mallock U2 Mk.14B Rowland

Source: 1976 Oceanair Formula Ford Start List

boy and school friend of Graham's who tragically lost his life in an air crash in 1964 whilst going on holiday to Austria. This air crash also took the life of Rex's wife, Sheila. Both the Normans were well-known Wraysbury residents and good friends to a number of villagers, in particular, Len and Avril Pearce. Len and Avril were due to go on that trip to Austria too but the person who was going to look after their paper shop let them down at the last minute, so they pulled out!

Motor Cycle INTERNATIONAL

500 mile race

Castle Combe Circuit, Chippenham, Wilts.

24th July, 1965

The Watmore brothers were a team, with Ray doing the racing and Reg the mechanics. Ray was exceptionally talented and set many a fastest time.

In the early 60s he won the Clubman's TT double at Oulton Park (350 and 500cc) but in 1965 he had a serious motorcycle accident at Castle Combe circuit and was paralysed from the waist down. Ray now lives in Lincolnshire and Reg still lives in the village, near The Green.

34.	1965 TRIUMPH T120 650 c.c.		Licence Number
Entered by	Kilbourn Motorcycles		C0224
First Driver	Raymond Watmore (24) A welder of Staines.		Z8194
Second Driver	John Hedger (21) A Toolmaker of Byfleet.		C716

Program from Castle Combe 1965
Source: ©Dave Riley-Weebly

Ray Watmore's entry
1965 Triumph Bonnyville 650cc

In 1956, Len and Avril Pearce moved to the village and took the job as manager and postmistress of the grocery stores and off licence at Sunnymeads. Built originally as a pub and owned by Courage brewery, it was refused a licence as the village already had five pubs.

Sunnymeads Stores and the Off Licence
Source: Wraysbury Archives

Permission was given though for an off licence. The previous tenant was Mr. White, who ran it as a grocer's shop (where Jennie Francis worked for a while). The Sunnymeads Stores was in a bit of state when the Pearces first viewed it but, helped by Courage and with sheer determination, it was soon sorted out. They have happy memories of those times, where their young children were brought up and of their customers' requirements! Len and Avril stayed there until about 1962 when they moved to the High Street and took over the newspaper shop, at one time owned by Charles and Mary Burr.

Len and Avril sold Sunnymeads Stores to the Willatts family, who were well-known grocers in the village, already having the two shops opposite the old school, which were knocked through into one.[42] They sold most groceries, fresh vegetables, and all manner of dairy products, they also had a milk delivery service, so it was a well-run family business. Selling to them, Len felt sure he was leaving his customers in very good hands.

Robert Willatts on his Milk Round c. 1964/5
Source: Willatts Family Archives

Amongst many things villagers have to be grateful to Len and Avril for is the setting up, with others, of The Magna Carta Wine Circle, The Jazz Club and, latterly, the Country and Western Club. See pages 90, 91 and 92.

---

[42] Now Wraysbury News and RK Leisure's office

Wraysbury Mothers' Club

1958 saw the start of the Wraysbury Mothers' Club, under the overall control of the County Medical Officer for Buckinghamshire and part of a nationwide movement to improve the health and nutrition of mothers and their children. The Wraysbury branch was formed with Rona Pitt as Chair, Pamela Bunn as Secretary and Ruby Oliver as Treasurer. By 1963, over fifty mums were members and they enjoyed a very active social calendar.

The first Annual Dinner was held in 1961 at the Manor Hotel, Datchet and a good time was had by all, judging from the wine bottles on the tables.

1961 First Annual Dinner
Manor Hotel, Datchet.
Source: Wraysbury Archives

Various events were held throughout the year culminating in the Annual Rally where plays, refreshment and talks were given on a variety of subjects. In 1962 for example, the Duchess of Bedford spoke on Woburn Abbey and its Treasures and in 1968, Fabian of The Yard addressed the Rally on his experiences at Scotland Yard. Two totally different subjects but both equally interesting.

Mums Needed – Early advert
Source: Horticultural Society,
Wraysbury Archives

1962 – Mothers' Club Rally
l to r – Ruby Oliver, B. Keene & Pamela Bunn
Source: Wraysbury Archives

APPLE FLUFF.

1½.lbs Cooking Apples. Grated rind & juice of ½ lemon.
3-4 tablespoons Water. 2.ozs Castor Sugar.
2 Egg yolks.
Meringue Topping.
2 Egg whites.   4.ozs Castor Sugar.

Wipe, peel and core apples and cut into slices. Cook in a saucepan over gentle heat with the lemon rind and juice and water until tender. Remove from heat and whisk to a smooth puree. Allow to cool, then stir in egg yolks and sugar and turn into a fireproof dish. Spoon prepared meringue topping over so that the apple is completely covered, then dust with castor sugar. Bake in a moderately slow oven (335°F. Mark 3) for about 30 minutes or until pale golden brown. Serves 6.
To prepare Meringue Topping.
    Whisk egg whites until stiff and standing in peaks. Add half the sugar and whisk until satiney. Fold in remaining sugar carefully with a metal spoon.

    This pudding is a great favourite with the children and is equally good served hot or cold.
                    Mrs. Gwen Clark.
                    (Wraysbury Club).

A Wraysbury Mothers' Club Recipe – Oct 1968 - Give it a try!
Source: Wraysbury Archives

The club slowly lost membership over the years and finally ended in c. 1974. Reflecting the change in society from stay at home mums to mothers who actively went to work to help with the mortgage and the rise in pre-school and child care facilities.

Wraysbury Mothers in A Touch of Eastern Promise
October 1966 – Village Hall.
l - r - ladies – Pat Brace, Sylvia Wait and Hazel Enoch
l-r - gents – Pat Bunn and Joan LeMarchand.
Source: Wraysbury Archives

Wraysbury Mothers take on the cricket club at rounders
July 1974
l to r rear– Eliz. Wood, Liz Collett, Pam Etheridge, Pat Brace,
Beryl Deevy and Jill Chadwick.
l to r front– Rona Pitt, Helen Martin, Hazel Knox and Ann Gore.
Source: Wraysbury Archives

Wraysbury Mums' Drama Section
January 1965 – Village Hall
Source: Wraysbury Archives

1968 – Mummy of the Year – Joan Sharp
of Mafeking Road.
Source: Wraysbury Archives.

The Village Fair

Entertainments

Judo	. . . . by Slough Social Centre
Wrestling	. . . . . . by Slough Community Centre
Fencing	. . . . . . by Boys of Beverley School, Malden
Hula Dancers	. . . . from Datchet
Gym Display	. . . . . by Slough Technical College
Comic Interludes	. . . by the Handlebar Club
Games	. . . . arranged by Scouts
Train Rides	. . . . by Slough Miniature Railway Circle
Donkey Rides	. . . . Horse Rides . . . Pony Rides

Plus various stalls

Fair Programme 1962 - Source - Wraysbury Archives

SPECIAL NOTICE has been given by Count de Quarte of Wraysbury, the invincible swordsman, that he will take advantage of the occasion of the Fair to meet the Marquis de Flach-e.
(Seconds will be provided by the Wraysbury Association and Doctor Deathwatch and Nurse Killem will be in attendance.)

First Fair Programme 1962

The lovely Bennett Girls - 2015

The village fair was brought back to life on the 15th June 1962, after an absence of over fifty years. A great programme of events was put in place, despite opposition from Mr. Albert Silver - a local builder who wanted to build on or near the village green, on what was ancient inclosure(enclosure) lands (Plot 279) over which the villagers had a right to hold an annual fair.

The Wraysbury Association, on finding out that these rights were in danger of being taken away, resolved to sue the builder and took their claim to the High Court. The gallant villagers were Mr. & Mrs. Balgarnie-Wyld, Mrs. Muriel Beale and Mrs. Christine Ord Mosley, all staunch supporters of village life and vigorous opponents of the builder's and Council's plans. The Wraysbury Association won the day and the fair has continued ever since. In those early years the Fair Committee was chaired by Jill Sarsby and the fair was held on the Memorial Ground behind the Village Hall. Certainly in 1975 it was held there and thanks to villagers like Eric Larcombe and Kit Aston, to name only a few, over 3000 people attended! There was an enormous tea tent with fabulous cakes and teas, *Jeux sans Frontieres* games, a donkey derby and an impressive soft toy stall, all handmade by the two Eileens: Aston and Laister.

The Raft Race was also a big hit, with teams coming from all over the country to compete. Anything that could be made to float was the order of the day, oil drums, scaffold poles, plastic containers and miles of rope and timber were lashed together with lots of style and a few prayers. Held in what is now the old swimming area behind the Village Club, contestants battled away with each other hoping to reach the end before either sinking or capsizing. Usually nothing could prevent the inevitable ducking but the Scouts always had a good attempt although everyone got soaked anyway!

A dance was usually held afterwards with the opportunity to quench one's thirst at the bar, and Sinclair Transport* supplied the lorries for the floats for the Playgroup, Jazz Club and others. The Fair has improved year on year, bringing all sorts of different entertainment to the village, with the Classic Car Concours d'Elegance organised by Frank Burry and also for 2017, the Mad Hatter's Tea Party brought alive thanks to Katie Morgan. There's always new ideas and a lot to look forward to. ***See Appendix 3**

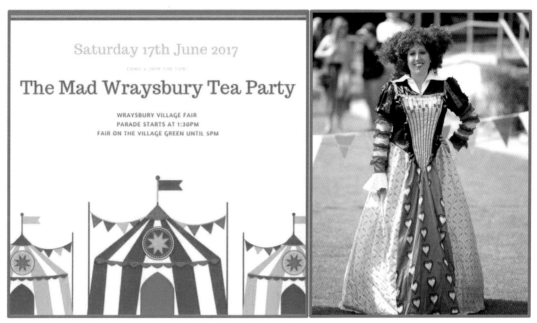

Wraysbury Fair Advert 2017
Source: Wraysbury Archives

Sarah Green from Pick 'n' Mix events as
the Snow Queen
Source: Wraysbury Fair

The Fair was a hard fought for event by fellow villagers long since forgotten by most but thanks to the Wraysbury Association, the present Fair Committee and residents who donate all manner of prizes and goodies, run tea and beer tents and work like Trojans, we still have our wonderful fair today. No wonder it's so popular, year after year.

Mad Hatter's Tea Party
Source: Wraysbury Fair

The Queen's Silver Jubilee

Celebrating 25 years of her reign, the year 1977 saw an upswell of patriotic fervour and Wraysbury residents were not going to be left out. Out came the bunting and the villagers put their heads together in numerous committees and meeting places to decide what to do. Much head scratching took place amongst the clink of glasses and silent munching as the wheels of organisation turned. What could they do, who would they ask, could it be done, how much would it cost, I know someone who.... Finally, a programme was decided upon and from the 7th May until the 1st July, the village celebrated as only Wraysbury could.

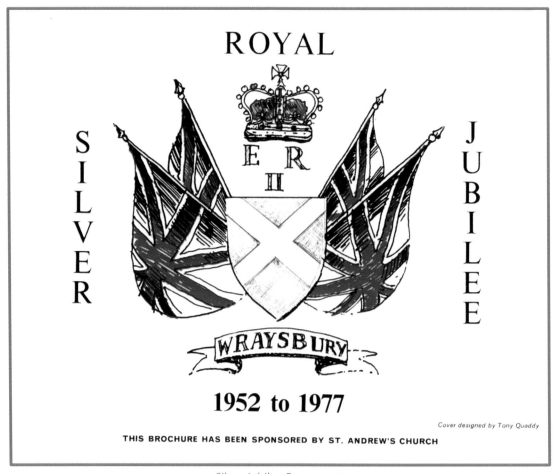

ROYAL

SILVER

JUBILEE

E R II

WRAYSBURY

1952 to 1977

Cover designed by Tony Quaddy

THIS BROCHURE HAS BEEN SPONSORED BY ST. ANDREW'S CHURCH

Silver Jubilee Programme
Sponsored by St. Andrew's Church with the support of local businesses.
Source: Wraysbury Archives

In addition to the programme of events, Wraysbury issued another commemorative mug to match that of the first one issued on the occasion of the Queen's visit to village when Her Majesty opened the new Village Hall in 1974. The cost then was £1 each and for the 1977 mug the cost was £1.50. The mugs were hand-made and were designed by village resident Tony Quaddy. Tony had what members of our Art Society have, that wonderful ability to draw and paint. He studied at the Royal Academy of Art in London and spent 26 years at the BBC as a scenic artist, becoming head of department at the BBC TV Centre. He and his wife ran a successful art gallery in Staines. He died aged 73 in 2010.

Every child in village who was under the age of thirteen at the time of each of these celebrations, was given one of these mugs. Designed as a pair, so that when on display, the handles were on opposite sides yet the design still faced forward. Now these are collector's items, in particular, the '74 mug. How many villagers still have theirs?

Out of all the celebrations and parties, and there were a great number, one stands out above the rest for its scale, grandeur, number of participants and attendees. This was of course 'The Legend of Wraysbury' - Son et Lumiere. Thanks are due to Jill Sarsby for her sterling work in making it happen, Mavis Froud for directing, Bob Anderson for the action and to Tony Quaddy, who again designed the programme and created all the scenery and props. Set on the Scouts boating lake behind the village club, this was a floodlit performance by players and dancers on a floating stage. It told the story of Wraysbury village from pre-history to the present (1977) in dance, song and glorious costume. I won't attempt to list the cast and crew save to say that they were in excess of 90 plus extras!! Here is a lovely photograph of the evenings performance.

The fabulous floating stage with its great dramatis personae!
Source: Wraysbury Archives

The Wraysbury and Horton mug along with the programme itself, are worthy of showing.

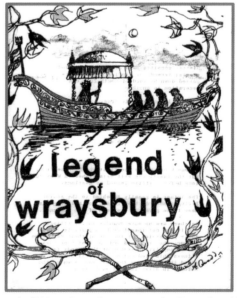

Do you still have yours?
Source: Janet Crame BEM

Legend of Wraysbury Programme by Tony Quaddy
Colour (not original) by GRM
Source: Wraysbury Archives

Best Kept Village

In 1984, 1990 and 2000, Wraysbury was awarded the accolade of the Best Kept Village in Berkshire (501 to 3000 souls) thanks to the efforts of villagers and the Parish Council. The hours of work put in to achieve this is not always seen by the casual observer, from the mowing of the village green and verges, to bulb and flower planting. Thanks are due to the Village Trust, Parochial Charities and all who helped. The certificates are on display in the Village Hall. If we could stop drivers throwing their litter out of the car on to our village roads, we might yet win again!

--ooo000ooo--

As can be seen with the Fair, the village green is at the heart of the community and many of the village activities and important buildings are located in this area. The Village Club, founded in 1894, is still going strong and a meal and a drink are available here most days of the week. The Village Hall and the Community Centre are also here and between them, they are used for a wide range of village activities. Here are just a <u>few</u> of the attractions and recreational amenities that help define our community, and take place in and around this idyllic part of the village.

The Village Hall

The Village Hall – Community Hub
Source: Wraysbury Archives

Where else is there to start than the heart and hub of village life the Village Hall. It lies next door to the Village Club and on the edge of the Memorial Field. Its planning goes back to as far as 1937 when the Parochial Charities (*P.C.*) were asked if they would release the land that Bridge Cottages used to stand on for a new Village Hall (to be called Coronation Hall). This they agreed to and a small committee was set up to raise funds and an account was opened in Lloyds Bank, Staines called the 'Village Hall A/C'. All of the sports clubs, Scouts, Girl Guides, WI and other groups in the village set about raising money for this exciting new project, and by 1939 work had started. It was soon realised that not enough money had been raised and things came to halt with the impending war.

After the war it seemed to stall and no further action was taken until about 1957, when it was decided that the answer might be for a new prefabricated building to be erected as the new Village Hall. The *P.C.* were approached but despite the old school having a similar extension, it was not felt appropriate, 'a proper job' being the long-term goal. The Village Hall Committee therefore decided that the remaining cash raised and still sitting in the bank, should be spent on improving the Scout Hut instead of an expensive new hall. The *P.C.* then made a donation to the committee of new chairs for the Scout Hut/Village Hall.

However, not long after, it was decided that a new Village Hall would be built, and the *P.C.* made a generous donation of around £5000 towards the cost. Helped by the fund-raising efforts of Sir Kit Aston and Eric Larcombe at the Fair and designed by wonderful Gordon Cullen, a local resident, it was officially opened by HM The Queen in October 1974 as part of Her Majesty's Royal Progress of the Thames, to mark the formation of the Royal Borough of Windsor and Maidenhead.

The Queen - Opening of the Village Hall
Source: Diana Hughes

Subsequently, two further rooms and an entrance were added. The first in 1978, courtesy of the *P.C.* and Wraysbury Village Trust called the Lake Room and in 1995, thanks again to the *P.C.* the large Windsor Room and entrance were built.

Here is a little remembered photo from a 1974 brochure used to publicise the new hall. The prices weren't bad either, a meeting for 50 people including coffee, lunch and tea was £3.40 per person and for a Dinner Dance for 100 people including band and dinner it was £3.70 per person. There was also a little-known group called the Colne Cooks who ran the early catering. They were Margaret Tracey, Jill Sarsby, Jackie Roper, Betty Husher, Betty Varian and June Blofeld. The menus were fantastic and so much in demand that they branched out into private catering. None of that 'cheese on a stick' stuff!

The Village Hall was managed in its early years by volunteers and then Henry and Cissie Summers. Followed by Lou and Mary Fee who stayed until 1993, when Pam and Ray Alletson took over and who helped make it the success that it is today. They retired in 2003 after ten years of hard work. The Hall is a continuing hit, used by all groups large and small and is the home of most of the clubs and associations that play an active part in village community life.

Source: Alletson Family

Ray spotted unwelcome guests in 1996 and they caused a right rumpus; how to get rid of them that was the problem, were court orders needed or could they just be thrown out? Well these guests were a little bit different, they were bats, yes bats, a whole roost of them had breached the defences and moved in, lock, stock and suitcase! The Bat Conservation Trust were called and no, they couldn't be thrown out or disturbed in any way. They were however, quite friendly little things and once the ladies had realised they weren't going to fly into their hair at the dinner dances, things settled down. Eventually a compromise was reached in that once the young had developed and they had left the roost during the evening, action could be taken to board up the entrances in the roof. Sad in a way to see them go but the effects of them living in the roof voids would have led to big maintenance problems.

The present management team of Mark and Jackie Keynes took over in around 2009 and the good work goes on, fitting in immediately and both proving to be an asset to the village. With Wi-Fi now installed it makes the hall even more attractive for any type of event. The present Village Hall Management Committee, have plans to refurbish the Lake Room patio area that overlooks the Memorial Ground, to make it even more user friendly. Roll on summer!

The Village Club

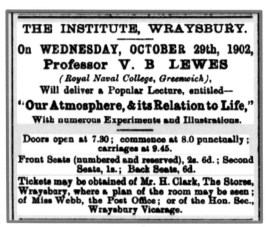

Opened on the 2nd of May 1894 by Lord and Lady Curzon, it is one of the oldest of our many village recreational attractions. Designed as an educational workingmen's club and institute it had regular lectures and slide shows on various subjects. In addition, it fielded both a football and cricket team under the name of Wraysbury Institute in the early 1900s.

Club and Institute Opening
Source: South Bucks Standard 4th May 1894

Typical Lecture
Source: Windsor & Eton Exp. 18th Oct. 1902

In line with the more liberal attitude of the time and relaxing of the licensing laws, it applied for and received its first licence to sell alcohol in 1933. It enjoys a great location adjacent to the Village Hall and amidst all the sporting and recreational activities of the village.

The club exists for the benefit of its village members and has an active Management Committee that ensures the club and its facilities are maintained to a high standard. It has a newly refurbished kitchen and hot food is available Wednesday to Saturday lunchtimes. This plus its well-stocked bar, ensure its members and guests are really looked after.

It has two bars. Firstly, the Lounge Bar which is the main hub of the club and is the scene of most entertainment events. Fitted with a large projection screen, it is available for coverage of major sporting events. Secondly, the Sports Bar or Member's Bar is the quieter of the club bars where *newspapers can be read in relative peace and it offers seclusion from any club functions taking place in the Lounge. It also has a wide-screen television for the use of members and smart/casual dress is actively encouraged in the club at all times. There is also a snooker and games room, which has two full-sized snooker tables and features other games such as darts, dominoes and cards. The club also has a darts team which is in the local league.

*As part of the Club's Constitution, newspapers and a library are provided and now include a computer. Initially for the education and betterment of the 'working man' but now staples of a modern society.

Ronnie Greenwood, Chief Steward looks
forward to welcoming you.
Source: Wraysbury Club

The Sports Bar
Source: Wraysbury Club

It normally has a full and varied programme of sport and entertainment, especially at the weekend and in addition organises occasional trips out, the Isle of Wight being a favourite. In the summer the club's garden is the place to be. Overlooking the sports field and lake, it's a great place for families and friends to have a relaxing drink and put the world to rights.

The Village Club – early 1900s
Source: Wraysbury History Group

The original clock presented to the club in 1894 by Mr. A. H. Benson Hangs in the snooker room

The Jazz Club

The Jazz Club was started in the Village Hall in 1979 by Len Pearce and Ron Oakman who, after a couple of trial runs, were delighted to find that the village loved it. With the small profit made from the initial sessions, the club was officially formed as the Wraysbury Traditional Jazz Club, with Ron as Chairman and Len as Secretary. It was made a members' only club and everyone paid a small membership fee.

Every month, Len with the help of his wife Avril, sold the tickets, booked the outings and sent out a newsletter along with a copy of the Jazz Guide. The club soon became a great hit. All of the performances made a profit and donations were made to local charities. By 1996, over £31,000 had been given to worthy causes and considerably more has been donated over these last years. Ron retired as chairman after a few years but Len carried on successfully attracting the best bands with the help of Tony Masterson as Treasurer.

The club soon had a great reputation and bands like Chris Barber, George Melley* and the Feetwarmers, Terry Lightfoot and Humphrey Littleton all played in Wraysbury, some more than once. The bands introduced new sounds taking jazz to a new level and with this the name of the club was changed and became simply Wraysbury Jazz Club.

After the decision to have a fish & chip supper in the interval, word soon spread round the bands and Wraysbury became known as the Fish & Chip Jazz Club. Whilst at Heathrow one day, Len bumped into Chris Barber who remarked, 'Len, from the Fish & Chip Jazz Club'. Fame indeed!

A great performer from the Chris Barber Band was Amy Roberts who brought her own band, The Magnificent 7, to Wraysbury for the summer hog roast a few years ago. She is an outstanding flute, clarinet and sax player and plays in venues all over the world. In addition to the normal monthly trad jazz performances, 'Jazz on the Side' evenings are now also a feature where alternative jazz styles are played. First tried a few years ago, they have proved very popular. One of the best in 2016 was an evening with Pete Long and his band and singers who, with covers of Peggy Lee, Duke Ellington and Benny Goodman, made the hall 'jump' all live no tapes or recordings!

More recently, the Big Band sound was tried and the stage at the hall was filled with a revival of the 1938 Benny Goodman Carnegie Hall concert, thanks again to Pete Long. With 140 members present, it was an evening to remember as the sound of 'swing' had everybody on their feet.

The Jazz Club is under the Chairmanship of Ralph Marsh who, with his hard-working committee, put on the best jazz possible with new bands and old favourites. A full year's programme of top quality music including the now famous fish & chip supper is provided and, in addition, in summer, a hog roast at the June concert, and a wonderful Silver Service Dinner at Christmas for the December concert.

*Somehow on the 18th October 1987, George's signature was entered into the Queen's Book which sits in the lectern in the Village Hall Foyer! The lectern was made by local craftsman Mark Baker.

Magna Carta Country Winemakers

Another fabulous club in the Village Hall, the envy of many now defunct winemaking circles, was started from an article in the local press about Slough Wine Circle. This gave Len Pearce and Denys Webb the idea that maybe Wraysbury could have its own wine club. Discussions were had with Norman Headon of Slough Wine Circle (also a village resident) and, with his encouragement, leaflets were handed out at Wraysbury Fair in the summer of 1972. A meeting was held in the September in the snug of The George pub and 13 interested people attended. From this small number an embryonic committee was formed with future meetings to be held in Champney Hall, Horton until Wraysbury's new Village Hall was completed in 1974.

From its very first meeting in October 1972, a monthly newsletter has been sent out and I don't believe a month has been missed since - a truly great achievement. Membership soon started to increase and by 1977 the numbers had reached 121 and to date the club has a very healthy membership that is always looking for new members and new ideas. This attitude of being receptive to changing trends, especially in winemaking, from members own fruit, to kits, to supermarket bottles, has undoubtedly kept the membership intact and interested. Anyone now can try a suggested wine 'off the shelf' so to speak, if they do not have the knowledge or inclination to make their own. This also has helped attract new members who can enjoy the social side of the club without the 'pressure' of having to make their own wine.

The social side is also one of its highlights, with monthly get-togethers with usually a guest speaker and new wines to taste (don't forget to bring a glass!), and regular dances throughout the year. In its earlier years one of the main social events was the annual music hall show (variety) which started in 1981, where members did turns or special productions were staged. A few of the ones still remembered are those of the late Arthur Walters who, with his wife Kay, did a wonderful impersonation of Charlie Chaplin and also of Vernon Gosling as Sherlock Holmes. The shows ended in c.1999 and, whilst a shame, they did require almost a full-time commitment to planning, organising, rehearsing and performing, which George Carroll, Vi Carroll, David Blight and Richard Carney (grandson of Kate Carney the music hall artiste) did with great aplomb. The Carneys, a great music hall family, had a number of relatives in the village, mainly in Wharf Road and Fairfield Approach. Who also remembers the talk given by Thea McIntire, one of the original Roly-Polys (Les Dawson show) and her American tap dance thrown in for good measure? Great names, great days.

Recently celebrating its 45th year in October 2017 with a Gala Dance, the Wine Circle goes from strength to strength. Donations to charitable causes from profits and raffles are still made, thanks to the generosity of its members and the Committee. The President for many years until 2018, was Maureen Rolfe who did a wonderful job. The new President is Ray Alletson, ably assisted by his team of long-serving members, some of whom go back to the club's inception! It still has a full calendar of talks, dances and wine tasting tips, no wonder members come from all over the local area just to be part of this happy social circle. Now looking forward to 2022 and its 50th anniversary, the club marches on to an assured future.

Fairfield Country Music Club

Jeannie Sinclair & Stateside
Source: RedPunk@45 worlds

Another regular at the Village Hall is the Country Music Club, formed in 1987 by Len Pearce and Harold Hutt. They discussed the idea and decided to call the Club, 'The Fairfield Country Music Club' as both of them lived in Fairfield Approach. A trial evening was subsequently arranged in the Village Hall featuring The Jeanie Sinclair and Stateside Country Band. The evening was a great success, and new bands were booked for the remainder of the year. More quality acts were booked such as Nashville Sounds, Cactus River, Tom Williams Band, Union Revival and The Gary Blackmore Band, all were a great success and often appeared many times over the years.

A supper is always provided and in the early years it was just bangers and beans with a jacket potato, prepared in the kitchen by Avril Pearce and Barbara Hutt. Things have changed since then but many old timers still remember those early meals with affection as being the best, rather like an impromptu BBQ.

Over the next twenty or so years, the club showcased some of the best acts in Country Music and soon developed a reputation as a happy place to perform in and where the bands were always assured of a good reception. Write-ups in the local papers and in the Country Music press soon established Fairfield Country Music Club as a top venue. In October 2012, the club celebrated its 25th anniversary by giving all the members a free meal and supplying wine on the tables. This special night drew over 190 members, the largest attendance ever, who danced the evening away to a band formerly known as Nashville Sounds but now reformed as Badger Country Band.

2013 was fully booked with favourite bands and the odd new ones who had received good reviews in Southern Country Magazine-the 'bible' for country music fans-and supper again was supplied at all events. By this time, both Len and Harold were getting rather tired of all the responsibility involved in running the club for so many years and they decided that time was approaching to take a back seat and let younger people take over - if they could be found.

By the end of 2013, no one had come forward and the club was in danger of closing. Word soon went around and into the breach stepped Frank and Joy Burry who, in a matter of weeks, threw the club a lifeline and agreed to manage it. So, from despair sprang great delight and a new name, Wraysbury Country Music Club. From the 28th February 2014 the new management team assumed responsibility for the club and has ensured that its traditions of great entertainment, dancing and good food, have never faltered. Here's to the next 25 years.

Wraysbury Players

A firm favourite at the Village Hall and, although thought to have been initially established in 1966, evidence exists to show that this is not the case. Wraysbury Players go back much

> Wraysbury Players. — "Far, far away." — The cook, Mrs. Fish; Queenie, Mrs. Sherriff; Penny, Mrs. Thompson; Mrs. Considine, Mrs. Sword; Nancy, Mrs. Hann; Mrs. Grimwade, Mrs. Goodfellow. Producer, Mrs. C. Hann.

Play and cast of Wraysbury Players
Source: Bucks Herald 1ˢᵗ April 1938

further, at least until 1938 and for sure even earlier. The thespians competed in the 1938 Buckinghamshire WI Drama Festival and were placed 3ʳᵈ with their play, 'Far, Far Away'. A cast list is shown here and some of our more senior readers may indeed recognise the names. Their existence is further supported by other reports from 1940 and 1942.

During these war years, it is known that members of the then Wraysbury WI were also members of the Players and they were heavily involved in War Work as can be seen from the section devoted to the WI in this book. It is thought that this, and the shortage of men, caused the Players to just fade away as its members were overtaken by more pressing events of the time. Once gone, of course, it becomes much more difficult to resurrect but long after the war this wonderful institution returned.

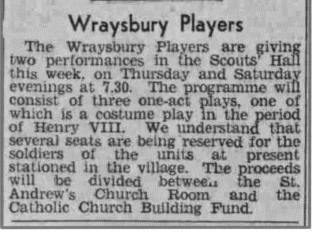

Wraysbury Players

The Wraysbury Players are giving two performances in the Scouts' Hall this week, on Thursday and Saturday evenings at 7.30. The programme will consist of three one-act plays, one of which is a costume play in the period of Henry VIII. We understand that several seats are being reserved for the soldiers of the units at present stationed in the village. The proceeds will be divided between the St. Andrew's Church Room and the Catholic Church Building Fund.

Wraysbury Players
Source: Mx. Chronicle 20ᵗʰ January 1940

The new Wraysbury Players was founded in 1966 by Dennis Williams and is affiliated to the National Operatic and Drama Association. Its first production was The Whole Truth in January 1966 and this immensely talented group has blossomed ever since. A range of shows has been staged from The Importance of Being Ernest to the fabulous production in 2016 of Allo, Allo for which Nigel Handyside and his team were awarded runners up for best scenery, and Group Chairman, Ben Wood, was awarded the best male actor award for his role as "Rene" by NODA for theatre production district 14. With currently c.30 members and always looking for more, they currently put on three productions a year: plays in May and October and, of course, the Pantomime in January, which in 2018 was Cinderella.

Here is a look at one of their early production of Aladdin in 1985, which shows the fun and enthusiasm that the Players had and still bring to their roles over 30 years on.

Beautiful Slave Girls – Alison Beckett and Nicola Fulljames
and
The great Tony Masterson as Abanazar
Source: The Observer 18ᵗʰ Jan 1985

Wraysbury Players undoubted success is down to the spirit of the cast and crew who enjoy great support from the village and who have developed over time their own 'groupies', who go to see them perform again and again. From their audience's spring volunteers who just want to help out a bit back stage, but before they know it they're putting on the greasepaint and having a great time. The Players have a wide cross section of actors from youngsters of 10 years of age to more senior thespians whose ages shall remain a secret!

It's not all glitz and glamour, someone has to do the work. You'll never believe the amount of tea that's drunk. Although from this photo it looks a lot stronger than that!

Seriously though, the wonderful job they do for the scenery, lighting, props and costumes is truly amazing, a host of talent in front and behind the stage. Where do they find the time to do all this as well as perform?

Source: Wraysbury Players Facebook

2018 Pantomime - Cinderella
Source: Wraysbury Players

Front of House – Sue Habicht-Britton and Lesley Minter
Source: Wraysbury Players Facebook

Tickets are on sale in Sai News, Wraysbury News and Pennyfields, while performances are always advertised in Bennetts and on the corner of The Green/Windsor Road. See you at the next show!

History Group

Group will record Wraysbury's past

WRAYSBURY village can claim many links with the past—it was even mentioned in the Domesday Book. But its past will not be allowed to fade, for a new history group is being set up in the village.

The group, which will meet at the George Hotel on the first Monday of every month, has already attracted plenty of interest—from young and old alike.

At its first meeting this week, there were nearly two dozen residents ranging from 20 year olds to pensioners. Their aim is to remain informal, and only a small committee has been formed under the temporary chairmanship of Mr Tom Sumner.

Its first task will be to compile the history of the parish during the last 100 years, with the aid of maps, relics and old documents. Members are also hoping to visit some of the older residents to record their memories of olde-worlde Wraysbury.

And when that is complete

there is plenty of scope for a deep dig into the past. Magna Carta was sealed in the parish, and King Henry VIII is reputed to have indulged in more than one amorous adventure under a yew tree there!

All the facts compiled will be first recorded in a file and possibly later produced as a book. Some of the donkey work has already been done by joint secretary Miss Nell Goodman, of Woodhall, Vicarage Lane, who has been an avid collector of historical data for more than 30 years.

Miss Goodman, who is sharing the secretarial work with Mr J. Jones, is hoping to hear from residents who want to join the group or are willing to lend them documents or maps for copying. She can be contacted at Wraysbury 2141.

First meeting
Source: Slough Express 14th Jan 1972

Also based in the Village Hall (how many more wonderful things happen there?) this friendly club was formed on the 10th January 1972, initially out of the work done by the then Wraysbury Association in its battle with Mr. Albert Silver and Plot 279 as mentioned in the article on the Fair. Its first meeting was held on the 2nd February and attracted twenty-five members. The initial meetings were held in The George, member's houses and then progressed to the church annexe, cricket club and ultimately to the Colne Room in the Village Hall. It soon became independent of the Wraysbury Association and since that time has attracted various speakers to attend on a monthly basis with topics that varied from 'A History of Heathrow' to 'Jack the Ripper', so it's certainly not dry and dusty as some would think.

Trips to interesting places have taken place over the years, and various projects have been undertaken in the village such as the Wraysbury Archaeological Dig at the rear of St. Andrew's Church, restoration of the Harcourt family graves, restoration of the Hargreaves family Celtic Memorial Cross, restoration of the Award Stone at Hythe End, and creation of the Archives Room*. The latter in particular, was due to Arthur Walters and Dennis Pitt, both long term members of the History Group.

***See Appendix 9**

Wraysbury Fair Display 1975
Source: History Group Archives

Displays at the Fair in 1975 brought in new members and in this photo is Jill Gray, Jim Newell, Wraysbury's vicar, and his wife Mabel.

The Group have held many displays in the village in aid of others, in particular St. Andrew's church where efforts to help others less fortunate is always a priority. It works both ways as it not only helps the fundraising but also shows off the work done by the Group which in turn attracts new members.

In 1982, the History Group again won the Annual Wraysbury Society Challenge Quiz, the only club to have won it twice up to then. Up against fierce competition from the Tennis Club, Jazz Club, Wine Circle et al, the History Group swept to victory and proudly collected the cup.

Way Marking in Douglas Lane 28th March 1976
Source: History Group Archives

The History Group also carried out sign posting of footpaths throughout the village and as can be seen from the photo it was a team effort. None of the lovely walks in the village would be way marked if not for the History Group. In the photo is Bernard Colton, Steve Gray, Len Rowlands and Jim Jones. Also, all of the footpaths were walked regularly and any damage or illegal blocking was either dealt with at local level or referred to the parish council for further action.

In 2012, the History Group celebrated their 40th anniversary with a party at the Cricket Club and a great time was had by all. Reminiscences flowed (as well as the wine) and past members were recalled with affection, such as Joan Dick, Margery Rowlands, Poppy Burtonshaw and Kay Walters, to name just a few, all of whom had added to the atmosphere and personality of the History Group.

40th Anniversary Celebrations at Cricket Club
Source: Margaret Rooks

Joan Dick with Margaret Rooks
The Grange 2006
Source: Margaret Rooks

A lot is owed to the Group for its commitment to preserving the village's historic sites. It is always looking for new members who can help preserve the past for the benefit of future residents. Special recognition should be given to Jill Hopkins, Margaret Rooks, Maggie Gardiner, Wendy Kessack, Jan Willis and Shirley Warner, all long-term members whose energy and enthusiasm have kept the Group going. There are many interesting, and often amusing speakers, who illustrate their subjects with skill and ease that keep the audience attentive. One of the more recent talks was 'The Rise and Fall of Skindles', the sad and derelict hotel on the riverside at Maidenhead that played an important part in the character of the 1930s through to the 1970s. It was a venue to be seen in for all the bright young things and hot pop groups of the time. The Talk brought alive the Rolling Stones and all our misspent youth! How nice to see the regeneration of this once run-down area.

Age Concern – Wraysbury & Horton

MAGNA CARTA W.I.
welcomes you
to
an afternoon **Tea Dance**
at the Grange
on
Saturday 3rd June 1989
from **2.30. - 5.00 p.m.**

Live Music   Browsing Stall   Cake Stall
Raffles   Craft Stall

Price: **£2** including refreshments

all proceeds in aid of **Westminster Age Concern**

Source: Magna Carta WI Archive

Meeting at the Village Hall every Thursday at 10am, today's Age Concern has come a long way since the early days of the 70s and 80s and in addition, the support for the then Westminster Age Concern, spearheaded by the two local Women's Institutes. One of the highlights was the annual tea dance held at the Grange where they were entertained by the Magna Carta WI thanks to the generosity of Mrs. Sams.

Now Wraysbury has its own branch, born out of the riverside tea parties in the early 70s given by Margaret Tracey, whose house was nicknamed 'The Scone Factory'! Officially formed in 1976 by Harry Walton*, Careen Temple and Jackie Roper, it was registered as charity in July 1977. It is supported by the other village charities, clubs and local commercial concerns.

Mr. Green of Burnham Garage hands the keys or the new Mini-Bus to Mayor Cllr. Ron Dyason. Chairman of Age Concern Cllr. Arthur Jacobs is standing behind Mr. Green

Handover of new Mini-Bus – Village Hall Oct 1980
Source: The Windsor Observer

Here in 1980, Mr. Green of Burnham Garage hands over the keys to new Mini-Bus, a scene to take place a few times over the coming years. Well used and well driven, it took the members of Age Concern to places far and wide, including Brighton, Bognor, Hampton Court and all places in between. Trips to London's theatreland were always popular with such shows as Hi De Hi, Hello Dolly and Me and My Girl, and parking for Age Concern was allowed in front of the theatre then, it's drop off only now and that's if you're lucky!

*Windsor Express 12th November 1976

At The Grange – 19th May 1984
Source: Wraysbury Archives

Always trying to raise funds for its own activities and others less fortunate, regular raffles are held plus a Spring Bazaar and Autumn Fundraiser. With stalls at all the local events, they provide a variety of things for sale and home baking is a strong feature. Within the group it has knitting circles and all manner of recreational activities. The kettle is always on and usually cake is not too far away; well attended by residents who enjoy each other's company, it welcomes members both old and new with its friendly and happy atmosphere.

The recent trip to Warners at Hayling Island in December 2017 for lunch and a panto, proved a great success. With a trip behind the scenes to see how all the lights and magic work and a three-course lunch, it was a great day out.

Sinah Warren Hotel, Hayling Island 17th Dec. 2017
Source: Warner's Hotels

The club has recently taken delivery of their newest bus to replace its ageing transport, bought out of its own funds and through the generosity of villagers, the hard work of the various fund-raising members, local businesses and, in addition, a donation from Wraysbury Village Trust*. The new bus features a wheelchair lift and is driven by a team of volunteer drivers who go that extra mile with a smile. If you can't make it to the Village Hall the Community Bus will take you there and bring you back, so there's no need to sit at home and miss out on any of the social mornings or outings. ***See Appendix 8**

Andy Davison of the Village Trust hands over the keys of the fabulous new bus to
Mike Williams of the Parish Council
Members of Age Concern Committee can't wait and are already aboard!
Source: Wraysbury News

Without this kind of support from the volunteer drivers and 'shotgun' riders, our senior residents would not be able to attend the weekly get togethers or enjoy the local trips out organised by Pam and Dennis Gabriel. Pam has been Chairman for the past year, taking over from Sandra Hopkins who also gave a lot of herself to this worthwhile cause. Pam is fully supported by a hard-working volunteer committee whose one objective is to ensure that the senior residents of Wraysbury and Horton have a great time and are not forgotten or side-lined in any way. Nothing seems to be a problem and they are always thinking of new things to do and how to improve the quality of life for its members.

Pam Gabriel – Chair of Age Concern
Source: ancestralresearch library

Dennis Gabriel – Age Concern
Source: ancestralresearch library

Wraysbury Art Society

Linda Kinsella in her Wraysbury studio
Source: W. Eton Express 21ˢᵗ May 1971

This very talented group started in 1971[43], in the old Village Hall or Scout Hut as it was then. Its main driving force was a Wraysbury lady, Linda Kinsella, an extremely talented painter of in particular, miniatures, of which she had a number exhibited at the Royal Academy and at the Paris Salon. Linda was trained at both Ealing and Isleworth School of Art. She taught twice a week in the Scout Hut, in between her short story writing and running a stall at Eton Antique Market, (*now no longer there*).

Her work drew great acclaim and inspired others who were just vaguely interested to pick up the brushes and get painting. The movement grew and now there is a dedicated group of artists who come together on a Monday morning at the Village Hall. Now under the wing of Reg Marsh and Lesley West, they work in most media including pen, pencil, pastels, acrylic, oil and watercolour. There seems to be no shortage of talent and enthusiasm in the village as everyone helps each other, and beginners soon feel at home and become more accomplished. The work produced is outstanding and exhibited for sale three times a year at the various exhibitions in the village.

Attention to detail, colour
and layout
Lesley West

Glorious wild flowers in a
triumph of colour
Wendy Kessack

Source: The Art Society

*See also rear cover

---

[43] Windsor, Slough and Eton Express 21ˢᵗ May 1971

Playgroups and Preschool

A playgroup was started for toddlers in the Scout Hut in about 1960, reflecting the move of more mothers going out to work. The group moved to the Village Hall and lasted till about the 90s when the new Community Centre was opened in place of the Scout Hut. The playgroup is now called Angels Preschool and has been in the Community Centre since 2005 and focuses on a fun, learning environment.

Another toddler group in the village today is called Pumpkins Preschool, and is to be found in St. Andrew's annexe. In the village since 2013, it has the same high standards of fun with learning. Pumpkins also has another school in the Baptist Church annexe and one in Horton.

Bowls Club

Bowls Pavilion
Source: Wraysbury Archives

Amongst newer clubs and societies in the village is the extremely popular Bowls Club. Opened in the late 90s, right next door to the Tennis Club, it has a beautiful pavilion built by Glyn Larcombe using reclaimed timber (Inc. some from Tilbury Docks) in a similar, attractive design to the village Windmill, another of Glyn's masterpieces.

The Bowls Club was formed[44] [45] out of a coming together of Bill Stewart, Nancy Fuller, Bob Marshall, Jack Pengelly and others, who were all originally involved with Short Mat Bowls (indoor bowls) in the village hall. The success of short mat* sowed the seed for a proper outdoor bowling rink and this small nucleus of like-minded enthusiastic villagers was formed. (*Short Mat Bowls was initially set up by the RBWM to offer communal activities to the borough's villages. Introduced in the village hall in 1988 it didn't take long to get going and it soon found a strong following in the village which continues to this day.)

Approaches to the Parish Council were made but, despite expressing support, funding was going to be an issue. However, it did allow the lease of a piece of land next to the tennis courts, which, after a great deal of work, eventually became the bowling rink.

The group through their hard work with others raised sufficient money to get things started. Various hiccups occurred along the way, in particular, "The Hedge War" with the Tennis Club, and the Planning Application for the pavilion, which seemingly attracted adverse criticism due to ancient inclosure(enclosure) regulations affecting the site, which stated that any building should be temporary and on wheels!

---

[44] Memoirs of Bill Stewart
[45] The Bowls Club 2002 Wraysbury Archives

In addition, the site was earmarked to provide overflow parking for the newly erected village hall, a condition applied at the outset. Things eventually calmed down and construction went on apace. It soon became apparent that more money was required. Thanks to Bob Marshall's personal generosity, a substantial sum was contributed towards the club's finances, which enabled a full 3 rink all-weather surface to be completed in 1998 with a celebratory match day on Sunday, 25th September. A year later the clubhouse (named the Marshall Pavilion) was finished and officially opened on the 18th September 1999 by the late Rt. Hon. Lord Archer of Sandwell, a Wraysbury resident, and the club has never looked back.

The club has many competitions and each is hotly contested by the members. Present Captain Alan Dell, who, along with other previous captains such as Harold Hutt (now Chairman) and Roger Painter, is always looking for that winning edge.

Bob Marshall – President and Tommy Wareham – Chairman Club opening 18th September 1999.
Source: Wraysbury Archives

Mixed Pairs Winners and Runners Up 2013
Ian Smith, Yvonne Gorrod - Eddie Wisby, Graham Sinclair
Source: Bowls Club Archive

Playing in the Berkshire Kennet KLV League Division 2 and also the Chilterns & Thames League, matches become very competitive. The biggest success was being nearly promoted to KLV Division 1 in 2013, losing out in a decider to Maidenhead Town B who won by just 7 shots!

Lambert Family 'Clean-Up' at 2017 Awards
Source: Bowls Club Archive

Season 2017

Wedding Party - Happy Days 2017
Source: Bowls Club Archive

Andy Doughton and Julia Cream
Winners Winter Cup 2016/7
Source: Bowls Club Archive

Denys Webb and Sue Bennett
Memorial Pairs Runners Up
Source: Bowls Club Archive

With an annual early season trip to Chess Vale Club near Chesham, the club team enjoys a top-quality game on a first-class surface used by the England team bowlers. In their third visit in 2017, Wraysbury Club won against this really top team. They hope to repeat their success in the 2018 season.

The club has an enviable site, right in the heart of the village near The Splash Windmill and also enjoys a clubhouse with full facilities, playing all year round on outdoor carpet. It has a friendly membership of about 42 active bowlers and is happy to welcome new members. It is not just for the older generation, younger players are also attracted to the sport, so whatever your age, experienced or beginner, have a chat with Fred Parsons, secretary, on a Friday or Sunday morning at the clubhouse, a friendly welcome awaits.

Our Fabulous Windmill

The glorious Splash Windmill[46] is a joy to behold, set in this picturesque part of the village overlooking the Bowls Club and village green, it looks as though it has always been there. But this is not the case, built in 1996/7 by Glyn Larcombe and his talented team at Splash Studios, it soars majestically upwards in command of all it surveys.

Splash Studios, better known for their advertising and promotional work, in particular stage back drops for some of the best music events and entertainers in the world, such as Live Aid, Queen, Tina Turner, Michael Jackson and Brian Adams, set to turning Glyn's seed of an idea into reality. His plan was formed out of a joint desire to enlarge his then family home and put back in the village some of what over the years has been lost in the destruction of the numerous beautiful old houses, and the mills that used to be on the Colne in the village and at Hythe End. A planning application was made, very much tongue in cheek and to Glyn's surprise, full permission was granted!

Source: ©Maxwell Hamilton - Flickr

Glyn studied a 17th-century smock mill at Lacey Green near Princes Risborough before drawing up his design. Once done he turned to reclaimed timber specialist, Ashwell Recycling, from Essex, for the eight, 50 ft. long posts for the main structure, each of which weighed two tons and once lined the Tall Ships sidings at Tilbury Docks.

To build the 60 ft. tall windmill and the 10 ft. high "boat" that sits on the top and turns on a series of giant castors, Glyn enlisted his engineer brother, Ewan. They used weatherboarding, screwed to a frame constructed from short pieces of old scaffolding boards, jointed and bolted together. Inside, the timber walls were obtained from various west London demolition sites and are festooned with lengths of rope, pulleys and pieces of old agricultural equipment that were collected over the years. There are five floors - three of them used for bedrooms. A bathroom occupies the third floor and there is gas central heating. The tiny kitchen, which resembles a galley, is alongside the octagonal dining/sitting room on the ground floor.

---

[46] Out & About Star FM 1996 and Daily Telegraph 2003 – Wraysbury Archives.

In addition to a family home and familiar landmark to aircraft landing at Heathrow, it has also been a romantic getaway and B&B, ultimately being featured on Out and About with Star FM in 1996, House Beautiful magazine in 2004 and on TV's '60-Minute Makeover' in 2005. Whereas they were only able to give a fleeting glimpse of this fascinating and beautiful structure, Wraysbury villagers can stand and stare and enjoy the wonder of it every day.

St. Andrew's Church

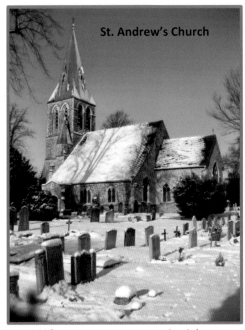

St. Andrew's Church

When a poor man came in sight

Moving on from this lovely setting to just up the road to St. Andrew's Close, let us look at that wonderful building, St. Andrew's Church, another centre of community life for over 900 years and along with Ankerwycke Priory, one of the very few witnesses to the sealing of the Magna Carta. They say walls have ears, if only they could talk as well, Egham and Runnymede's claim to the sealing of the Magna Carta would have been scotched long ago! Set on rising ground and possibly the highest place in the village, well chosen by our village ancients, the church lies on what was long ago considered to be a sacred site. Its relationship with our ancient Yew cannot be ignored and it is thought that the tree attracted Druid and Celtic worshippers here in ancient times and why down through the ages, this site including Ankerwycke Priory, has had religious significance.

Our St. Andrew's story has been left until now so that we may celebrate this lovely church in the modern era and not talk about its past or construction, about which more than enough has been said and written and not always complimentary…'Wraysbury (Church) is the worst in the country. Two windows were dammed up in the Chancel and several in the North Aisle and all were broken in the glass. The South Aisle seemed to have been removed altogether!'[47] And again – '1637, Wraydisbury(sic) – 3 bells – frames broken, bell frames in decay, bells cannot be rung; steeple in great decay and braced round with timber and iron pins.'[48] This must have been a very sad sight.

Nevertheless, it has withstood the bad maintenance and bad press over the years and all has been put right. What has emerged, is this lovely aged-coloured stone church with beautiful stained glass that we all know and love, and this is why we will concentrate on its modern image, and how it punches above its weight for a small village church, representing us all in a more meaningful way than the fabric of the building, irrespective of faith.

'There will always be poor people in the land. Therefore, I command you to be openhanded toward your fellow men who are poor and needy in your land'.[49]

---

[47] Victoria County Hist. of Bucks 1637 – St. Andrew's Church Guide – Dennis Pitt
[48] Church Bells of Buckinghamshire
[49] Deuteronomy 15:11

St. Andrew's Church Today (2017 CE)

Lovely St. Andrew's in the morning sun
Source: Wraysbury Archives

There is so much already said and written about the history of St. Andrew's, its foundation, modifications and bells that to do so again would become rather repetitive. If you would like to know about its ancient history there is a very good little book by the late Dennis Pitt and Tony Kimber, available from the church.

What is also very interesting and not often spoken about is its 'human face', its place in the modern world and society and what it does on behalf of villagers and the wider community in general. These are things that go quietly on behind the scenes and as such deserve greater recognition.

One of its longer-term financial commitments is to the bore-hole project run by the St. John's Mission in Gwelutshena, Zimbabwe. Gwelutshena is in north Matabeleland and it is underdeveloped with poor water and school facilities. Transport is variable to say the least and road safety is not a priority, accidents are common. Therefore, the bore-hole project is of prime importance to this area and its people, who are mainly subsistence farmers, as without it no irrigation is possible for crops nor for the basic necessities of life. Hand in hand with this project is also financial assistance to buy maize and seed for crops, with which to, hopefully, become self-sufficient. Whilst water is the prime concern, one relies very much on the other to make a difference to their quality of life.

The Better Portion is a ladies' lunch group sponsored by St. Andrew's who meet monthly and support financially deserving causes. The current charity is Love Russia, founded by Noel Doubleday in 1993. Noel found that just handing out Bibles to the children in the orphanages wasn't enough (he worked for the International Bible Society) as this did nothing to alleviate their living conditions or improve their prospects. Consequently, the charity was born and St. Andrew's and the Better Portion support the orphans and young mothers and enable them to have a better life.

The graphic images of children living on the streets in different capitals of the world is all too familiar to us. St. Andrew's does what it can to help these children and has chosen a charity called Operation Restoration in Santa Cruz, Bolivia. Established in 1991 by Roger and Isha Hulford, it aims to get the kids off the streets and into some meaningful way of life. Santa Cruz is one of the fastest growing cities in Latin America, having grown from a population of less than 700,000 in 1991 to more than 3.4 million in 2016. As a result of this population explosion, the poor always seem to get left behind and the number of children abandoned to the streets exceeds 5000. Trying to give them life-changing opportunities is a constant battle with inadequate resources. Thanks to St. Andrew's a little of the pressure is relieved.

Some years ago, the Revd. Colin Gibson's youngest son Ben, spent a GAP year working with this charity and in 2014, Roger and Isha Hulford paid a visit to Wraysbury to talk about their work in Bolivia. It's nice to see that contacts and help are still established. Ben married his work colleague from Bolivia, Kathryn Rowe, on the 29th August 2015. Both Ben and Kathryn trained as missionaries and are actively seeking placement at the moment.

Ben Gibson, Roger Hulford
Isha Hulford, Kathryn Rowe
The Front-Line staff in Bolivia – Operation Restoration 2014
Source: St. Andrews Church

STITCH is another group set up in St. Andrews whose volunteers provide feminine hygiene products for girls in underdeveloped countries such as Nepal, Ghana and Uganda. Whereas they would miss school or other days in their lives due to their bodies natural cycle, STITCH empowers girls to take control, prevents them being marginalised and helps them to equally participate in their communities.

On the lighter side, a 60th birthday treat at Duxford, a present from the family - Revd. Colin Gibson.
Source: St. Andrews Church

Working closer to home, Slough Food Bank receives the Harvest Festival offerings and there is also a box in the church for food donations to this worthy cause. It does seem so strange that in modern day Britain there has to be such things as Food Banks.

In addition to its regular church services, The Church also sponsors support groups within the local community such as 'Pop In', a weekly meeting for tea, cake (there's always cake!) and a natter, for the more elderly residents who fancy some time and space. Also, held about every four weeks or so, on a Saturday morning, is what is termed 'Men's Breakfast', and by the size of the breakfast the title's certainly correct! It is a 'men only' (sorry ladies) gathering and gives men the opportunity to meet and discuss in company of their peers, the subject of the day. There are a number of very interesting talks with which men can identify with such as motor racing, local photography, film production and many others. All are welcome at these very friendly gatherings, just bring an appetite!

Within the congregation of the Church and the wider community in general, lies a very important group of villagers known as "The Friends of St. Andrew's", its role is to ensure that the basic fabric of the church, the actual building itself, which is now over 170 years old, is maintained and repaired to a satisfactory standard for the benefit of all. They do this by in addition to the annual membership of £10, organise a number of fund raising schemes (there is no help from central or local government) throughout the year, amongst which, the most well-known to villagers, is the annual garden party at The Grange. Now in its fourteenth year since being resurrected, it reflects the glorious days of a summer idyll long since past, when in 1931, The Grange* first opened its Italianate gardens in support of St. Andrew's, by its then owner Major H. E. Meade.

*See page 41

What a lovely photo – very evocative and 1950s in Black & White
l to r : Wolf Heiner, Alan Powell and Cyril Giles
Source: Tony Kimber

An example of the funds required would be the repairs to the church tower, of which a most dramatic photograph is shown here. This was completed in 2002 and was the biggest maintenance project since the church was rebuilt in 1862. The earlier tower was made of wood, and considerably shorter than the current stone tower which was added at the time of its 1862 restoration.

A very expensive job completed with the assistance of Wraysbury Village Trust, 'The Friends of St. Andrew's' and local villagers. From the photo, Wolf was supervising the work, whilst Alan and Cyril were Church Wardens. Their names now locked in time within this History for the work they did on behalf of us all.

The importance of these funds is clearly obvious, and without the congregation and 'The Friends', the church would be in a parlous state. For such a small sum per year, so much can be done and new 'Friends' are always welcome.

In addition to those previously mentioned, there are other good causes that St. Andrew's supports and I suppose it's fair to say there will always be a long queue but as long as we have our lovely church St. Andrew's, working together with the Baptist Church, helped by their congregations and the village in general, they are doing their best to help those less fortunate. Apart from spiritual guidance to all, this heartfelt caring for others by 'putting its money where its mouth is', is what makes St. Andrew's relevant in the village today. Something we can all identify with and what Wraysbury has always been proud to do*.

*See Appendix 3

Millennium Celebrations

Wraysbury played its part in these festive occasions and put on a number of shows and a variety of entertainment for villagers and their guests. All too easily forgotten about, they are worth recording for the effort put into them by many in the village, especially Mike Smith whose vision it was to make the Millennium a success for everyone.

This fun filled evening was followed later in the year, by on Saturday 15th July 2000 at the Village Hall, where Magna Carta Winemakers hosted a 'Cockney Cavalcade', an evening of comedy, singing and dancing complete with a sausage and mash supper all for £8 per ticket! Any profits made, and there were, thanks to the number of people that turned up, went to providing a Silver Service lunch for the senior residents of the village.

This was followed on Sunday the 16th July at 2pm outside the Village Hall, by the Consecration of the new War Memorial Stone. The Stone was not without its critics, but the day went off without incident. Attended by church groups, Scouts and the British Legion, and despite being part of a celebration, it was nonetheless a day for reflection and remembrance.

Thursday 20th July saw the day of the Silver Service lunch for Wraysbury senior residents, made possible by donations and sponsorship from the Jazz club, Country & Western Club and Magna Carta Winemakers. The big tuck-in began at 12.30pm at the Village Hall and a great time was had by all.

Fairfield Country & Western Club kicked off Friday 21st July with music, dancing and a fish and chip supper at 8pm in the Village Hall. The fabulous James Twins supplied the music and all for £7 a ticket! Again, all profits made went towards the Silver Service lunch.

The following Tuesday 25th July, saw villagers in the Village Hall at 8pm for a fabulous concert given by Wraysbury & District Musical Society, supported by the Kidwells Park Recreational Trust on behalf of the RBWM. It was an evening of Gershwin music with Jack Gibbons on the piano. Described by the BBC as 'The Gershwin pianist of our time', Jack is an acknowledged expert with sell out concerts both sides of the Atlantic.

Friday 28th July again at the Village Hall (where else!!) at 7pm, a Fashion Show for all Ages was held sponsored by WISE*. Clothes for all ages were on display and the models weren't bad either, thanks to local volunteers.

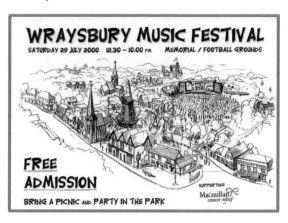

Then on Sunday 30th July at 2pm on the Memorial Ground there was a fantastic non-stop Music Festival and BBQ, with music covering all spectrums. Villagers could enjoy the BBQ's or bring a picnic. With acts like Wraysbury Schools Pop'N'Dance, AbbaLike and The Tippen Family's American Bluegrass to mention only few, it was great day. Again, all profits went to others in need, this time they went to Macmillan cancer relief. Here is the fabulous programme designed by Splash Studio.

*Wraysbury's Intellectual and Sagacious Eccentrics – who shall remain anonymous!

The following week, Tuesday 1st August, the Jazz Club presented John Meehan and the Savannah Jazz Band, one of the most popular bands in the UK. Always a great success, they went down to a lot of foot stomping and great applause. All this and supper included. Here they are as jazz fans would remember them.

That same week, Friday 4th August, was deemed to be Children's Day and sponsored by The Village Trust. At the Village Hall from 2pm-7pm, the day was packed with many exciting and interesting things for the children to do. Professional entertainment, fun and games and football coaching organised by Montem Leisure Centre. All this followed by a buffet tea.

--ooO0oo--

What is obvious from this History is that Wraysbury villagers know how to have a good time and any excuse for a party is seized on, even more so when a Royal celebration is in the offing! Planning Committees swing into action, venues are found and villagers come together to produce all manner of fantastic goodies followed by that very acceptable four-letter word CAKE. Let's look at some of these wonderful Royal occasions that have brought fun and goodwill into villagers lives and help make Wraysbury the special place it is.

HM The Queen's Diamond Jubilee

Sunday the 3rd June 2012 was the day Wraysbury celebrated with a lunch at The Grange. With only a slight shower to dampen the day, the lunch was great success with many attending including The Mayor Cllr. Colin Rayner and Mayoress Samantha Rayner. Here are few photos of the memorable day.

Lunch at The Grange
Sunday 3rd June 2012
Source: Wraysbury News

Lunch at The Grange
Sunday 3rd June 2012
Source: Wraysbury News

In addition to the lunch, villagers were also involved in a special tree planting ceremony. To mark this Diamond Jubilee, the Tree Council had presented a Persian Ironwood tree (Parrotia persica 'Vanessa') to the village. Assisted by the local Scouts, Cubs, Beavers, Guides and

Brownies, the Tree Wardens William Perez and Diana Hughes, planted this magnificent tree in front of the Village Hall. It is particularly prized for its beautifully coloured autumn foliage.

Wraysbury's Youth Groups at the Tree Planting
Source: Wraysbury Archives

William Perez and Diana Hughes
Tree Wardens

The village photographs, write-up, poems and prose were also included in a book to be presented to the Queen before the end of this Diamond Jubilee year, called 'Jubilee Diamond Trees'.

Magna Carta 800th Celebrations

The year 2015 saw the 800th anniversary of the sealing of the Magna Carta and Wraysbury residents were not going to let this pass without some special recognition. In addition to the numerous celebrations that were planned, such as the River Relay Pageant in conjunction with the Royal Shallop "Jubilant" and the Royal barge "Gloriana, there were other 'smaller' events which may not have caught villagers' attention so much. Let's look at these celebrations and three that may have slipped under the radar, so to speak.

There was a *Peal of Cambridge Surprise* rung on the bells of St. Andrew's on the 6th June 2015 and here is a photo of that heard but rarely seen group, the St. Andrew's bell ringers.

St. Andrew's Bell Ringers - 6th June 2015
Source: Wraysbury News Facebook

Magna Carta at the Fair

Happy Summer Days

Jayne Kennedy and children
Source: Magna Carta Fair

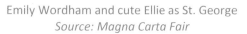

Emily Wordham and cute Ellie as St. George
Source: Magna Carta Fair

Polly Chan and Beryl Williams
Source: Magna Carta Fair

Where does all this talent come from?
What a delight the children are.

There was also a wonderful Flower Show at St. Andrew's. Lucy Foster found herself volunteering to make something happen and between her and her team, 'Kew Gardens' appeared in St. Andrew's! What a triumph of colour and variety, rather like the old days of the fabulous Horticultural Society Flower Show, truly beautiful arrangements. Here are a few photos of this colourful show.

Main Alter Flowers by Anne Munday, Carolyn Humphries and Lucy Foster
Source: Lucy Foster

'On a Summers Day in 1215'
By Christa Adams
Source: Lucy Foster

'Light Penetrates the Dark Ages'
By Beryl Walters and Janet Baxter
Source: Lucy Foster

Magna Carta River Pageant

Windsor Boys rowing the Gloriana to Runnymede - *Source: Graham Sinclair*

Captain Butt's boat 'The Jolly Brit'   Captain Henry Butt of Hythe End

The Wraysbury Magna Carta Plate – Designed by Tony Kimber
Source: ©Antony McCullum of Wyrdlight Photography

Finally, the pièce de résistance was the wonderful Magna Carta Tapestry, now to be found hanging in St. Andrew's Church. In the planning since 2012, thanks to Margaret Lenton's determination that Wraysbury should do something *special* and Margaret Perkin's idea of a Tapestry, it brought together a dedicated group under the guidance of Art Society leader, Lesley West. This very talented group, now with the memorable name of The Wraysbury Stitchers, had their inaugural meeting in February 2013, where it was decided to divide the work between the 'Stitchers', each being responsible to bring it to a satisfactory finish. Eventually, Lesley's house was being used twice weekly and it remained that way for over a year, the dining table only seeing the light of day for her family's Christmas lunch!

What about this colour? - At Lesley West's house
Source: Julia Coram

On completion, the tapestry measured approximately 84cm x 119cm (2ft 9" x 3ft 10") and was sent to The Frame Workshop in Egham who did a great job of mounting and framing this glorious piece of hand-made story telling. In so few words it is difficult to convey to the reader, the hours of work and dedication, spread over two years, that was put in to this wonderful work of art. Here are a few photos of this dedicated group and the tapestry itself.

Coming together nicely – Lesley West's house
Source: Julie Coram

Wraysbury Stitchers - The Team

June	Blowfeld	Julie	Coram	Celia	Cotter	Tom	Farr
Barbara	Hearne	Benta	Hinckley	Anne	Kemp	Wendy	Kessack
Anne	Lasiaux	Pat	Miles	Jenny	Owen	Avril	Pearce
Margaret	Perkins	Katherine	Rayner	Gladys	Sauro	Kessie	Sauro
Deborah	Shepherd	Lesley	West	Carolyn	Wheeler	Lesley	Willis
Alex Wood							

Sealing of the Magna Carta – Wraysbury Stitchers 2015
Source: Lesley West

HM The Queen's 90th Birthday

The highlight of 2016, was the celebration of the 90th birthday of Her Majesty the Queen on the 21st April 2016. With the Scouts helping to manage the evenings fireworks, bonfire and barbeque, it was all a great success. The fireworks and the beacon were visible for miles and marked a truly historic day.

The Queen at 90
Source: ©Press Association/Danny Lawson

Wraysbury Village Hall 12th June 2016 – Queen's Birthday Party
Some of the wonderful cakes on display
Source: Wraysbury News Facebook

This was later followed on the 11th and 12th June, to mark her official birthday, by a variety of celebrations ending on the 12th with a jazz band and picnic on the green. Due to the rain, the jazz band and picnic both transferred to the Village Hall where a great time was had by all.

Some wonderful cakes were on show, all were home-baked and donated by talented villagers, various village clubs and organisations. Nine cakes had been asked for (one for each decade of her life) but such was the baking fever, that more than a few extras were supplied! There was also a children's entertainer who used a Harry Potter, Hogwarts theme. Several hundred residents and their children enjoyed the festivities, which due to the inclement weather were all held indoors.

Some Famous Names

Wraysbury has had a generous quota of celebrities, especially in the period after the war up to, say, the mid 60s, and one major incident stands out from that time. It concerned a firework party on the 5th November 1961 at Riverhome, a Thames-side bungalow at Hythe End. It was the home of the late American Impresario John Kennedy, the manager of Tommy Steele and Sidney James, of Carry On fame. An unknown person threw a firework into the bungalow and it landed in a box of fireworks, the resulting explosion and fire gutted the bungalow and three people died: two were burned to death and one suffered a heart attack.[50]

At this party, amongst many were Diana Dors, Sidney James, Sara Leighton and a chap called Tommy Yeardye, an associate of the Kray Twins. He was an actor-come-stuntman and one-time squeeze of Ms. Dors (or so it was said). During the panic that ensued, Yeardye managed to drag out Sara Leighton and pushed Diana Dors out of the window, saving her life.

Tommy Yeardye met Vidal Sassoon at around that time and went on to mastermind his business and made them both multi-millionaires. In 1996, Tommy put up the money for his daughter, Tamara, to buy the business of Jimmy Choo, the couture shoemaker. With Choo's designs and Tamara's business flair, money and society connections, the combination worked perfectly, making Jimmy Choo Ltd., a world fashion icon and Tamara millions of pounds. Tommy remained chairman of Jimmy Choo until he died in 2004. Jimmy Choo split from Tamara in 2001 and now makes his own bespoke shoes at Jimmy Choo Couture, under licence from Jimmy Choo Ltd. which is the ready-to wear-range. Tamara resigned in 2011.

Another of our 'residents' assisted by John Kennedy was Christine Keeler of Profumo fame (*see page 32)* her mother being a near neighbour of his. He afforded Christine the odd introduction to show biz personalities and attended some of Ms. Keeler's mad parties at Dolphin Square, London. Christine, born in Slough in 1942, moved to Wraysbury in 1946. She lived with her mother during her formative years at Hythe End, in two railway carriages joined together side by side. Her parents divorced in 1948.

Barbara Mullen (9 June 1914 – 9 March 1979) was an American actress well known in the UK for playing the part of Janet McPherson, the housekeeper, in *'Dr Finlay's Casebook'*. Although the role of Janet brought her fame in later years, she had already made her mark in the theatre.

She appeared on television in America and Britain in programmes such as *'Juno and the Paycock'* and *'The Danny Thomas Show'* before being offered the role in *'Dr Finlay's Casebook'*, which began on the BBC in 1962. Her character, Janet McPherson, was the ever-efficient housekeeper to Doctors Finlay and Cameron at Arden House in the fictional Scottish village of Tannochbrae. When the series finished on television nine years later, it transferred to radio, running until 1978. She was the subject of *'This Is Your Life'* in March 1964 when she was surprised by Eamonn Andrews in central London. Barbara Mullen died of a heart attack in London, England, on 9 March 1979.

---

[50] Illustrated London News 11th Nov 1961

Beryl Elizabeth Reid, OBE (17 June 1919 – 13 October 1996) was a British actress of stage and screen. She had no formal training but despite this, she had success with the 1950s BBC radio show *'Educating Archie'*, in which she played the naughty schoolgirl Monica and later, the Brummie *'Marlene'*. She won a Tony Award in 1967 for *'The Killing of Sister George'*, the 1980 Olivier Award for Best Comedy Performance for *'Born in the Gardens'*, and the 1982 BAFTA TV Award for Best Actress for *'Smiley's People'*. Her film appearances included *'The Belles of St. Trinian's'* (1954), *'The Killing of Sister George'* (1968), *'The Assassination Bureau'* (1969), *'Entertaining Mr. Sloane'* (1970) and *'No Sex Please, We're British'* (1973).

Always a big personality, character actress and gifted in comedy, she appeared in many situation comedies and variety programmes on TV including BBC TV's long-running music hall show, *'The Good Old Days'*. She lived in Honeypot Cottage with her beloved cats.

Charles Gordon Mosley – FRSA (14 September 1948 – 5 November 2013) was a British genealogist who was among the foremost experts on British nobility. Born in west London, the son of George Gordon Mosley and Christine (*née* Dowland) he grew up in Wraysbury, Berkshire (Old Bowry House, now demolished).

He attended Eton College from 1962 to 1967, having been elected a King's Scholar. He then went on King's College, Cambridge. From 2008 to 2010 Mosley was a Fellow of the Royal Society for the Encouragement of Arts, Manufactures & Commerce. He was an author, broadcaster, editor, and publisher, best known for having been Editor-in-Chief of *Burke's Peerage & Baronetage* (106th edition)—its first update since 1970—and of the re-titled 107th edition, *Burke's Peerage, Baronetage & Knightage* (2003). He was thought to have been related to Sir. Oswald Mosley of Blackshirt infamy but it turns out that this is not so.

Gary Numan – singer, record producer and musician, was brought up in Wraysbury on the Staines Road. He first entered the music industry as lead singer of the new-wave band, Tubeway Army. After releasing two studio albums with the band, Gary released his debut solo album *'The Pleasure Principle'* in 1979. His biggest hit singles were *'Are Friends Electric'* and *'Cars'*.

Gary achieved his peak of popularity in the late 70s and early 80s, but maintains a loyal cult following. In 2013 he released his 20th studio album, *'Splinter'* (Songs from a Broken Mind). The album reached the U.K. Top 20 and Numan embarked on a worldwide tour to support the release throughout 2014. The following year he started writing his 21st studio album and set about funding the album via fan pledges. This was done with the fund amount exceeding its target. Focusing on the album and his personal life in 2016, Numan also found time to collaborate with Jean-Michel Jarre on his album, *'Electronica 2: The Heart of Noise'*. That same year he was also awarded the Moog Innovation award as well as the Ivor Novello award for inspiration. 2017 saw the release of Numan's 21st album, *'Savage'* (Songs from a Broken World).

Geoffrey Whitehead (b. 1st October 1939) is an English actor. He has appeared in a range of television, film and radio roles. In the theatre, he has played at the Shakespeare Globe, St. Martin's Theatre and the Bristol Old Vic, formed in 1946 as an offshoot of London's Old Vic.

His many film appearances include *'The Raging Moon'*, *'Kidnapped'*, *'Titanic'*, *'Inside the Third Reich'* and *'Shooting Fish'*. He was married to Mary Hanefey the actress, who is featured on page 122.

He is seen regularly on television as well as filling many roles on radio. His television appearances include *'Z-Cars'* (1964–1965 and 1972–1975) and playing two different regular characters as Sherlock Holmes in the television series *'Sherlock Holmes and Doctor Watson'* (1979–1980). He has also starred in *'Little Britain'*. He has starred on BBC radio in many comic roles, including *'Bleak Expectations'*, featuring as five entire families between 2007 and 2012. He appeared in two series of the BBC's remake of *'Reggie Perrin'* as Reggie's Father-in-Law, William and more recently as Mr. Newbold in *'Still Open All Hours'*.

Jess Conrad, was a young repertory actor with the famous Charles Danville Company. He also played seasons in Barnsley and Derby before being discovered by television producer Daphne Shadwell who saw him appearing in an advertisement for the Daily Sketch Newspaper. She felt he was right for the part of 'Barney Day' in the TV play *'Rock A- Bye Barney'*. Jess landed the part and was seen by the now legendary TV and stage producer Jack Good. Because he "Looked like a pop star" Jack immediately put Jess on television in the original *'Oh Boy!'* show. He then went on to become a 'teen idol' and armed with a Decca recording contract hit England's pop charts with *'Cherry Pie'*, *'Mystery Girl'*, *'This Pullover'* and *'Pretty Jenny'*.

Voted England's Most Popular Male Singer in the 1961 NME annual poll, Jess played the London Palladium, Wembley Pool and went on to tour around the globe with fellow British and American rock 'n' roll and pop stars of the day including, Eddie Cochran, Gene Vincent, Brenda Lee, Billy Fury, Marty Wilde, Joe Brown, Eden Kane and Johnny Kidd to name a few.

Lord Peter Archer of Sandwell (20 November 1926 - 14 June 2012) lived in Hill View Road, off Welley Road. Lord Archer was born and raised in Wednesbury, Staffordshire, the son of a toolsetter, Cyril, and his wife, May. After the local high school, he was a clerk in the Ministry of Health until he was called up under the Bevin Boy scheme. Emerging four years later with his newfound political enthusiasms, he enrolled at the London School of Economics and University College London. He qualified as a barrister in 1952 and, practising on the Oxford circuit, had a distinguished legal career parallel to his political life. He became a QC in 1971, was a crown court recorder from 1982 and used his legal expertise to assist in his numerous campaigns.

He was particularly concerned with the plight of Soviet Jewry; was responsible for a legislative amendment to abolish the death penalty for treason and piracy with violence; and in 2007 chaired the independent inquiry into the contamination of blood with HIV and hepatitis C in the 1970s and 80s. He was a founder member of Amnesty International, a leading figure in the Society of Labour Lawyers and an office-holding member of the Fabian Society.

Mary Hanefey is an actress, known for amongst other theatrical performances, *'Alfie'* (1964 written by Bill Naughton) with Terence Stamp, *'Moll Flanders'* (1975), Unnatural Pursuits' (1992), *'Middlemarch'* (1994), 'The Knock' (1994), and *'Samson and Delilah'* (1996).

She was married to Geoffrey Whitehead (see page 121) and she is the daughter of Mr. Hanefey, the schoolteacher who taught at the old Scout Hut during World War 2.

Sarah Harding – singer with *Girls Aloud* - was born in 1981 Sarah Hardman and brought up in Windsor Road, Wraysbury. Girls Aloud was created through the ITV talent show *'Popstars: The Rivals* in 2002' and comprised singers Cheryl Cole, Nadine Coyle, Sarah Harding, Nicola Roberts and Kimberley Walsh. The group achieved a string of 20 consecutive top 10 singles in the United Kingdom, including four number ones. They also achieved seven certified albums, of which two reached number one. They have been nominated for five Brit Awards, winning the 2009 Best Single for *'The Promise'*.

As a young girl Sarah loved to 'put on a show' for anyone who'd watch. Her set list of shower songs included Sheryl Crow's *'All I Wanna Do'*. Sarah's dad and brother were both musical, having a small music studio in the village and she owned her own guitar and tiny amp.

Susan Melody George (born 26 July 1950) is an English film and television actress, film producer, and champion Arabian horse breeder. In the early 1970s, she came to be associated with rather provocative, sometimes (as in *Straw Dogs*) controversial roles and became quite type-cast. Her lighter side was apparent in some of her TV appearances, such as in an episode "The Gold Napoleon" of *'The Persuaders'* (1971) with Roger Moore and Tony Curtis. In 1988, Susan marked her film-producing debut with *'Stealing Heaven'*. She had a 4-year relationship with American singer Jack Jones before she later married British actor Simon MacCorkindale in 1984. Simon died from cancer on 14 October 2010. They had no children.

Therese "Bunty" Bailey (born 23 May 1964) is an English model, dancer and actress. Bunty started her career as a dancer in the dance group *Hot Gossip* in the early 1980s. She became known as the girl in the music videos of A-Ha's singles *'Take on Me'* and *'The Sun Always Shines on TV'* made in 1985; she met Morten Harket (the lead-singer and voice of A-Ha) on the set and became his girlfriend.

She has since appeared in several films, with her most recent role in 2008 as a Gypsy Momma in *'Defunct'*. She also used to work as a children's dance teacher at Wraysbury and Datchet Village Halls. She was listed by Fox News as being one of *The Hottest '80s Video Vixens*. She was one of the first people to take advantage of the UK government car scrappage scheme and was invited to breakfast with the Prime Minister at the time, Gordon Brown. In September 2012, she appeared as the mystery guest on Channel 4's *Big Fat Quiz of the '80s*, with her appearance in the A-Ha videos being the correct answer.

Thomas Gordon Cullen (9 August 1914 - 11 August 1994) lived in Wraysbury from 1958 until he died in 1994. He was an influential English architect, urban designer and a key motivator in the Townscape movement. He was responsible amongst other things for the Village Hall and the Children's Playground. His techniques consisted largely of sketchy drawings that conveyed a clear understanding of his ideas which had a considerable influence on subsequent architectural drawing styles. He also illustrated several books by other various authors, before writing his own book in 1961, based on the idea of Townscape, called *'The Concise Townscape'*. It has subsequently been republished around 15 times. In 1972 he was elected Honorary Fellow of the RIBA. In 1975 he was awarded with an RDI for Illustration and Townscape and in 1976, he was awarded a gold medal from The American Institute of Architects. In 1978 he was awarded the CBE for his contribution to architecture.

William Mervyn (3 January 1912 – 6 August 1976) was an English actor best known for his portrayal of the bishop in the clerical comedy All Gas and Gaiters, the old gentleman in The Railway Children and Inspector Charles Rose in The Odd Man and its sequels.

Usually cast as a wealthy upper-class gentleman, he also featured in The Ruling Class (1972) and around the same time, he appeared as Sir Hector Drummond, Bt., in the British TV series The Rivals of Sherlock Holmes in an episode entitled "The Superfluous Finger" (1973).

Mervyn was married to Anne Margaret Payne Cooke, a theatre designer and architect who survived him with their three sons – one of whom, Michael Pickwoad, became the production designer on Doctor Who. William Mervyn's granddaughter Amy Pickwoad, became an art director and standby art director for Doctor Who.

*__Judy Leden__, MBE (born 1959) is a British hang glider and paraglider pilot. She has held three world championships, twice in hang gliding, once in paragliding. She was awarded an MBE in 1989 for her services to hang gliding, and has received many other awards, including the Royal Aero Club Gold Medal, and Sportswoman of the Year from *Cosmopolitan* magazine and Middlesex county. She also received the Hussein Medal for Excellence in recognition of her flight to Jordan by microlight, and the Star of the First Order by King Hussein.

For the Channel 4 documentary *Cotopaxi Dream,* she climbed and flew from the top of Cotapaxi, at 19,600 feet the world's tallest active volcano. In early 1992, Judy took part in the Flight of the Dacron Eagles, a 1000-mile, three-week microlight and hang glider expedition down the rift valley in Kenya, filming for the BBC1 *Classic Adventure* series with cameramen Sid Perou, microlight pilots Richard Meredith-Hardy and Ben Ashman and hang glider pilots, Mark Dale, Tim Hudson and Louise Anderton.

In 1996, Judy's autobiography *Flying with Condors* was published. This title was also used for a BBC1 *Natural World* documentary, in which Judy and her husband Chris Dawes, travelled to Patagonia to fly with Andean condors using hang gliders, paragliders and paramotors.

* See also Appendix 1

Judy's father Thomas, was one of the children saved by Sir Nicholas Winton prior to the outbreak of World War II. She has taken Sir Nicholas flying in a microlight on a number of occasions including his 98th and 100th birthdays.

For a more complete list of Celebrities, *see Appendix 5*

In Conclusion

In more recent years, the village has slowly lost its ability to offer local employment as the tentacles of suburbia stretch ever nearer, bringing larger and more varied employers within commuting distance, in particular Heathrow. This, in turn, has made the village more affluent and house prices have soared.

Whilst many changes have been seen over the years, not least the movement of people, and whilst some have come and gone, many have chosen to stay for generations and feel happy being part of our inclusive community.

There is much to praise the village of Wraysbury for as is confirmed by those who have wanted to live here. From its tranquil setting by the Thames, social life and amenities, transport links, friendly villagers, local shops, Post Office and excellent schools, all boxes are ticked. In my opinion, Wraysbury remains as one of *the* places to live in England today.

---oo000oo---
Further information on particular subjects featured in this narrative may be found in Wraysbury Village Archives in the Village Hall. Open most Thursdays 10am – 12noon

The lovely Glenmore
now sadly gone and replaced by amongst
others the Telephone Exchange

Appendix 1

Wraysbury News

"On August 20th a particularly low-flying aircraft caused a ceiling to collapse in the home of Mr. and Mrs. John Denison in Whitehall Lane. We have evidence that the aircraft concerned was belonged to Pan-American who say they are holding an enquiry into the matter. We are making vigorous protests to the airline".

From the first edition – September 1971
Source: Wraysbury Archives

Wraysbury News is the 'Voice' of the village and it has campaigned on behalf of the village for 47 years. There have been other magazines and monthly newsletters but none has stood the test of time so well as the Wraysbury News. One of the earliest parish magazines was called St. Andrew's Parish Magazine and Monthly Record and it was started around 1924/5 and there have been others, such as the Echo and The Villager but Wraysbury News is by far the best, having a good format, nicely produced and always current.

Started by Jill Sarsby in 1971 as the 'Local News', it was typed by her onto those unforgiving stencils where any mistake meant that it all had to be redone. Our more senior readers will remember those awful hand turned Roneo drums where the stencil was placed and with luck, blot free copies emerged! Jill's background as a ghost writer for Corgi books helped her with this task as did her family and her friend Gay Bazelle, who made less mistakes on the stencil! Artwork was also produced 'in house' and again Jill's background came to the fore. She studied art and calligraphy in Paris before WW2 and she produced in addition, many of the programmes, flyers and posters for village events. The magazine was produced by the Wraysbury Association, with whom a number of early village enterprises were linked, such as the History Club and The Fair (see Plot 279, page GM85 and GM92). It was distributed free of charge (and still is) to all villagers and was hand delivered by a group of early volunteers, some of whose families still have village connections, like the Traceys, Pinions, Blofelds, Beales and Varians whose names turn up time and time again when things needed to be done.

Thanks to a number of volunteers like Mike and Rosemary Smith, Susie Pond, Glyn and Debbie Larcombe, Alice Hopkins, Christine Benefer and Anne Blake who between them, did all manner of jobs, Wraysbury News is still with us today. Published in the June and December of each year and edited and published by Maggie Gardiner (another of the Wraysbury ladies who gets involved for the benefit of all) from 2006 until Christmas 2017, when Mike Williams took over, the magazine has evolved to become the 'must have read' every six months. Full of local news, sometimes not so good but compensated by news of Wraysbury youngsters and their exploits in the Scouts, Brownies, Rainbows and Guides etc. News of all the local clubs and associations, in particular, the outings to sunny climes by the Horticultural Society and days out by Age Concern. Now hopefully, we should also have news of the Women's Institute (WI), restarted after an absence of many years.

The Wraysbury News is well supported by local businesses and Wraysbury Parish Council, without whom the magazine would be lost to the ravages of expenses and costs. It is thanks to the villagers using their local services, that these advertisers keep advertising and help to keep the magazine 'in the black'.

Issue 40 – Wraysbury News
December 1983
Source: Wraysbury Archives

The magazine is delivered to the door by about 20 volunteers and it is also in the local shops: it is free to all villagers. Where else is there such a useful publication to keep the villager involved and in touch with all local events. All local goings-on are reported, some are topical whilst some hark back to years gone-bye and involve the reader in the village's history, such as the record breaking flight of our own *Judy Leden, champion hang glider and paraglider. Shown here is the December issue of 1983, which covered her flight of July that year.

*See also page GM123.

Here also, is the 100th edition from December 2013, there are not many free publications of the quality of the Wraysbury News that last until the 100th issue.

Please support the Wraysbury News and its advertisers, without it as Jill Sarsby said at the beginning "Nobody in this village will ever know what's going on". Thanks to all the wonderful volunteers who make it all possible. Long may it continue to the 200th edition, I wonder what it will be reporting then?

Issue 100 – Wraysbury News
Front Cover by Bill Stewart
Source: Wraysbury Archives

Appendix 2

Page 40 - RE. Miss Bertha Herring 1940 - The author is indebted to Ms. Shrabani Basu, author and correspondent of the Calcutta-based newspaper Ananda Bazar Patrika and The Telegraph for the background to the story, which I have paraphrased below:

Miss Bertha Herring – Wraysbury Heroine

The background to this story starts in WW1, when over 1 million Indians were persuaded to enlist and fight for the Empire. They were encouraged by their own leaders in the hope that after the war, India would be given Dominion status.

When the war ended, Indian deaths were over 70,000 and thousands upon thousands more were coming home crippled or blind. The general feeling among the Indian population was they had more than deserved to be accorded Dominion status, after all Canada, Australia and New Zealand were given it, so why not India? Being the largest country and having the largest population, it felt deprived and let down that it was still not allowed to have more say in its own affairs. The people showed their unhappiness by a series of strikes or hartals, where across the Punjab, cities ceased to function as labour was withdrawn. Two of the senior members of the Congress Party were arrested and issued with Deportation Orders. This led to growing resentment and outbreaks of public disorder across the Punjab, in particular Amritsar, resulting in the deaths of a number of Europeans. As a result of which, a ban on all meetings was put in place. However, no steps were taken to ensure all parts of the city were made aware of this.

On the 13th April 1919, it was the time of the Sikh New Year festival and most people were brightly dressed in orange and yellow, the colours of the festival. A meeting was to be held at 4.30pm in the public park, Jallianwala Bagh, next to the Golden Temple. This park was enclosed on all sides by walls and buildings with only a few small entrances between them.

Brigadier General Reginald Dyer arrived with troops, blocking the main entrance with an armoured car. He took 50 soldiers onto the high ground either side of the entrance overlooking the park and ordered the troops to fire into the crowd. Over 1560 rounds of ammunition were fired and English figures stated there were 379 dead and 1200 wounded. The Indian Congress Party, however, stated that 1000 had died and 1500 were wounded, many women and children among them. Approximately 15-20,000 people were estimated to have been at the park. So barely 5 months after the end of WW1, when over 400,000 volunteers from that area alone had fought for the Empire, British guns had been turned on them, a cruel reward, it was felt, for their loyalty.

In the subsequent enquiry, led by the former governor of the Punjab, Michael O'Dwyer, Brigadier Dyer was acquitted of any blame and never backed down or regretted the incident. It was felt by most Indians that O'Dwyer had just 'whitewashed' the whole terrible event.

There was at this time a 10-year-old boy, Udham Singh, who was in Amritsar at the time and was deeply affected by the shooting. Fifteen years later, after bathing in the waters at the Golden Temple, he vowed to restore honour to the humiliated Punjab. He travelled to London and blended in with the Indian workers. On 13th March, 1940, he got his opportunity. At a meeting of the East India Association, he entered, dressed soberly, and carried a revolver hidden inside a book. At the end of the meeting he calmly shot O'Dwyer, killing him outright.

His escape was blocked by **Miss Bertha Herring** and he coolly waited to be arrested. He was hanged on the 31st July 1940 at Pentonville Prison.

India was finally given Independence by Royal assent on the 18 July 1947, which came into effect on the 15th August 1947. The same time as the official recognition of Pakistan.

Bertha Herring – 14th March 1940
Source: Daily Herald

Appendix 3

The Giving Village

Leading by example is what Wraysbury does well. Taking the lead from St. Andrew's and the Baptist Church and their open-handed approach to charitable causes, both villagers and clubs have risen to the occasion as has been mentioned in numerous articles in this work. Here are two examples that exemplify the very nature of the act of giving to those less fortunate. No excuse is made for their inclusion.

Action Aid, an organisation to improve the living of those less fortunate in Third World countries had a stall at Wraysbury Fair some years ago and they made quite an impact on those who came into contact with them. So much so that the then committee of the Jazz Club donated to them the proceeds of one of their raffles.

The committee then decided to take a little more positive action and arranged to sponsor a child in Nepal for 4 years. This sponsorship meant that at least one child would have some basic education, clothes to wear and a meal a day. Details were later received of the child sponsored and her name was Musaini Tamang and she lived in a village called Masan Tole, about 8000ft up in the foothills of Kathmandu. She was 12 years of age and had never had the opportunity to go to school. Both parents were illiterate and owned just 0.12 of an acre of land, one buffalo and a calf. From this they had to provide for a family of five.

Len with Musaini Tamang
Learning to colour
Source: Pearce Family Archives

Avril and Len
Happy Days in Nepal
Source: Pearce Family Archives

This sponsorship was subsequently followed up by two members of the Jazz Club, Len and Avril Pearce, who happened to be planning a trip to Southern India and decided to make a detour to Nepal! Numerous adventures followed as they made their way overland and trekked to visit 'Their Girl', who had by now learned letters and numbers. They made it to the local school Jaleshree Primary, built from wood and cow dung with help from Action Aid. No desks or chairs, all pupils sat on the polished mud floor. With the help of the local Action Aid rep. the girl was found and, amongst tears, she was given some little gifts of crayons and pencils, which after a while induced a smile.

After this visit Len and Avril now knew why 65% of little children die before the age of five, why adult literacy is only 19% of the whole population and why only 9% have access to safe water. On their return to the UK they made a full report to the Jazz Committee and arranged for the Wraysbury News to print what they had seen to try and increase awareness of this neglected part of the world. Subsequently, due to this local publicity, three more children were sponsored by Wraysbury residents, with a caveat that part of the money was to be used for Adult Education on Growing and Marketing produce.

The Jazz Club today, still donates to worthy causes (*as do most of the village clubs and the Fair*) but now tends to support Wraysbury Parochial Charities in aid of local needs.

In Aid of Poland

In 1981 and 1982, Wraysbury held a number of fund-raising events to aid our wartime friends as the communist government of Poland made drastic cuts in food and all other necessities of normal life. Virtually all products were lacking, including bread, meat, coffee, laundry detergents, sugar and cigarettes. In the capital Warsaw, buses had no spare tyres and the company announced that only main routes would be kept, adding that the public has to get used to the situation, in which "there is shortage of meat, soap, cigarettes and the decent transportation system". The situation was summarized by a grim Solidarity poster that appeared on Polish streets in early summer 1981. It showed a black skull with a crossed knife and fork under it. '*The first result of the ninth party congress: a cut in food rations',* the poster said, referring to the 20 percent reduction in meat allotments.

Wraysbury residents and in particular, Graham Sinclair and the late Commander John Husher of the Royal Canadian Navy responded by forming a Polish Aid Group, organising collections and donations and raised over £2000 for the children of Poland and, in addition, collected food parcels, clothing, sweets and toys etc., all packed by Wraysbury schoolchildren.

In the December of 1982, Sinclair Transport and Windsor and Slough Lions, arranged the hire of a large lorry to try and get vital supplies direct to the children of Poland. Goods being sent through normal channels seemed to being stolen by criminal gangs operating a Black Market. 10 tons of supplies were loaded on to the lorry and with Graham Sinclair at the wheel, assisted by John Husher, they set off on the hazardous journey to Poland. Written on the lorry's side in Polish was '*England helps Polish Children*' – Their aim was to get through to Krakow and Warsaw, in particular the children's orphanages whose suffering was particularly acute.

They had some frightening border crossings and numerous scary adventures along the way with cases of hidden contraband, and narrow escapes from armed guards with dogs 'as big as bears!'[1] But they eventually made it, and the joy and delight of the Nuns and the children made the risks all worthwhile.

Another example of Wraysbury residents' generosity for others in their time of need.
All villagers should be proud of what they do for others less fortunate.

_____

[1] My Polish Adventure – Graham Sinclair

Appendix 4
Wraysbury Voluntary Care

Originally started by Jill Sarsby and Jackie Roper and supported by local volunteers, it was later 'inherited' by Janet Crame BEM and re-formed in 2014 by Simon Carter and Katie Morgan with Janet Crame as Chair. Its aim is to render assistance to Wraysbury and Horton's more vulnerable residents who require help with their every-day living. From fixing the shower to a trip to the Doctors, they can normally find an answer. In 2017 the most received request was for Datchet Health Centre.

Meals on Wheels are an integral part of this and was originally started in the 1960s by Jill Sarsby, Jackie Roper and Betty Cuming. The meals being prepared at the Welley Café (now a Chinese restaurant) and delivered by volunteers. Now organised by Janet Crame, they are still delivered by a great team of volunteers. There is now also a Thursday Lunch Club, set up by Janet Crame and the team, they aim to provide a 'home-cooked' two course meal for those who are on their own, cannot cook for themselves or just fancy a meal with company. The cost at the moment is £5 per person and there are currently 40 places available, allocated on a first come first served basis. Bookings can be made with Tim Whittick on 01784 482515 the dedicated WVC helpline, at the latest on the Wednesday of the week you wish to have lunch.

Transport can be provided to and from the Village Hall, courtesy of the new Community Bus for those who no longer drive or are unable to make their own way to the Village Hall. The bus is equipped with a wheel chair tail-lift, so no problems here if you need your wheel chair.

WVC is run solely by unpaid volunteers who have a few hours to spare to help out. They are always looking for more help as in this respect many hands make light work. If you can help by offering your free time for something really worthwhile please do. You'll be very welcome.

Wraysbury Action Group (WAG)

Wraysbury Action Group (WAG) was the idea of Su Burrows in February 2009, in response to Thamesfield and Coppice Field going up for sale in several hundred small plots. Its main purpose initially was to make buyers aware of the problems they may encounter and hope to prevent the loss of community open spaces that have been used and crossed by footpaths for decades.

It didn't take long for a committee of concerned residents to be formed and WAG then in conjunction with RBWM managed to prevent the random fencing off of odd plots in Thamesfield and Coppice Field, and also, Public Footpath Orders were submitted in an effort to preserve these open spaces for the village.

It was felt that better progress might be made if these open spaces were termed as 'Village Green' and in early 2010 the necessary paperwork was submitted. This application had over 150 supporting evidence forms to preserve Thamesfield as Open Space, and as a Village Green for continued use as a recreational area for the Village. This application was later rejected and rejected again at a Judicial Review in 2014. The Village Green application now no longer feasible, the original footpath claims were resurrected and the RBWM wished to recognise some of the footpaths. Due to objections this brought, there will now be a Public Enquiry in 2018. So watch the local press, if it wasn't for WAG, these open spaces would be long gone!

Appendix 5

Some Celebrities who made their home in Wraysbury

Robert	Anderson	King Johns Close	Olympic Fencing Coach
Peter (Lord)	Archer	Hill View Road	M.P. & QC
Bunty (Therese)	Bailey	The Avenue	Dancer/Actress
Peter	Black	The Avenue	Daily Telegraph
Peter	Brace	Old School Court	Actor & Stunt man
Jess	Conrad	Kingswood Creek	Singer
Reginald	Conway	Ferry Croft, Welley Road	Orchestra - Covent Garden
Henry & George	Cooper	Park Avenue/Ouseley Road	Boxer
Gordon	Cullen	The Drive	Urban Architect
James	Doulton	Oast House	Potter family
Buster	Edwards	Hythe End	Gr. Train Robber
Andy	Ellison		Singer
Derek	Franklin		Hedley Ward Trio
Susan	George	Park Avenue	Actress
Fiona	Gillies		Actress
Peter	Goodwright	Magna Carta Lane	Comedy/Impressionist
Mary	Hanefey	The Green	Actress
Sarah	Harding (Hardman)	Taylor's Folly, Windsor Road	Singer – Girls Aloud
Marcus	Harris		Actor
Philip	Hinchcliffe	Thatched Lodge, Staines Road	Producer/Director
Alfie	Hinds	Ferry Lane, Hythe End	Jewel thief & Robber
Francis (Capt)	Inch	Ouseley Road	Hero of the ship Volturno
Jack	Jones	Park Avenue	Singer
Christine	Keeler	Hythe End	Model
Judy	Leden		Hang glider/Paraglider Champion
Simon	MacCorkindale	Park Avenue	Actor
George	Melvin	Littlemore, Kingswood Creek	Music hall Star
William	Mervyn	Barleymow, Station Road	Actor
Charles Gordon	Mosley	Old Bowry House	Editor Burke's Peerage
Barbara	Mullen	Whitehall Stables	Actress
Gary	Numan	Staines Road	Singer
Henry	Perkins	Douglas Lane	Dancer
Beryl	Reid	Honeypot Cottage	Actress
Tommy	Trinder	Welley Road	Comedian/Film Star
Gareth	Van den Bogaerde	Staines Road	Dirk Bogaerde's brother
Robert	White	Whitehall	Lemonade maker
Geoffrey	Whitehead	The Avenue	Actor
John	Wilcox	Kingswood Creek	Anna Neagle's brother-in law
Emyln	Williams	Holm Island	Actor
George	Woodbridge	Ouseley Road	Actor
Joan and John	Young	Tythe Farm Cottage	Actors

With thanks to Ann Blake for compiling the names.

Appendix 6

Village Clubs and Organisations for You to Join & Enjoy			
Name	Contact	Phone	Email
Age Concern	Pam Gabriel	01753 685842	pgabriel@live.co.uk
Angels Pre-School	Jane DeCecco	07944 848347	info@angelspreschool.co.uk
Art Society	Lesley West	01784 482812	lesleywest125@btinternet.com
Badminton	Brian Holloway	01784 482419	brian@dhholloway.co.uk
Baptist Church	Revd. Carolyn Urwin	01784 482553	enquiries@wraysburybaptist.org.uk
Bowls Club	Harold Hutt	01784 482944	wraysburybowls@gmail.com
Bowls Short Mat	Steve Boschen	01753 684390	boschenfest@btinternet.com
Christmas Fair	Mark Foster	07788 413030	wraysburychristmasfayre@gmail.com
Cricket Club	Tom Dibley	07775 587633	wraysburycc@hotmail.com
Disabled Water Ski		01784 483664	bdwsa.org/regional-centres/heron-lake
Dragon Boats – all types			info@hurricanes-dbc.com
Fair	Katie Morgan	07921 679311	katie@bsbennett.co.uk
Football Club	John Stephenson	07831 132311	ltc.uk@virgin.net
Girl Guiding	Giovanna Cochrane	07914 673278	giovanna.cochrane@btinternet.com
Greyhounds in Need	Carolyn Davenport	01784 483206	info@greyhoundsinneed.co.uk
History Group	Maggie Gardiner	01784 482520	maggie_gardiner@btinternet.com
Horticultural Society	Pam & Ray Alletson	01784482545	alletson@aol.com
Jazz Club	Mrs. R. Smith	01784 483452	micro500@btinternet.com
Library (Container)	10.00-13.00 and 1400-19.00		Village Hall car park Wednesday only
Magna Carta Book Club	Wendy Kessack	07990 643140	stott.kessack@btinternet.com
Magna Carta Winemakers	Maureen Rolfe	01784 483947	maureenrlf@yahoo.co.uk
Meals on Wheels	Mrs. J. Crame BEM	01784 483528	janet@thegardenhouse.uk.com
National Trust	Runnymede	01784 432891	runnymede@nationaltrust.org.uk
Parkinsons Disease	Richard Tyner	01628 671635	www.parkinsons.org.uk
Pop-In Social Club		01784 482520	St. Andrew's Annexe Tuesdays 2-4pm
Pumpkins Pre-School	Kellie Fairhall	07500 224115	pumpkinspreschoolwraysbury.wordpress.com
Silverwing Sailing Club	Roger Bennett	01784 482985	rogerbennett110@hotmail.com
Skiff & Punting	Imogen Jones	01784 437206	wraysburyskiffandpuntingclub.com
Slimming World	Nicky	07469 935565	Village Hall, Tuesdays 9.30am
St. Andrew's Church	Revd. Colin Gibson	01784 481258	vicar.hortonandwraysbury@gmail.com
Swan Lifeline	Wendy Hermon	01753 859397	wendyhermon@btinternet.com
Swan Sanctuary	Mrs. D. Beeson	01932 240790	www.swanuk.org.uk
Tennis Club	Ros Nockles	01784 483001	wraysburyltc@yahoo.co.uk
Thames Hospice Care		08456 128812	www.thameshospice.org.uk
Tree Warden	Diana Hughes	01784 482729	diana@wraysbury.net
Village Club & Institute	Steve Lewis	01784 482804	steven.lewis27@btinternet.com
Village Halls	Mark & Jackie	01784 483240	mail@wraysburyvillagehalls.com
Village Trust (250 club)	Marylyn Ferguson	01784 482198	www.wraysburyvillagetrust.co.uk
Wraysbury Action Group	Su Burrows	07816 777416	wraysburyag@outlook.com
Wraysbury Archives	Anne Blake	01784 481310	
Wraysbury Association	Maggie Gardiner	01784 482520	wraysburynews@hotmail.com
Wraysbury Country Music Club	Frank Burry	01784 483383	frank.bury587@btinternet.com
Wraysbury Parochial Charities	Sue Chapman	01784 483186	s.k.chapman@btinternet.com
Wraysbury Regatta	Bob Silvey	01344 627040	www.wspc.org.uk/egham
Wraysbury Scouts	Andy Bouch	01784 483493	wraysburyscouts@btinternet.com
Wraysbury Players - theatrical	Nigel Handyside	01932 247856	secretary@wraysburyplayers.com
Wraysbury Voluntary Care		01784 482515	
Get involved with your village activities, you are assured of a warm welcome everywhere.			

Appendix 7

Wraysbury Parochial Charities

No History of the village can be written without deferring at some point to the contribution Wraysbury Parochial Charities have made to the betterment of villagers' lives, and for their support for local causes. Mentioned in this work a number of times in connection with their help and assistance to the needy of the village, and support for local enterprise, WPC are an amalgamation (c1898) of six old parish charities, all of whom were set up solely for the benefit of Wraysbury villagers. One of the oldest charities merged dates from the 16th century, and is known as the Bridge Lands Trust, where Andrew Lord Windsor left around 10 acres of land to the villagers of Wraysbury. This land was subsequently compulsory purchased for £41,000, which transformed the WPC's finances and enabled them to contribute more to the village. This generous act of Andrew Lord Windsor is commemorated in the naming of the Village Hall extension – The Windsor Room, made possible by a donation from the WPC.

As they generally perform below the radar so to speak, their contribution to village life can often go un-noticed and un-remarked or forgotten. Therefore, in recognition of their work, detailed here are just some of the projects helped by the WPC in the last year (2017).

1. Financial contribution to the Village Hall's running costs.
2. Cost of repairs to the Baptist Church tower clock.
3. Football team coaching facilities.
4. Donation to Thames Valley Hospice.
5. Provision of Lifelines (40+) for our most vulnerable residents.
6. Support to enable expansion of the Craft Show.
7. Support for young members of the Karate Club.
8. Support to the Wraysbury History Project (A more up-to-date view of Wraysbury)
9. Financial support to those in need.

The WPC's guidelines, administered by its trustees are quite wide and in general are:
"To relieve distress, sickness and the poor: to give support for social welfare, recreation and leisure, and to offer other financial support as they see fit"

They cannot however assist with help for such things as rates, taxes or where help should come from public funds.

Most of the clubs and associations mentioned within this work make donations on behalf of their members to the WPC and in addition, WPC hold the donations given to Wraysbury Voluntary Care so as to support their future activities.

They can be contacted by calling in confidence the Secretary Sue Chapman on 01784 483186.

A vote of thanks on behalf of the village is given to the trustees for the work they do on behalf of so many.

Appendix 8

Wraysbury Village Trust

Again, this work would not be complete without acknowledging the work this charity has done for the village. It is dedicated to support the social and environmental life of the village, by raising funds to support various initiatives. The inaugural meeting was held on the 6th February 1972 at Kit Aston's house 'Longfields' on the Staines Road, who became Mayor and was later knighted for his services to the Borough. Meetings were then held at alternate committee member's houses. Initial members being Kit Aston, Jill Sarsby, Mrs. Blofeld, Lord Craighton, Mr. Dailey, Mr. Cuming, Mr. Jacob and Mr. Hanaford. The trust also came to be known as The 250 Club, as its aim was to have 250 members financing the Trusts activity.

Its main objectives are:
1. To stimulate and support public interest in the beauty, history and character of Wraysbury.
2. To assist in providing, equipping and furnishing the Village Halls at Wraysbury.
3. The improvement of the conditions of life for the inhabitants of Wraysbury in the interests of social welfare.

Some of the very early grants, for example 1973, were £100 towards a piano for the Village Hall Thames room, £60 towards a piano for the Colne room and £500 towards the curtains for both. There is only one piano in the Hall in 2018. What's happened to the other one?

The Trust has helped village amenities such as the cricket club and the fair, badly affected by flooding, to carry on and is also amongst other things, responsible for the Christmas tree and lights. Our more senior members may remember the Christmas lights that used to be in the large beech tree[2] outside Jewsons the chemist, these again were supplied by the Trust. They also decorate the Village Hall so that all that use it may enjoy the Christmas decorations.

Many of the local groups, clubs and amenities have cause to thank this charity for its generosity. Even things that residents might think have happened naturally such as roadside bulbs, have been *planted by the charity to give our village that uplift on the verge of spring. Here are just a <u>few</u> of the clubs and organisations that they have helped over the years.

Wraysbury Scouts
Wraysbury Bowls Club
Wraysbury MacMillan nurses
Wraysbury Cricket Club
Wraysbury School

Wraysbury Village FC
Wraysbury Canoe Team
Wraysbury Brownies
Wraysbury Fair
Wraysbury Village Hall

The present Chair is Marilyn Ferguson who along with her committee do a wonderful job. It can't be easy deciding who to help out of the many requests they must receive. Over the last 14 years, their Christmas and summer dinner dances have been the highlight of the village social calendar and with their draws, raffles and donations, over £51,000 has been donated to worthwhile causes for the benefit of Wraysbury residents.

*See also page **id** of the Timeline

---

[2] Cut down in 1998 due to disease

Appendix 9

Wraysbury Village Archives

This veritable treasure chest of information about the village and its place in history, owes its existence to the 1973's Parish Council's determination, that all the old records lying mouldering in the then clerk's garage would be saved. This tin trunk full of records, was given to Anne Blake for safe keeping and eventual sorting. When Anne moved from English Gardens to Garson Lane the new storage area wasn't considered safe enough to house this treasure drove, so an alternative had to be found. The History Group had by this time been running about a year and Anne being a member, mentioned these documents to its then chairman Arthur Walters, who expressed a desire to have them and they speedily found their way to Arthur's house. Fortunately, the document haul began to grow as more and more villagers brought all manner of photos, records and 'do you want this?' until Arthur's house was creaking at the seams! The haul of documents was now quite impressive and by 1981, they had seeped out of windows and under doors into other villagers' houses as Arthur and the History Group pleaded for more space. Thankfully the Parish Council had asked for an Archives Room to be included in the 1995 extension to the Village Hall, and slowly the documents were transferred over.

■ HISTORICAL: Arthur Walters studies an old photograph.

The past goes on record

AN ARCHIVE room containing photos, records and maps detailing over 200 years of Wraysbury's history has been opened to the public for the first time.

The facility, at the village hall, has finally thrown its doors to interested villagers after former parish councillor Arthur Walters laboured to prepare the room for two-and-a-half years.

After uncountable hours of sorting, filing and organising, Mr Walters proudly unveiled the results of his work at the parish's annual meeting last month.

He said: "I think it's very rare for a parish to possess its own archive room. Hopefully, now it's open we can encourage more people to part with items of local interest."

The room contains parish council records dating back to its foundation in 1895 and reports from the village's police constable from as early as 1784.

Source: Observer 7th May 1998

It took a long time for all the documents to be indexed and referenced and all the while more and more items were being donated. Arthur had great help from Dennis Pitt, Frances Burton and Anne Blake in these early years and was finally able to announce that the Archive Room would be open to the public/visitors in May 1998.

Since this time there have been many visitors, both locally and from abroad, all anxious to find out about their relatives who used to live in the village.

Work in the Archives is a continuing programme of sorting, indexing and filing and the end is never reached! There is now so much more material that a larger storage and working facility is required and it is hoped that this will be addressed in the not too distant future. It cannot be emphasised enough how important the village records are and how unusual it is for a small village to have its own archives. Usually, any records if they exist, have long since been sent off to some centralised record office, out of sight and out of touch to the people they mean the most to and never see the light of day again.

Appendix 9 - continued

A major project for the Archive Room staff will be the re-indexing and digitalisation of the records so that they are available via an online catalogue. This obviously will be a labour-intensive task and will take some time to complete. However, the benefits to all when done will be enormous.

Now that Wi-Fi is available, enquiries can now be answered by email, and likewise, documents and photos sent via the internet. Visitors will have the advantage of being able to have information send to their phone or laptop or indeed 'hard copies' to take away.

Some of the original Archive Room staff
Kay, Dennis, Arthur (sitting) and Anne-2007

Of the original staff, only Anne now remains, but now with the addition of Graham Morley and Janet Pugh, the work continues. Here are just some of the vast range that we have: - Maps of all types, Photographs, Electoral Registers, Record of Churchwardens, and local Constable's report books going back to 1734, Minutes of various clubs and associations and oral histories of older residents. The 'Oral Histories' are an ongoing project and will be continued for as long as possible.

The Archives Room offers a useful service to local residents and they are happy to deal with any enquiries they may have. If you would like to more about Wraysbury's history then the Archive Room is the place you ought to visit. Usually staffed on a Thursday morning from 10am till 12pm, you'll be assured of a friendly welcome, so please do pop in.

Appendix 10

Further Information

In addition to this work, the writer has conducted numerous taped and recorded interviews with village residents. These interviews have then been transferred to CD and form the new 'Talking Heads' section of the Parish Archives. The recordings are of good quality throughout and are recorded as mp3 files. In addition, in each of the CD cases, there is a photographic record of the Interviewee which also dated. These CDs will play only on new cd players and in computers. The later part of the recording with Henry Butt of Hythe End, was in true outside broadcast style, recorded in the rain outside his property on the river whilst running to rescue his boat! So, it's a bit stormy in parts but it was fun. They may only be played in the Archives, they must not be taken away.

1. Henry Butt,	7. John Sleep
2. Elsie Joan Cole	8. Ann Blake
3. Ruby & Vic Oliver	9. Roger Willatts
4. Maureen & Frank Burr	10. Brian Reeves
5. Jennie Francis	11. Rita Brutnell
6. Joyce Histead	12. Graham Sinclair

CDs – Compiled by ancestralresearch.org.uk - see CDs for more detailed information.

Wraysbury History Group – August 1972, June 1977, September 1977 and July 1984.

Wraysbury History Group – History of Wraysbury 1984 & Out and About with Star FM Nov. 1996

Basil Masterson – My War Years & Wraysbury Reminiscences – Oct 1988 and Dec. 1997

These CDs have been compiled from recordings on old cassette tapes. There are faults with the recordings and tapes and in some cases, too many people are speaking at once which makes understanding sometime difficult. However, they have been cleaned up as best as possible and transferred to CD for the benefit of all.

Films that feature Wraysbury in some way or another have also been researched and copies placed in the Archives.

Films

The Piccadilly Incident (1946) – filmed in part at Ankerwycke House – shows the outside and some of the inside.

Séance on a Wet Afternoon (1964) – film sequences at Wraysbury/Staines Greyhound Track – shows it in its derelict state with the circuit, floodlights and the betting offices.

Stock Car (1955) –and - *Smashing Through* (1960) – both with filmed sequences at Wraysbury/Staines Greyhound track which was also used for Stock Car racing. Shows the stadium in its heyday of the 50s and 60s.

Do You Remember?

More than happy to be singing in the rain

WRAYSBURY'S summer fair celebrations were drenched by sudden downpours of rain on Saturday, but one lucky group came well prepared for the occasion.

Wraysbury Jazz Club umbrella twirlers Jennie Hannam and Avril Pearce proved there is more to jazz than saxophones and trumpets with their elaborately decorated brollies.

I bet the musicians wished they had remembered to bring their umbrellas too!

● Our picture shows Wraysbury jazz club umbrella twirlers, Jennie Hannam and Avril Pearce, keeping the punters entertained

Wraysbury Jazz Club Parade – 21st June 1997
Source: Avril Pearce

Gillett's Butchers window – Queen's Coronation 1952
this is where the Dentist is now
Source: Wraysbury Archives

A great view of Gem's Stores – now Bennett's Estate Agents
Source: Wraysbury Archives

In straw bonnets and frilly summer dresses, hoping for a hot summer day, are the pretty programme sellers of Wraysbury. The girls will mingle with the crowds the Wraysbury Association hopes will be drawn to the fair being held on the village green this afternoon and evening.

The first Wraysbury Fair for 50 years– June 1962
The Bonnet Girls – just like the Bennett Lovelies of 2015
Source: Wraysbury Archives

More photos from the Festival of Britain 1951
Do you recognise anyone?
Source: Wraysbury Archives

*See also page **iF** of the Timeline and the Bibliography

Wraysbury Stores - opposite The Perseverance
Source: Wraysbury Archives

Early view of Ouseley Road
Source: Wraysbury Archives

Wonderful drawing by Gordon Cullen – The High Street - undated
Source: Wraysbury Archives

Water colour of the old swimming area by the Club
Source: Wraysbury Archives

The High Street from the 70s
Source: Wraysbury Archives

The High Street from the late 90s
Source: Wraysbury Archives

Bibliography and other records of Interest

1918 - Year of Victory – Imperial War Museum

1841 – 1911 Census and the 1939 – Identity Card Census

A Child's War – Mike Brown

Battle of the Atlantic – HMSO 1946

Between The Wars – Julian Symons

Brief History of St. Andrew's Church 1965-Revd. Coates. Re-issued 1990 D. Pitt & Tony Kimber

Britain's Conquest of the Mediterranean – HMSO 1947

British Newspaper Archives

Civilian War Dead

Comments on the 8 Yards - John Sleep Leg D'Hon - 2010

Commonwealth War Graves Commission

English Place Name Society – The Place Names of Buckinghamshire 1925

Extracts from the Domesday Book 1086 (aka The Great Survey)

History & Antiquities of Buckinghamshire V4 – 1847- George Lipscombe

History of the Parish of Wraysbury 1862- Gordon Gyll

Historical records of Wraysbury Archives - various

Historical records of Wraysbury History Club – various

Jubilee Diamond Trees – The Tree Council 2015

King John's Hunting Lodge 1973 - Buckinghamshire County Planning Survey

Notes of Arthur Walters – various

Notes of Graham Sinclair – various

Place Farm House and Lands – Maps – Bodleian Library

Recollections of Cyril F Brants - 1974

Records of the Church Parochial Council – Bucks County Record Office

Reffell Family Archives

Royal Aero Club Certificates – National Archives

Silver Jubilee Programme 1977

Sir Thomas Smith – A Tudor Intellectual in Office 1964 - Mary Dewar

Son et Lumiere Programme 1977

St. Andrew's Parish Magazine 1932 – Origins of Place Names

Bibliography and other records of Interest - cont

St. Georges Chapel Windsor 1348 – 1416, A Study in Early Admin. 1947- AKB Roberts Ph.D. –

at the Royal Library, Windsor Castle

The Baptist Magazine 1871

The Diary of William Thomas Buckland

The First World War – Hugh Strachan

The Memoirs of Bill Stewart

The Memoirs of Len Pearce

The Records of T.H. Mawson, Landscape Gardener – Cumbria Archives

The Story of the Wraysbury Wall Hanging – Lesley West

The Western Front – Prof. Richard Holmes

War Diaries of the 56th Brigade Royal Field Artillery – National Archives

War Diaries of the Kings Royal Rifle Brigade 11th Service Battalion – National Archives

War Diaries of the Royal West Surrey Regiment – 1/5th Battalion-Surrey Archives

Wirecesberie (Wraysbury) A Chronology – Dennis Pitt 2011

Wraysbury News – back issues

Wraysbury Windmill – Glyn Larcombe

*1951 – Festival of Britain Parade
Source: Wraysbury Archives
*See also page **if** of the Timeline and page 3 of Do You Remember

Rear Cover Pic – Old Windsor Ferry in Old Ferry Drive